DATE DUE

MAY 30 2008			

DEMCO 38-296

D1603555

The History of Sex
in American Film

JODY W. PENNINGTON

Westport, Connecticut
London

Library of Congress Cataloging-in-Publication Data

Pennington, Jody W., 1959–
    The history of sex in American film / Jody W. Pennington.
        p. cm.
    Includes bibliographical references and index.
    ISBN-13: 978-0-275-99226-2 (alk. paper)
    1. Sex in motion pictures. 2. Motion pictures—United States. I. Title.
PN1995.9.S45P437 2007
791.43′6538—dc22   2007016352

British Library Cataloguing in Publication Data is available.

Library of Congress Catalog Card Number: 2007016352
ISBN-13: 978-0-275-99226-2

First published in 2007

Praeger Publishers, 88 Post Road West, Westport, CT 06881
An imprint of Greenwood Publishing Group, Inc.
www.praeger.com

Printed in the United States of America

The paper used in this book complies with the
Permanent Paper Standard issued by the National
Information Standards Organization (Z39.48–1984).

10 9 8 7 6 5 4 3 2 1

To my family, friends, and colleagues

Contents

Photographs follow page 108.

Introduction

An enormously important aspect of interpersonal relationships in the contemporary world, sex has come—over the course of the twentieth century—to occupy an elevated status as an element of human experience. Sexuality also has an institutional aspect: it has been confined to marriage by law in earlier periods and regulated by age. Commercial versions such as pornography (if obscene) and prostitution have been or are still illegal. The legal control of sexuality makes clear another aspect of human sexuality: it is often very contentious. Sex, in its complexity, unites and divides people. Some of sex's most common—and divisive—cultural manifestations are its representations in cinema.

The analyses that follow go beyond explicit nudity or on-screen sex and conceive sex broadly, looking at the cinematic representations in their social and historical contexts. Otherwise, a collection of stills with nude actors and actresses and shots of people engaged in any variety of sex acts would suffice. In order to examine the representation of sexual behavior as it occurs in narrative as well as social, cultural, and historical contexts, the analyses that follow recreate these crucial elements of the sexual imagery and its larger meanings in intimate relationships and society.

To understand the interplay between film narrative and social and cultural history, the analyses not only provide correlative explications of *why* sexual behavior is in a film; they also illuminate *what* is on-screen and what is not. It is important to bear in mind that film is an aesthetic medium, and the way in which particular filmmakers choose to represent sexuality in specific narratives is immensely important and must be considered, as is done in detail. The analyses go beyond the aesthetic to consider the social and cultural preconditions at various periods in American history. Rather than draw on, for example, psychoanalytic theories to elucidate sexual representations in cinema, this work draws on social and cultural history, as well as non-Freudian psychology and sociology. To that end, the book is divided into two sections. The first section surveys the historical development of sex and nudity in film from cinema's beginnings until today, as well as the corollary growing recognition of the sexual diversity in American society. Integrating narrative analysis with a historical survey provides a more subtle view of how Hollywood's depictions of sex changed over the course of a century and shows how different genres have evolved alongside changing sexual values and behavior patterns in American society. The second section examines four specific sex-related themes—historical sexual revisionism, gay and lesbian sexuality, adultery, and pedophilia—in greater detail.

The first chapter traces the history of sexual representations and their regulation in American cinema from the industry's earliest years to the middle of the 1960s. The focus is on the film industry's self-censorship regimes, their enforcement, and their effect on nudity and sexual behavior in mainstream films until the mid-1960s, and the industry and social conditions that contributed to first the adoption of the Production Code, the industry's first set of self-censorship regulations, and then the Code's gradual undermining. Finally, the chapter traces the development of state obscenity law as the ultimate limit on constitutionally protected sexual expression in motion pictures.

In order to provide a more complete picture of the representation of sex in American cinema before the 1970s, the second chapter goes beyond the mainstream film industry to the films most affected by obscenity law. On the margins of the American film industry, sexual content suppressed by the mainstream industry's self-censorship and state censorship laws managed to thrive in several genres. The chapter looks at sexploitation, pornography, European movies, and American underground cinema. It concludes by tracing the important liberal realignment in sexual behavior patterns in the United States over the course of the decades following World War II.

Chapter three begins with an analysis of the sexual themes in films acclaimed as the final nails in the coffin of the Production Code. Next, it examines the development and structure of the ratings system that replaced the Code in 1968. Finally, the chapter surveys the role played by sex in the development of New Hollywood, one of the American film industry's periodical renewals, during the late 1960s and early 1970s. The brief flowering of pornography known as *porno chic* is discussed as part of a larger discussion of the extent to which once marginal genres gained greater acceptance and influenced mainstream production.

Chapter four picks up the thread of the changes in sexual behavior patterns in the United States, which continued through the 1970s and into the 1980s. The chapter then examines a thematic development that drew on the changes in Americans' attitudes toward marriage and intimate relationships that emerged along with the sexual realignment: in movies, characters that remained faithful to unfulfilling relationships were now no more common than characters whose first allegiance was to themselves rather than their relationships. To exemplify this development, the chapter analyzes shifts in the representation of intimate relationships and sexual themes. The chapter concludes with an examination of the way filmmakers handled sex in teen films.

The fifth and final historical chapter considers the impact of the conservative counterattack on the liberal sexual realignment of the postwar era and the representation of sex in mainstream American cinema from the late 1980s until today. The social-historical account dovetails into an examination of the introduction of a new rating category, NC-17, and the growing success of independent filmmakers. These dichotomous developments paralleled divisions between conservative efforts to limit sex in the public sphere and the continued liberal recognition and acceptance of sexual pluralism in the United States. To give a sense of the sexual dichotomy as it played out in movies, the chapter examines representative films from the romantic comedy and the erotic thriller, two genres that could be taken as representing the polar ends of the spectrum of sexual representations that have come to populate American movie screens.

The book then shifts from its historical review of sex in American film and looks at major sexual themes. Chapter six considers how Hollywood revised its representation of the past to include sexual behavior after the demise of the Production Code. Limits on sexual candor imposed by the Code clearly led to the creation of an image of people's sex lives that did not correlate with the roles sex played in society. Under the ratings system, American films revisited the past and portrayed the sex lives of earlier generations.

Chapter seven begins by examining the suppression of homosexuality under the Production Code as well as how more or less coded representations appeared in numerous films. It then examines the use of the gay bar as an iconic space in films depicting homosexuality as a marginalized sexual orientation. The chapter also looks at American cinema's representation of antigay sentiments in its films and the gradual emergence of homosexuality in mainstream films.

Chapter eight looks at adultery, in many ways the quintessential sexual topic for cinema. It also highlights a basic shortcoming with Production Code–style film censorship: although film is arguably first and foremost a visual medium, it does not have to show things for the audience to "see" them. Infidelity in general and adultery in particular are interesting tests on the limits of metaphors concerning how motion pictures reflect the attitudes and values of society. While unfaithful partners became common in Hollywood films and were often portrayed as sympathetic, adultery has never become a surefire box office magnet.

The ninth and final chapter looks at incestuous and nonincestuous pedophilia in American society and cinema. Incest and pedophilia have been included to provide the reader with an overview of how film has represented a criminal form of sexual perversion that perpetrators have kept highly concealed from public view.

Many more films were analyzed than could be squeezed into this work. The final choices reflect an effort to balance several criteria. Some were box office successes while others were landmark films. Others are independent films as well as critical successes that did not necessarily do well at the box office. The sheer number of movies that include nudity or sex is so large that any list can only exemplify the trends, the highlights, and scale of this phenomenon over the last one hundred years. Overall, the films chosen, several of which are in the United States National Film Registry, are representative of the variety of ways that sex has appeared on American movie screens.

I thank my editor at Praeger, Daniel Harmon, whose positive and timely feedback revamped an occasionally sagging spirit and helped me find the right tone and thematic shape for the book. Finally, I would like to say thank you to my wife, Pernille, an impoverished expression that does not begin to repay her invaluable input and patience while this book was being written.

1

Drawing the Line: Codes and Laws

EARLY AMERICAN FILM CENSORSHIP

Motion pictures appeared at the end of the nineteenth century. They immediately attracted large audiences, especially among the poor and working class, many of whom were immigrants. Increased leisure time had slowly emerged in the wake of industrialization and urbanization, two major outcomes of modernization. An array of social problems such as overcrowded tenements and crime accompanied urbanization. Reform organizations such as the American Social Hygiene Association poured energy into combating sex-related problems believed to accompany urbanization: sexually transmitted diseases like syphilis, premarital sex, and prostitution. Because modernization also brought with it secularization, many conservative Protestants felt they were in the throws of a social and cultural revolution that threatened to undermine public morality. Worried variably by the age, ethnicity, or social class of the audience and the bawdy content of some films, middle- and upper-class conservative Protestants viewed the burgeoning medium as a threat to family values, the latest "cheap" lower-class entertainment like saloons, vaudeville, and penny arcades. They attempted to stem the tide of change by regulating or forbidding nickelodeons, expanding older theater licensing laws to encompass the new medium.

The licensing approach to film censorship began in 1907 when Chicago required exhibitors to secure permits from the chief of police before showing films. The ordinance prohibited "the exhibition of obscene and immoral pictures."[1] Jake Block, who owned a chain of nickelodeons, challenged the ordinance by screening two Westerns, *The James Boys in Missouri* (1908) and *Night Riders* (1908), after they had been denied permits. Block's case reached the Illinois Supreme Court. In *Block v. City of Chicago* (1909), the court upheld the ordinance and legitimized local governments' power to censor or prohibit obscene or immoral films.[2] The industry took note of *Block* since it established a legal precedent legitimizing film censorship.

Six years later, in *Mutual Film Corp. v. Industrial Commission of Ohio* (1915), the United States Supreme Court ruled film censorship constitutional.[3] The Court cited *Block* as having sustained the use of the police power to censor films. Most importantly, the Court determined that the First Amendment did not protect motion pictures because they were "mere representations of events, of ideas and sentiments published and known, vivid, useful and entertaining no doubt" but also "capable of evil, having power for it, the greater because of their attractiveness and manner of exhibition."[4] The medium's *potential* to construct stories and show images that some Americans found immoral was enough to deprive it of constitutional protection.

The Court voiced concern with motion pictures' effects during a period of significant social transformation. The growth of the film industry paralleled changes in Americans' sex lives. Progressives' concerns about sex hygiene kept sexual concerns in popular magazines. Women's movements secured women the vote and kept issues such as birth control and marital sex on the national agenda. Rises in both the divorce rate and rates of premarital sex alarmed many Americans who were anxious about the vitality of the institution of marriage. Efforts to insure its survival included promotion of companionate marriage and manuals explaining the importance of the sexual compatibility of husbands and wives. Urbanization engendered greater individual freedom, undermining the Victorian social norms that governed sexuality.

Conservatives believed the weakening of traditional sexual values and the increased sexual opportunities in cities for men and women were directly related to increases in prostitution, miscegenation, abortions, and birth control use. Conservative reformers were especially vexed by female sexuality. Many filmmakers, by contrast, continued to make female sexuality central to their narratives. The social issues that caused reformers anxiety provided filmmakers with stock figures: the naive country girl unwittingly seduced by a big-city scoundrel or the fallen woman who became a prostitute. Filmmakers showed nudity in their films, despite the lack of First Amendment protection, because a substantial market existed. As Richard Randall notes, in the first decade of the twentieth century "the portrayal of vice and immorality seemed well on its way to becoming a multimillion-dollar business."[5]

The growing market for films with sexual content alongside increased calls for censorship delineated clear cultural divisions. Conservatives cheered when New York City mayor George B. McClellan, Jr., revoked the licenses of the city's nickelodeons in 1908 because he believed motion pictures were immoral. In reaction, to avoid governmental censorship theater owners and film distributors established a ratings board that would become known as the National Board of Review of Motion Pictures. As conservatives and liberals debated what was permissible, some filmmakers sought a middle ground by connecting sexuality—from on-screen nudity to adulterous relationships—to an uplifting moral message. For example, *The Hypocrites* (1915) did so quite literally with recurring shots of a fully nude character known as "The Naked Truth" (Margaret Edwards).

More commonly, sensationalism lured audiences into theaters by embedding sex in social contexts where immoral actions clustered together. Vice films were set in the underworld of crime syndicates, in the decadent leisure time of the wealthy and their mistresses, or in brothels. For example, *The Voice of Satan* (1915) followed the experiences of a woman forced into prostitution. Prostitution also figured in *A Mother's Ordeal* (1917). In *A Romance of the Underworld* (1918) a young woman leaves the convent she grew up in and winds up in the nether world of New York City's Lower East Side. White slavery drives the story lines of films like *The House of Bondage* (1914) and *The House of Silence* (1918), driving vice suppression groups into action.

The darker side of sexuality also had its female stars, beginning with the Fox Film Corporation's successful marketing of Theda Bara as a seductress. Bara became a star playing the Victorian stereotype, the vamp, a woman who lured men to their ruin, in Fox's first film, *A Fool There Was* (1915). Fox repeated the vamp formula in *The Devil's Daughter* (1915) and *The Vixen* (1916). In *The Vixen*, the main character, Elsie Drummond (Bara), is a nymphomaniac. Vamp films typically had risqué titles like *Flames of the Flesh* (1920). The Victorian dichotomy between vamps and virgins frequently shaped early film narratives, but most filmmakers believed characters should abide by dominant sexual morals. In most films, they did, not least because the boom in popularity meant large numbers of films had to be produced quickly, and filmmakers adapted existing plays, novels, and short stories based on Victorian moral codes.

The industry's first superstars did not challenge traditional sexual norms. In D. W. Griffith vehicles like *The Birth of a Nation* (1915) and *Broken Blossoms* (1919), Lillian Gish's characters—and in the eyes of many of her fans, Gish herself—personified Victorian sexual values such as innocence and the equation of virginity with virtue, and, with the films' rejection of miscegenation, racial purity. In *Way Down East*

(1920), an *urban* con man, Lennox Sanderson (Lowell Sherman) exploits Anna Moore (Gish). A young man from the country, David Bartlett (Richard Barthelmess), saves Anna from moral and physical ruin. While traditional sexual morality did not disappear, it now coexisted with modern values, a division that characterized films, audiences, and state governments.

While some Americans flocked to such films as Universal's white-slavery tale *Traffic in Souls* (1913) or Fox's *Cleopatra* (1917), starring Theda Bara, others found such fare shocking. Many of the offended, organized in women's clubs, religious groups, and antivice societies, called for greater censorship. By 1921, Pennsylvania, Ohio, Kansas, Maryland, and New York had established censorship boards to ensure that films exhibited within their borders met moral standards established by the state legislatures. Although some states and numerous municipalities empowered censorship boards, others did not. The industry confronted a complex distribution and exhibition web in which some states might alter or prohibit a film while other states let the same film play unedited. After the *Mutual* court case, the industry had no recourse to challenging censorship on constitutional grounds.

To add to its woes, a string of scandals generated massive negative publicity. Mary Pickford, who had become "America's Sweetheart" with her depiction of sexually innocent youth in films like *Rebecca of Sunnybrook Farm* (1917), divorced her husband in 1920 to marry her lover, Douglas Fairbanks. Fairbanks divorced his wife to marry Pickford the year she starred as a twelve-year-old orphan in *Pollyanna*. That same year, Pickford's sister-in-law, Olive Thomas, committed suicide. Roscoe "Fatty" Arbuckle went on trial for manslaughter in 1921. The following year, sordid intrigue surrounded the unsolved murder of director William Desmond Taylor. Hollywood's tarnished public image intensified the campaigns for censorship.

The Production Code

Partly to curb the influence of pro-censorship movements, the largest production companies in the industry, now located in Hollywood, formed a trade association, the Motion Picture Producers and Distributors Association (MPPDA), in 1922. Among its many tasks, the MPPDA assumed responsibility for ensuring the moral standardization of popular films. To that end, the MPPDA recruited a cultural conservative, Will H. Hays, to be its first president, a position Hays occupied until 1945. To counter movements among state legislators, religious groups, and newspapers that chafed at either explicit or implicit sex in films, Hays initially convinced members to adopt voluntary self-regulation.

Compliance was not fast coming. Given the success their films were enjoying, many studio heads waved off demands for censorship as the griping of a small, if vocal, minority. The complexity of the clashes over sex in film is illustrated by the success of Erich von Stroheim's *The Merry Widow* (1925). MGM edited *The Merry Widow* after pressure from Hays and conservative groups, even though the film had passed muster with censorship boards across the nation. Edited to placate the MPPDA, the film still included an orgy and clear indications of a foot fetish. Inspired by the film's success at the box office, other filmmakers produced lurid fare.

The studios also promoted stars as sex symbols. Greta Garbo repeatedly played women who violated traditional sexual norms in films that scored box office successes. MGM starred Garbo in the melodrama *The Temptress* (1926), in which the Swedish beauty played a married woman who is a mistress to other men. She costarred with John Gilbert in her next film, *Flesh and the Devil* (1926). Two lovers, Felicitas von Kletzingk (Garbo) and Leo von Sellenthin (Gilbert), exchange their first kiss in a scene that fades out and then fades in to the couple lounging together in her boudoir. Elliptical editing would remain Hollywood's preferred technique for implying sex.

Hollywood also discovered the sexually liberated flapper, the iconic modern young woman of the 1920s who enjoyed greater freedom than earlier generations of women. These middle- to upper-class single women lived in the city or its suburbs. The anonymity of city life allowed them to live on their own in small apartments and frequent clubs and theaters. They participated in dance crazes. They dated. They wore short skirts, sheer blouses, and revealing swimwear. They raised eyebrows and were targeted for repression by the legal establishment. They personified a rebellion in manners and morals and were personified in turn by the "It" girl, Clara Bow, exemplified by her character Betty Lou in the huge box office hit that made her a star, Paramount's *It* (1927).

The studios failed to meet Hays's expectations, so he formed the Studio Relations Committee in 1927 and drew up a list of "Don'ts and Be Carefuls." Hays took the threats of boycotts from organizations such the National Congress of Parents and Teachers seriously. The studios continued to worry him as well. Recognizing the ineffectualness of his list, Hays followed up on a initiative from Martin Quigley, Sr., a Catholic layman and publisher of the trade magazine *Motion Picture Herald*, and called upon Quigley and Daniel A. Lord, a Jesuit drama professor at St. Louis University, to draft "A Code to Govern the Making of Talking, Synchronized and Silent Motion Pictures." Quigley and Lord composed guidelines cloaked in quasi-religious language reflecting a conservative Christian view of human sexuality and marriage.

The Production Code reflected not only Quigley and Lord's religious values but also their assumptions about what various censor boards and religious organizations around the country would or would not permit. Both men preferred industry self-regulation, and they wanted to prevent the emergence of new censor boards. This interested the MPPDA as well, since the web of conflicting censorship laws impeded national distribution and exhibition. To avoid confrontations with censors, the Code incorporated self-censorship into the production process. The MPPDA consciously placed the Studio Relations Committee between filmmakers and the public, claiming to protect artistic freedom even while setting strict limits to expression.

The Code expressed conservative beliefs about media effects that were one of the motivating factors behind calls for censorship. Motion pictures were believed capable of exerting tremendous influence on behavior, especially that of youths. Quigley and Lord were concerned that members of a film's audience might imitate what they saw on-screen. Motion pictures' ability to mold attitudes and behavior and their tremendous popularity burdened producers with a special responsibility. The General Principles statement that accompanied the Code argued that immoral images were not allowed because they would "lower the moral standards."[6]

Although the Code proscribed nonsexual matters, it devoted considerable attention to expunging sex. It promulgated the conservative view that any relaxation of traditional sexual morals would precipitate a loosening of marital bonds. Nonmarital sex was not only wrong in and of itself; it also threatened the marital institution. Thus, the main objective with the ban on sex was to maintain the "sanctity of marriage and the home." The studios were also prohibited from implying that "low forms of sex relationship" were "accepted or common" because that misconception could potentially undermine the "sanctity of the institution of marriage." These "low forms" included adultery, passionate acts such as "[e]xcessive and lustful kissing, lustful embraces, suggestive postures and gestures," seduction or rape, "sex perversion," white slavery, miscegenation, sex hygiene and venereal diseases, childbirth, and children's genitals. The prohibition against "sex perversion," which encompassed homosexuality and pedophilia, was absolute, forbidding "any inference to it."

Provisions barring implications appear frequently, reflecting the drafters' awareness of narrative strategies for representing sex. Although the Code prohibited on-screen representations and narrative implications of the sexualized or eroticized body, its wording actually encouraged filmmakers to manipulate its restrictions by introducing situational justifications as narrative devices. Well aware of filmmakers' ability to create situations and settings that ostensibly called for characters undressing, the Code's drafters stipulated that "[u]ndressing scenes should be avoided, and never used save where essential to the plot." Plot relevance turned out to be a relative criterion. Rather than elide over changing clothes for the evening, inventive filmmakers might set a scene with important dialogue in the bedroom and let the clothing hang over the edge of a screen. Nudity unseen was better than no nudity at all.

After negotiations, the MPPDA adopted the Production Code in March 1930, but the studios largely continued to ignore Hays's commandments. In between Gilbert films, Garbo played a prostitute in her first talkie, the heavily promoted *Anna Christie* (1930). Garbo's sexually active characters and her star status proved to the studios that audiences generally did not want the same limits on sexuality in films that reformers and regulators desired, a view reinforced by the popularity of Paramount's *The Sign of the Cross* (1932). In Cecil B. DeMille's box office success, Mercia (Elissa Landi) rejects the seduction efforts of a lesbian temptress, Ancaria (Joyzelle Joiner), as well as the romantic overtures of Marcus Superbus (Fredric March). Although ostensibly a religious epic, DeMille's film helped refine the Hollywood approach to embedding sex in stories in which sex played a minor thematic role but had a significant screen presence. Debates over DeMille's epic raged over whether the film had a moral message or not, but it played uncut in New York, Kansas, and Pennsylvania and slightly edited in other locales.[7]

The recalcitrant studios continued to see sexual themes as a way to entice audiences into theaters. Studios relied on negative female archetypes like Jean Harlow's gold digger in *Red Headed Woman* (1932). *The Story of Temple Drake* (1933) included the implied rape of the title character (Miriam Hopkins). Disagreements among members of the MPPDA over concern about censorship were evident in the Advertising Code, which banned studios from exploiting censorship decisions when promoting films. One studio's legal obstacle was another's advertising copy.[8]

Once again, an attempt at industry self-regulation failed. The threat of censorship and boycotts increased, especially after the debates sparked by the publication of the multivolume Payne Fund Studies on Motion Pictures and Youth in 1933. In Hays's view, as he would recall in his autobiography, the "biggest factor bringing obloquy upon the industry was sex. There were other causes of public displeasure," he noted, "but ... sex pictures were the prime cause."[9] The bankers who financed film production demanded stability and pressured Hays. To mitigate the dangers of censorships, boycotts, and balking financiers, Hays reorganized the Studio Relations Committee into the Production Code Administration (PCA) in 1934, and gave the PCA the authority to interpret and enforce the Code. Hays appointed Joseph I. Breen, a culturally conservative Catholic, head of the PCA, a position Breen held until 1954. Under Breen, the Code succeeded for a number of reasons.

First, the industry was an oligopoly (the form it would have for roughly twenty years) dominated by the eight largest companies in the industry, known as the Majors (Paramount, MGM, Twentieth Century-Fox, Warner Brothers, and RKO) and the Minors (Universal, Columbia, and United Artists). Vertically integrated, the Majors owned production studios, international distribution operations, and theater chains. The Minors owned production and distribution facilities, but few or no exhibition outlets. Vertical integration made enforcing compliance easier.

Second, the Catholic National Legion of Decency, also founded in 1934, instituted a rating system to advise Catholics on the propriety of films. Ratings ranged from A (morally unobjectionable) to B (morally objectionable in part) to C (condemned), the latter forbidding Catholics to see a film. Studios feared Catholic boycotts if their films did not abide by the norms of the Code. The PCA and the Legion did not always see eye to eye in their evaluation of films, but the threat of boycotts by Catholics or other groups led to a prevalent belief that any film released without a Seal of Approval could not be profitable.

Third, and lastly, Hays instigated a number of changes to increase the effectiveness of the Code. To avoid the pitfalls of its predecessor, the PCA only gave its Seal of Approval to films that abided by the conservative normative standards stipulated in the Code. It could levy a $25,000 fine on any MPPDA member that sold, produced, or distributed a film without a Seal, which members agreed not to do. Producers had to submit screenplays to the PCA board for approval before the studios began production and films for final approval, with the PCA often exacting editorial changes at each step of production. If a studio adapted a literary work considered too sexy for the screen, it had to change the title, edit out the offensive material, and leave out references to the original in advertising. For example, Samuel Goldwyn released Lillian Hellman's Broadway play *The Children's Hour* as *These Three* (1936) and, most importantly, without the play's references to lesbianism.

Although the PCA and the studios managed to keep most of their disagreements to themselves until the 1940s, numerous films sparked considerable debates. The PCA condemned Jane Russell's cleavage in Howard Hughes's *The Outlaw* (1943). Re-released in 1946, *The Outlaw* went on to become a box office success without a PCA Seal of Approval or the blessings of the Legion of Decency and despite being banned in New York City. The Code was open to interpretation since its restrictions were quite general, and when the PCA and filmmakers disagreed, each side often interpreted the Code to its own advantage. When studio executives and the PCA negotiated snippets of dialogue, settings, or editing, the studios' interpretations sometimes prevailed, but more often the PCA's interpretation prevailed. Studios assigned the responsibility of conforming to or evading Code restrictions to writers, editors, and directors.

Filmmakers frequently worked around the Code by manipulating it. As a result, an unintended consequence of the Code was the institutionalization of ambiguity in the representation of nudity and sex. According to screenwriter Ben Hecht, writing a screenplay was a juggling act that included "censors to be outwitted."[10] As Lea Jacobs has shown, the PCA paid close attention to numerous filmic details, prohibiting scenery that explicitly established a brothel, narrative cues edited to imply adultery, or allusions and double entendres in dialogue to off-screen transgressive sexual practices.[11] Ambiguity aside, under Hays and Breen's leadership the conservative sexual norms embedded in the Code prevailed in popular films until the mid-1940s.

In 1945, Eric Johnston replaced Hays as president of the MPPDA, now renamed the Motion Picture Association of America (MPAA). Johnston, more moderate than Hays, would head the MPAA until his death in 1963. Although Breen still headed the PCA, the PCA relaxed its standards. For example, in David Selznick's *Duel in the Sun* (1946), Pearl Chavez (Jennifer Jones) watches in horror as her father (Herbert Marshall) shoots her mother (Tilly Losch) and the man she has taken to their bedroom. The film makes clear this was hardly the first time Pearl's mother entertained a caller. *Gilda* (1946)—as did numerous *film noirs*—insinuated adultery and homosexuality.

Johnston's appointment coalesced with several developments during the early years of the Cold War that weakened enforcement of the Code. In 1948, the U.S. Supreme Court handed down a ruling that was a serious blow to the industry structure that had secured compliance with the Code. *U.S. v. Paramount Pictures, Inc.* forced MPAA member companies to divest themselves of their theaters; to cease joint ownership of theaters and theater pooling agreements; and to end the practices of clearances and runs, block-booking, formula deals, master agreements, price-fixing, and discrimination between distributors.[12] Besides coming as a tremendous financial blow to MPAA member companies, the decision meant the PCA could not as effectively enforce the Code since MPAA members no longer monopolized first-run theaters and theater chains. Vertical integration would take the Code with it to its grave.

Four years after the *Paramount* decision, the Supreme Court provided the Majors and Minors with another impetus to circumvent the PCA: motion pictures finally received First Amendment protection in *Burstyn*.[13] Joseph Burstyn, a motion picture distributor and exhibitor, screened the Italian import *The Miracle* (*Il Miracolo*; 1948), the story of an unwed young peasant girl, Nanni (Anna Magnani), who is pregnant with a child she believes is a second Christ. Burstyn had his license to exhibit revoked after the New York Board of Regents (the state's censorship authority) had the film reviewed by a three-judge panel that found it to be "sacrilegious." Burstyn appealed, arguing the statute violated his First Amendment right to freedom of expression. The Court ruled unconstitutional the New York statute authorizing the state censorship board to deny a license to exhibit any film that, in whole or in part, was "obscene, indecent, immoral, inhuman, sacrilegious, or ... of such a character that its exhibition would tend to corrupt morals or incite to crime." The Court determined that films constituted "a significant medium for the communication of ideas."[14] The Court had created a legal opening through which nudity and sex would gradually enter the mainstream of American cinema. By reducing the threat of censorship, it had given filmmakers less reason to comply with the Code. Around the same time, studios received economic incentives to take the Code less seriously.

At United Artists in 1951, New York business executives Robert Benjamin and Arthur Krim took over the film company and brought in independent stars, directors, and producers to make movies. Otto Preminger effectively challenged the power of both the PCA and the National Legion of Decency in *The Moon Is Blue* (1953). The PCA denied the film a Seal and the National Legion of Decency gave it the dreaded "C" rating because the script had contained the words *seduce*, *pregnant*, and *virgin*. United Artists released the film without a Seal believing there was an audience for "mature" films that went beyond the Code. The Kansas State Board of Review banned the film because it found "Sex theme throughout, too frank bedroom dialogue: many sexy words; both dialogue and action have sex as their theme."[15] The United States Supreme Court reversed the decision.

In 1954, Geoffrey Shurlock replaced Joseph Breen as the head of the PCA. Shurlock confronted studios emboldened by liberal courts and greater use of independent directors who resorted less and less to ambiguity and began to challenge the Code more directly. Furthermore, the Majors were losing market share to a new medium. As Americans moved to the suburbs in the 1950s, television quickly overtook Hollywood's position as the largest provider of entertainment in the United States. Theaters began closing. The industry reduced the number of films produced annually from around four hundred to two hundred. They released stars from their contracts and cut back on star-building publicity campaigns. These measures proved insufficient, so the studios tried to regain market share by introducing wide-screen formats to differentiate motion pictures from television.

Because indecency laws for broadcasting were stricter than the Code, studios could also differentiate their product by marketing some films as *mature* or for adults. The Majors adopted the *Adults Only* marketing ploy in the late 1950s and early 1960s, both as a warning and as an enticement on their lobby posters for mature films. Equating explicit sexual representations with maturity had been a common high culture motif in public discourse, together with the label *sophisticated*. Film reviewers and social commentators consistently ascribed films that emphasized sexual revelations and self-disclosure with such qualities as being *adult, mature, frank,* or *candid*. These qualities were associated with greater realism and perceived links between maturity, tolerance, sophistication, and sexuality. In *Indiscretion of an American Wife* (1953), starring Montgomery Clift and Jennifer Jones, an American woman has an adulterous affair. *Indiscreet* (1958), with Cary Grant and Ingrid Bergman, mocked the injunction against adultery. Saucy comedies like Billy Wilder's *Some Like It Hot* (1959) included cross-dressing and hints of homosexuality.

Hollywood found the material for mature films by buying the rights to bestsellers with relatively explicit treatment of sexual themes. Titles included James Jones's *From Here to Eternity* (1951), which was purchased by Columbia and directed by Fred Zinnemann (1953). Grace Metalious's *Peyton Place* (1956) was brought to the screen by Twentieth Century-Fox (1957). Columbia produced Robert Traver's story of a man who commits murder to avenge a rape, *Anatomy of a Murder* (1958), directed by Otto Preminger (1959). Broadway proved to be a particularly rich vein. The works of Tennessee Williams were especially important for bringing sex into Hollywood film. Williams's plays adapted to the silver screen include *A Streetcar Named Desire* (1951), *The Rose Tattoo* (1955), *Cat on a Hot Tin Roof* (1958), and *Suddenly, Last Summer* (1959).

The studios invariably diluted the Broadway versions for the big screen, but faced with a shrinking market, studios pushed the limits of ambiguity, releasing films only marginally acceptable to the PCA. The introduction of mature themes into film could only occur at the expense of reopening fissures within the industry. The maturity of films increased proportionally to the decline in the effectiveness of the Code. In 1956, the PCA revised the Code to permit other formerly taboo topics: prostitution, abortion, miscegenation, and some mild profanity.

Throughout the decade, films began to treat sexuality more directly, but changes within Hollywood were neither unidirectional nor unimpeded, a development affected by growing market diversification. Studios targeted age-segmented markets. They looked to the youth market since parents tended to stay home and watch television. *A Place in the Sun* (1951), starring Montgomery Clift as George Eastman and Elizabeth Taylor as Angela Vickers, was popular with young audiences. The film skirted on the edges of the Code. Eastman is involved in a love triangle with Vickers before he gets his girlfriend Alice Tripp (Shelley Winters) pregnant. The youth market became even more attractive after the box office success of *The Wild One* (1954), starring Marlon Brando, and *The Blackboard Jungle* (1955), starring rock-n-roll.

The success studios enjoyed from targeting age-segmented markets would continue through the early 1960s and eventually help usher in greater aesthetic plurality within Hollywood films by softening the industry's objection to an age-based classification rating system to replace the Code. The Legion of Decency adopted an age-based rating system in 1957, changing its categories to classify films as acceptable for adults or for adults and adolescents.

The studios undercut the Code further with another form of market segmentation. They began to produce and distribute different versions of the same film for domestic and international release. Nudity in European releases was left out of American releases. For example, United Artists released two versions of *The Ambassador's Daughter* (1956). In one scene, the two main characters Joan (Olivia de Havilland) and Danny (John Forsythe) watch a Parisian nightclub revue perform brassiered in the American version and topless in the European. Hollywood studios took advantage of overseas markets that allowed them to include nudity and sex in a way that would have been illegal in some jurisdictions in the United States.

While not pushing the boundaries as far in their domestic releases, studios nonetheless enjoyed more freedom of expression by the end of the 1950s than they had since the introduction of the Code. The success of films distributed without PCA Seals or with Legion "C" ratings convinced filmmakers that there was a divergence between the attitudes and values of censors and the general public, a view that had also led directors to push the envelope between 1930 and 1934.

As the 1960s began, filmmakers poked more holes through the Code. In the opening sequence of *Psycho* (1960), Alfred Hitchcock wryly established the illicit nature of their tryst through images and dialogue. The camera intrudes on the privacy of a Phoenix, Arizona, motel room to find Marion Crane (Janet Leigh) in her bra and half-slip together with her shirtless lover, Sam Loomis (John Gavin). Wanting to bring their relationship from the shadows, Marion chides Sam, "You make respectability sound disrespectful." Sam's perspective on respectability hinted at a value pluralism that was becoming visible, not least in movies. Divorced, Sam says he has "heard of married couples who deliberately spend an occasional night in a cheap hotel." The sanctity of marriage and the family enshrined by the Code was absent in the cosmos of *Psycho* even if a hotel would be Marion's doom when Norman Bates (Anthony Perkins) transformed from mild hotel clerk to a homicidal transvestite replica of his mother. By tying Bates's murderous impulses to his confused sexual identity, the film strained the Code.

On October 3, 1961, the MPAA again revised the Production Code and dropped the ban against homosexuality and other nonnormative sexual behaviors. The revised Code reflected the PCA's concession to the growing visibility of marginal sexuality in other media. The MPAA conceded that "[i]n keeping with the culture, the mores and values of our time, homosexuality and other sexual aberrations may now be treated with care, discretion and restraint."[16] Hollywood wasted no time in exploring the new boundaries. In December, United Artists, which had pressured the MPAA to revise the Code, released *The Children's Hour* (1961), a remake of *These Three* that retained the play's lesbianism. *Advise and Consent* (1962) represented male homosexuality while Stanley Kubrick's *Lolita* (1962) charted the pedophiliac relationship of a middle-aged man and a fifteen-year-old girl. In 1965, *Sylvia* starred Carroll Baker as a woman who endures rape and prostitution. Studios included nudity during the production stage of several films, including *Splendor in the Grass* (1961), *Of Human Bondage* (1964), and *The Carpetbaggers* (1964), but the PCA and the Legion managed to apply enough pressure to keep the scenes out of the final prints.

In 1965, *The Pawnbroker*, directed by Sidney Lumet, a veteran of stage direction and of TV kitchen-sink dramas in the 1950s, included a scene with female nudity. Jesus Ortiz (Jaime Sánchez), who works for Sol Nazerman (Rod Steiger), the pawnbroker of the film's title, needs money. His girlfriend (Thelma Oliver), a prostitute, visits Nazerman, a survivor of the Holocaust, one day when he is alone in the shop. She tells him, "I'm good, pawnbroker. I'm real good. I've done things you haven't even dreamed about before. Just twenty dollars more. I'll make you happy, like you never know." He sits down in front of her with a hand to his face. She is framed with bare shoulders in a medium shot, from a slightly low angle. Her facial expression shows pride at her appearance. Her bare breasts trigger Nazerman's memory of the tragic fate of his wife Ruth (Linda Geiser) at the hands of Nazi rapists. As she says "look," a series of clips shift between close-ups of her, the pawnbroker, and his flashbacks, including flashbacks of Ruth topless, although they are very brief. Nazerman then has a lengthy flashback to the concentration camp during which a German soldier asks, "Willst du was sehen?" (Do you want to see?), which can be read literally in terms of the cruelty Nazerman is forced to witness and metaphorically—since it parallels the prostitute's question— as a question to the audience in viewing the sexual as traumatic. The flashback makes clear that after this experience sex has become dark and evil for Nazerman. He snaps back to the present, covers the young woman with her raincoat, and gives her a twenty-dollar bill. During the production phase of *The Pawnbroker*, Geoffrey Shurlock had told Ely Landau that nudity would "call forth a great amount of protest from pressure groups."[17] Nonetheless, the scene was not cut, and *The Pawnbroker* was released with both a Seal and nudity, but only after the PCA's Review Board overturned the PCA's denial. Allowing nudity in *The Pawnbroker* was tantamount to a revision of the Production Code. It signaled the industry's recognition of the numerous currents in filmmaking with which Hollywood filmmakers had to compete.

While the revisions to the Code reflected an awareness of the fluctuations of the normative boundaries of nudity and sex within commercial entertainment, they also exposed the diminished power of the PCA to enforce the Code. The PCA had been weakened further in 1963, when Ralph Hetzel became interim president of the MPAA following Eric Johnston's death. The PCA's grip on studios was further loosened by changes in the ownership within the industry, which further modified the enforceability of the Code. MCA (Music Corporation of America) acquired Universal Pictures when it acquired controlling interest in Decca (which had overtaken Universal in 1952) in 1962. Gulf & Western Industries bought Paramount Pictures in 1966. In 1967, Seven Arts Productions, Ltd. bought Warner Brothers, which was sold to Kinney National Services, Inc. in 1969, becoming part of Warner Communication, Inc., Kinney's entertainment subsidiary. Transamerica Corporation bought United Artists in 1967. Kirk Kerkorian acquired the majority of stocks in MGM in 1968. Changes in ownership had diminished the ability of the MPAA to regulate film through the Production Code. As Mike Frankovich told the *New York Times* upon becoming head of Columbia in 1964, he and other studio chiefs had become "expendable" and "obsolete."[18] Now, greater power was concentrated in the hands of directors, a shift that worried Shurlock since directors tended to approach it even more capriciously than producers. The corporations increased their overseas production and drew on international financing, both of which furthered film production from regulators.

It was not necessary to confer with the new executives at the apex of the industry to confirm the datedness of the Code or to demonstrate that conservative norms were losing strength within the industry. In Los Angeles, a "Methodist bishop compared the rules of the Code to 'a maiden aunt's fussy regulations,'" write Leonard J. Leff and Jerold Simmons, who note that even Walt Disney resigned from the MPAA, seeing "the group as an unneeded anticensorship lobby."[19] Producers, directors, screenwriters, cinematographers, and others involved in film production were well aware of the transformations in censorship laws brought on by the courts largely through changes in obscenity law. Those changes would ultimately relegate censorship of Hollywood films to the past and also lead to a greater presence of sex in American film, from Hollywood to pornography.

Obscenity Law

Until 1957, obscenity was not a constitutional issue. There had been antiobscenity laws such as that enacted in Massachusetts in 1712, making it a criminal offense "to publish 'any filthy, obscene, or profane song, pamphlet, libel or mock sermon.'"[20] The major legal precedent for American obscenity doctrine in the nineteenth and early twentieth century was an English case, *Regina v. Hicklin* from 1868.[21] *Hicklin* guided lower courts throughout the United States since there was no Supreme Court precedent.

On April 22, 1957, the Supreme Court heard the appeal of Samuel Roth, a New York book, magazine, and photograph publisher and seller charged with violating the Comstock Act. Roth's appeal, which failed, took up the constitutionality of obscenity for the first time. Justice William J. Brennan wrote the Court's opinion. *Roth* established a new set of standards for determining whether material was obscene or not, moving American obscenity doctrine beyond the criteria established by *Hicklin*. To classify certain representations of nudity and sex as beyond First Amendment protection, Justice Brennan needed to define *obscenity*. His definition bridged the intrapersonal (appeal to prurient interest), the social (contemporary community standards), and the textual (the dominant theme of the material taken as a whole). Drawing on *Ulysses* (1933), Justice Brennan concluded that the "standard for judging obscenity . . . is whether, to the average person, applying contemporary community standards, the dominant theme of the material, taken as a whole, appeals to prurient interest."[22]

The ruling set two conflicting standards. Upholding federal and state obscenity legislation, *Roth* sustained the division of protected and unprotected expression by ruling that obscenity was unprotected by the First Amendment. Because it had no social value, obscene material did not fulfill the aims of freedom of thought and expression in a democratic society. Nonetheless, *Roth* created a more permissive environment for the production, distribution, and consumption of sex in film (as well as magazines and books) by ruling that "sex and obscenity are not synonymous." Sex, the Court admitted, was a legitimate topic for literary and scientific works, and sex itself was "one of the vital problems of human interest and public concern."[23] This meant that the First Amendment protected at least *some* representations of nudity and sex. Confusion about obscenity law led the Court to modify *Roth* repeatedly.

First, it added the criterion of *patent offensiveness*. Ruling on the alleged obscenity of three gay magazines *MANual, Trim,* and *Grecian Guild Pictorial*, the Court found the magazines could not "be deemed so offensive on their face as to affront current community standards of decency—a quality that we shall hereafter refer to as 'patent offensiveness.'"[24] The Court formally added the requirement that materials offend *current* standards in *Jacobellis* (1964), which also modified the social importance requirement. By rephrasing it as "utterly without redeeming social importance," the Court made it more difficult for courts to apply it. The justices often seemed mystified by obscenity. In a brief concurring opinion, in reference to the alleged obscenity of Louis Malle's *The Lovers* (*Les Amants*; 1959; France), Justice Potter Stewart offered his famous nondefinition: "I shall not today attempt further to define the kinds of material I understand to be embraced within that shorthand description; and perhaps I could never succeed in intelligibly doing so. But I know it when I see it, and the motion picture involved in this case is not that."[25] None of the justices commented on the implied cunnilingus in the film, although Chief Justice Earl Warren, in dissent, pointed out that the advertising for the film had promoted its sexual content: "The frankest love scenes yet seen on film."

In 1966, in *Memoirs*, the Supreme Court reaffirmed *Jacobellis*'s definition of obscenity.[26] Justice Douglas concurred with the plurality opinion in *Memoirs* in 1966, but he assailed media effects theories about the negative social consequences of sexual materials, which he called "the most frequently assigned justification for censorship." In his view, any purported relationship between sexual materials and social behavior remained unproven. He championed an expansive liberal position that contrasted with the restrictive position of the conservative: "The censor is always quick to justify his function in terms that are protective of society. But the First Amendment, written in terms that are absolute, deprives the States of any power to pass on the value, the propriety, or the morality of a particular expression."[27] By the mid 1960s, liberals articulated their desire to take the power of passing judgment on expression away from social institutions and majorities and place it in the hands of consenting adults. Hollywood took note and the battle over expression on American movie screens entered a new phase.

2

Shifting Boundaries

Standard approaches to film history begin with the Production Code. To grasp fully the history of sex in American cinema, though, it is necessary to look beyond mainstream films to genres that existed beyond and challenged the shifting boundaries of film regulation: sexploitation, pornography, European imports, and American underground cinema. Each of these genres provided historical antecedents to the nudity and sex that appeared in Hollywood movies in the 1960s and 1970s. Both the movies and the audiences may have been marginal, but the sheer existence of both the production side—from producers and directors to the actors and gaffers—and reception side—the audiences—for these genres evinces a plurality in cultural tastes in the United States that existed long before their greater visibility in the 1960s. Given that these movies either always (pornography) or often dealt with sex, it seems fair to conclude that these audiences also held a plurality of sexual values.

SEXPLOITATION

The Production Code's mid-1960s demise supposedly signaled a revolution in nudity and sex in American cinema. Yet entrepreneurs and small independents from Ivan Abramson to Louis Sonney had produced, distributed, and exhibited movies with potentially illegal representations of nudity and sex acts since the early years of motion pictures despite official sanctions. As far as these maverick producers were concerned, the regulations of the Production Code and censorship boards guaranteed them a market vacuum they were happy to fill.

To profit from that void, *celluloid gypsies* like Sonney, Dwain Esper, Kroger Babb, and others with backgrounds in carnivals and burlesque, traveled the back roads and small towns across the country during the 1930s and 1940s, renting run-down theaters or putting up tents. During the 1950s, drive-ins joined road shows and carnivals as an outlet for their sexploitation fare, which grew out of the sex hygiene and nudist films of earlier decades.

As early as the 1880s but with renewed vigor during the years surrounding World War I, Americans were quite concerned with what was then called *social hygiene*, not least the spread of venereal diseases by returning veterans. Capitalizing on the publicity generated by health campaigns as well as the growth of sexual education courses in schools, filmmakers like Ivan Abramson produced movies such as *Enlighten Thy Daughter* (1917) about the "facts of life," a phrase rich in its contradictions. While official America worked tirelessly to repress the sexual from the public sphere and from the nonmarital private sphere, one of modernity's major social developments was an augmented faith in and demand for scientific knowledge. Sexploitation filmmakers incorporated this desire to know into their marketing campaigns as their movies often promised viewers knowledge and insights into behavior otherwise concealed. Thus early nudist films like Bryan Foy's *Elysia* (1933) purported to inform viewers about an alternative lifestyle and its ramifications for health at a real Californian nudist club, Elysian Fields, and staring Constance Allan (as Prudence Kent), a nudist Foy recruited from the club. Although *The Unashamed* (1938) included sex in its story line, most nudist films were asexual, exploiting the notion of informing viewers. Later sexploitation filmmakers honed genre and promotional conventions that allowed them to partially adhere to and partially transgress the Code's sex norms as well as the legal norms enforced by censorship boards, the police, and the courts.

By manipulating genre conventions, filmmakers like J. D. Kendis could ostensibly adhere to the Code and remain near or within the boundaries of the law. They borrowed traditional elements of plot and dialogue from melodrama to construct a conservative message that the attitudes and conduct on the screen were reprehensible. They were also duplicitous in their claims to educate viewers. Narratives were often driven forward by investigations by law officers or health care officials, some of which were modeled by contemporary national or state campaigns against various forms of crime. The investigator's penetration into an underworld of vice provided narrative motivation for showing what otherwise went unseen in public. At the same time, the films breached those same conservative norms by representing nudity and sex acts ranging from a seduction scene to simulated sexual intercourse. Sexploitation filmmakers placed females in situations, such as a backstage changing room or a bedroom that warranted undressing, but they went further than the PCA would have ever permitted. Employing a variety of delaying ruses, the characters slowly removed articles of clothing until only a final layer separated the viewer from the titillation promised in the trailers or on the posters. Then, there would be a cut to the next scene, and the narrative would again begin raising viewer expectations.

Hucksters that they were, sexploitation distributors such as K. Lee Williams and Albert Dezel understood the importance of drawing patrons into the theaters with vaguely concealed promises of violating American sex norms. Lurid titles such as *Sins of Love* (1932), *Road to Ruin* (1934), *Slaves in Bondage* (1937), and *Human Wreckage* (1938) blended promises of disclosure with moral disdain. Lobby cards depicted women with fallen straps, racy scenes from the movie, taglines such as "Can a Beautiful Model Stay Pure?" for *Secrets of a Model* (1940). Posters virtually shouted "Adults Only!" Lobby posters were laden with drawings of women in torn dresses or their underwear captioned by rhetoric describing conduct that was "shocking" or a "story" that "revealed the truth" of "wild parties" and "unreleased passions" that ended in "shame," "horror," or "despair" for the guilty parties. Trailers and other promotional materials frequently used the same rhetoric of exposure, telling of "exposés," that revealed what others only "whispered about."

The adherence/transgression dichotomy formed the basis of the sexploitation genre and market. Besides being a marketing ploy, a highly moral message about actual (or popularly feared) social problems such as prostitution, sexually transmitted diseases, or unwed mothers sometimes helped the filmmakers circumvent censorship or arrest. Although the Supreme Court had castigated motion pictures in 1915, censorship was never absolute. Censors decided on a film-by-film basis whether any particular film actually warned against *moral depravity*, as explicitly stated in a voice-over or through the punishment of characters that had sex, or whether it encouraged moral depravity, despite explicit admonitions. The legal room for maneuver could quickly vanish; sexploitation filmmakers worked dangerously, as they balanced promising too much and delivering too little.

Other times sexploitation filmmakers distributed and exhibited material that no message could redeem in order to secure their market position. Balancing the threats from potentially harsh censors or disgruntled audiences, they often resorted to subterfuge. They would supply exhibitors with two copies of a film, one "cold" and the other "hot," the former shown to local officials, the latter to customers. In some markets where audiences became recalcitrant if teased too long or too often, distributors went even further. They would supply the exhibitor with an extra reel, which usually included nudity, called the *square-up reel*. This tactic involved considerable legal risks.

Sexploitation was far from a strictly small-town phenomenon. In cities that did not ban them, sexploitation movies were mainly exhibited in run-down theaters called *grind houses*. Because skid rows supplied most of the urban audience, media accounts often equated the audience for sexploitation movies with white male, lower-class skid row loners and misfits. This marginal, impoverished urban space and its marginal inhabitants buffered sexploitation filmmakers from the constant threat of legal prosecution and ensured that their movies attracted less attention. Filmmakers and audiences also took advantage of inconsistency in the laws. Some states and cities either edited out offending scenes or banned films completely, but viewers who wanted more explicit material could cross state lines into states where the movies could be screened unedited since not all communities had censorship boards or obscenity laws. For example, residents of Philadelphia could drive across the Delaware River into Camden, New Jersey, and watch movies that would have been cut or banned in Pennsylvania.

Sexploitation filmmakers were emboldened by a court case involving the 1954 nudist-camp film *Garden of Eden*, shot in color by Boris Kaufman, who had recently been the cinematographer on Columbia's *On the Waterfront* (1954). In the *Garden of Eden*, a young woman, Susan Lattimore (Jamie O'Hara), becomes involved in the nudist lifestyle after the death of her husband. Her conservative father-in-law, Jay Lattimore (R. G. Armstrong), adopts the lifestyle as well after first attempting to dissuade her. The film had the approval of the American Sunbathing Association, and although it had been screened in over thirty states, the film encountered censorship problems in some states, including New York, where censors ruled it obscene and denied it a license.

The case ended up in the New York Court of Appeals in 1957 where Judge Charles S. Desmond, citing *Roth*, ruled the film could not "lawfully be banned since it [was] not obscene in the sense in which the law has used that term for centuries.... Nothing sexually impure or filthy is shown or suggested ... and so there is no legal basis for censorship." The *Garden of Eden* decision effectively undermined the morality of the Production Code and narrowed the scope of what constituted obscenity. In distinguishing between "obscenity, real, serious" and obscenity "imagined or puritanically exaggerated," Judge Desmond contributed significantly to a widening chasm in organizations regulation film.[1] On one side, the MPAA, the National Legion of Decency, and censorship boards persisted in enforcing the conservative morality that still predominated. On the other side, the Warren Court and numerous lower courts increasingly gave priority to liberal conceptions of freedom of expression over conservative community standards.

A wave of nudist-camp films came after the *Garden of Eden* decision. Doris Wishman rode the nudist-camp wave, producing *Hideout in the Sun* (1960), *Diary of a Nudist* (1961), *Nude on the Moon* (1962), and *Gentlemen Prefer Nature Girls* (1963). Herschell Gordon Lewis filmed a series of nudist-camp films in Florida, such as *Daughter of the Sun* (1962) and *Nature's Playmates* (1962). The production of a nudist-camp film was relatively simple and inexpensive. The movies were either shot on outdoor locations with models in the roles of nudists or compiled from footage of real nudists at real nudist colonies or a combination of the two approaches. The nudist-camp theme provided sexploitation filmmakers with a pretext for their on-screen nudity. Friedman, Lewis, Wishman, and others complied with unwritten genre conventions that kept their movies within range of the shifting legal boundaries of protected expression. These filmic conventions permitted showing women's breasts and buttocks on-screen, but genitals were concealed, usually by objects typical of the diegetic world of the nudist camp such as volley and beach balls, towels, and guitars.

Even before nudist-camp films ebbed in popularity, the *nudie-cutie* appeared with better-constructed story lines than nudist-camp films and promptly dominated the sexploitation circuit. One of the most innovative and successful practitioners of the nudie-cutie genre was Russ Meyer. A successful *Playboy* photographer, Meyer began working in the late 1950s with the owner of the El Rey Burlesque Theater in Oakland, Pete DeCenzie, who had supplied him with contacts to burlesque dancers willing to be models. It proved to be an opportune moment. The Supreme Court had recently handed down its *Roth* decision. The door to nudity and sex in marginal films was opening as censorship boards and courts struggled to interpret the Supreme Court's position on obscenity. In this climate of legal uncertainty, Meyer and DeCenzie released a low-budget sex comedy entitled *The Immoral Mr. Teas* (1959).

The female nudity in *The Immoral Mr. Teas*—promoted as "A French Comedy for Unashamed Adults"—remained easily within the guidelines established by *Roth*, hardly appealing to the prurient interest of the average person or offending national community standards. The only sex in *The Immoral Mr. Teas* was an involuntary voyeurism on the part of the protagonist, a hapless Mr. Teas (Bill Teas), who suffers a side effect from a dental operation that causes him to see nude females, a condition he tries unsuccessfully to have corrected. As a comedy, *The Immoral Mr. Teas* made nudity the punch line of a joke.

Meyer and DeCenzie distributed the film on the regular grind house circuit, where it encountered few difficulties with local censors. To their astonishment, it eventually played in art house theaters. In its January 1960 review of the film, the *Los Angeles Times* described the mainstreaming of the audience for sexploitation: "Last Friday evening the Peep

Show finally moved across the tracks from Main Street. And, to judge by the concourse of solid-looking citizens, presumably all aged 18 or over, the show is going to be a great success."[2] With new exhibition outlets open to it and with the attention of the press, the film surprisingly grossed $1,000,000. Meyer and others moved into the art house and college circuits that European filmmakers had utilized during the late 1950s. The success of *The Immoral Mr. Teas* brought sexploitation out of the shadows of its grind house existence. The tolerance buoyed by the popularity of foreign movies and Supreme Court rulings compensated for the loss of the protective cocoon of skid row areas and inconsistent enforcement of obscenity laws.

Meyer's success sparked imitations such as *The Adventures of Lucky Pierre* (1961), *The House on Bare Mountain* (1962), and *Pardon My Brush* (1964). Nudie-cuties were invariably low-budget copies of *The Immoral Mr. Teas*, which had found a way to represent nudity on-screen in a manner that got past censors and courts if not the PCA. Each of these movies followed Meyer's formula (derived from the nudist-camp genre) of providing ample long and medium shots of female breasts and bottoms. The voyeuristic motivation for the nudity in the film was also similar but went further: the females were nude in locations and engaging in actions that "justified" their nudity—they were showering, changing clothes in their bedrooms, sunbathing or skinny-dipping, or some other nonsexual situation that required nudity or partial nudity.

Eventually, nudie-cuties declined in popularity, so Meyer and marginal filmmakers such as Doris Wishman, David F. Friedman, and Herschell Gordon Lewis tried a different approach. They simply abandoned comedy and returned to the traditional ambivalence of the sexploitation genre—partially adhering to while still transgressing conservative moral codes. By the middle of the 1960s, the Supreme Court had practically institutionalized this approach by allowing "redeeming social importance" as a way to avoid an obscenity conviction. So voice-overs intoned excerpts from literary works or Bach played on the soundtrack or "scientists" or "psychologists" explained sexual aberrations, any narrative device that might give a film at least a hint of redeeming social worth. The burden of proving a lack of redeeming social importance fell upon prosecutors, who had to convince juries that a work lacked *any* redeeming social importance.

Sensing that it had become more difficult to enforce censorship laws, sexploitation filmmakers began featuring simulated sex in their movies. Nonetheless, just as their predecessors had done in the 1930s, sexploitation filmmakers in the middle-to-late 1960s framed sexual deviance or perversion in a context governed by a strict conservative moral code to avoid antagonizing local law officials or state censorship boards that might ban the film outright, even in the increasingly liberal social climate. They continued to integrate dialogue, plot developments, or voice-overs to claim or imply the vileness of the sex depicted in the film. Narrators were invariably shocked and disgusted by sex, and sexually active characters were often punished, especially if they were female. In three new subgenres—*roughies*, *kinkies*, and *ghoulies*—punishment became more violent and central to the films' story lines.

In roughies, titles such as *The Defilers* (1965), *Bad Girls Go to Hell* (1965), and *Hot Spur* (1968) raised viewers' expectations that they would see some combination of sex, violence, and moral degeneracy. Russ Meyer's *Lorna* (1964) was a typical roughie. A "Man of God" (played by longtime Western character actor James Griffith) appears at the film's start, its conclusion, and various points in-between, and intones that one must pay for one's sins. His admonitions serve to explain the death of the title character (played by a Las Vegas dancer named Lorna Maitland) at the hands of her husband, Jim (James Rucker). Coming home early from work, Jim discovers his wife with an escaped convict (Mark Bradley), whose fatal fling with Lorna had begun as a rape before she "gave in" and "enjoyed" the forced sex and took him home with her. A fight ensues, and the convict and Lorna (accidentally) are killed. Its pretense to a moral message notwithstanding, *Lorna* was banned, but the Maryland Court of Appeals overturned the ban in 1965.[3]

Parallel with the roughies was the development of a similar subgenre, the *kinkies*, which emphasized nudity and deviant sex. As did the roughies, the kinkies nearly always presented sadomasochism, lesbianism, and castration as being morally wrong or as contemporary social problems. They echoed the concerns—and negative characterizations of suburbia—that had filled the media for over a decade. For every article that championed the nuclear family and its virtues, there seemed to be one inventorying its sexual deviations, ranging from adultery to wife swapping to prostitution rings. Stories from the media became fodder for the sexploitation branch.

Kinkies modified the traditional sexploitation story of the perils of an innocent country girl lost and debauched in the city by portraying suburbia as a community that generated social pathologies. In *Sin in the Suburbs* (1964), lesbianism and a sex club drives its members to alcoholism and the brink of insanity because of feelings of guilt. *One Shocking Moment* (1965) features bisexual seduction, infidelity, and masochism, as well as attempted rape. *The Swap and How They Make It* (1966) is structured around the activities of a middle-class wife-swapping club that extend beyond infidelity to lesbianism and incest. *Suburban Confidential* (1966) tells the story of a psychiatrist opening the files of housewife patients and exposing confidential private information to the viewer, including details about lesbianism, rape, fetishism, and transvestitism.

While some filmmakers sought greater realism, others in the sexploitation market combined the sexual violence of roughies and the sexual aberrations of kinkies with the violence and gore of horror movies such as Roger Corman's *A Bucket of Blood* (1959). Knives, meat cleavers, and implements of torture cluttered the mise-en-scène of these movies. Filmmakers combined depictions of murder and blood with nudity and sex to achieve their narrative (and marketing) goals and in the process created the *ghoulie* subgenre. In these forerunners to the slasher film, women were the victims of extremely violent sexual abuse and often murdered. David F. Friedman and Herschell Gordon Lewis made the first ghoulie, *Blood Feast* (1963), the initial entry in Lewis's "Gore Trilogy," which also included *Color Me Blood Red* (1964) and *Two Thousand Maniacs* (1964). Russ Meyer contributed with *Faster, Pussycat! Kill! Kill!* (1966). While their audiences remained relatively small, they were larger and more similar to Hollywood's productions than anytime in their history, not least because of screenings in drive-ins.

PORNOGRAPHY

Pornographers, with some exceptions when pornography first became visible in public, did not misrepresent the conservative norms underlying the Production Code and censorship laws as had Hollywood or sexploitation filmmakers to avoid censorship. Pornography, understood here as films that portray explicit sexual behavior that is not simulated, pushed the boundaries between the imaginative and real in sexuality further than any other film genre. Until the 1970s, pornographic movies would invariably be judged obscene if the filmmaker, distributor, or exhibitor were prosecuted.

Although pornography first became pervasive in public in the late 1960s and early 1970s, the genre itself and its market are as old as the film medium. Indeed, photographs of nudes and sex acts predated cinema. Historians date pornographic photographs to around the middle of the nineteenth century. Explicit sex had been recorded on film for commercial purposes in the United States for decades when it caught the nation's attention in the 1960s and 1970s. Already at the beginning of the century when the earliest pornographic movies were produced, many in Argentina, their narrative line was firmly established. One of the oldest extant American pornographic movies is *A Free Ride* (or *A Grass Sandwich*) from around 1915. In the film, two women and a man who are driving in the countryside stop so the man can urinate. The women become sexually excited upon viewing the man relieve himself. He then watches the two women urinate and then has sexual intercourse with each of them (implying the paraphilia *urolagnia*). The film then ends. Narratives in stag films were more one-dimensional than those of sexploitation movies, since there was little or no narrative development, not least because the vast majority of stag films were one-reelers that lasted only a few minutes. If there was a narrative, it developed quickly and moved solely toward the explicit sex, which invariably required little more than the sight of the body to spark sexual desire.

The films were "primarily the work of what we might call the professional purveyors of sex—that is, houses of prostitution, independent prostitutes, pimps, and the like" and were accordingly most often shot in "brothels or cheap hotels or motels."[4] Based on his extensive viewing of stag films, Frank Hoffmann surmised that the actresses were prostitutes. Their ages ranged from young to late thirties or early forties, and they ranged in appearance from attractive to homely. The actors, their faces often concealed by a disguise or mask, were usually older than their female counterparts. Although the movies were tailored to the sexual predilections of a heterosexual male audience, that audience's preferences went beyond heterosexual sex. The titles were often indicative: *The Pick Up* (1923) and *The Casting Couch* (1924) suggest what little plot there might be to create a context for having sex, while *Wonders of the Unseen World* (1927) hinted at the illicitness of what would be shown on-screen.

In their content analysis of over a thousand stag films that had been produced since the 1920s, Knight and Alpert found that heterosexual fellatio was in nearly 70 percent of the films and heterosexual cunnilingus was in nearly 50 percent. They also noted that female bestiality (most often a woman and a dog) was in just over 2 percent of the films. They remarked, "While woman-animal activity is relatively uncommon in our society, such ideas are quite common in the history of male pornography—even being reflected in Greek mythology." Indeed, pornographic films represented female bestiality slightly more frequently than exclusively gay sex (less than 2 percent of the films). Lesbian sex, by contrast, was not uncommon, appearing in nearly 20 percent of the films, with nearly 7 percent of the films representing exclusively lesbian sex.[5]

Narratives often placed men and women together in a place with enough privacy to have sex (unless voyeurism was a motif). Occupations often brought a man or a woman into the other's home. One common occupation for males in American stags is doctor, which provides character motivation for the woman to undress and gives the couple privacy. Salesmen were not uncommon, with women portrayed as housewives and the encounter occurring while husbands were at work. Women might be babysitters. Some stag narratives implied longer-term relationships, with a couple meeting in a motel room. Other stag films dispensed with plot altogether and simply had people engage in sex. These films can be considered nonnarrative pornography, unless one takes sex acts themselves to include some sort of narrative trajectory.

Because of its graphic sexual representations, pornography remained outside the film industry since it was illegal even if thoroughly commercial. The pornography market differed historically from sexploitation's in that the pornography market was covert while that of sexploitation was generally overt (except for the square-up reel). Of necessity, pornography circulated outside the public sphere. Until pornography emerged into public view in the late 1960s, it was largely confined to small (almost exclusively all-male and all-white) audiences. Pornographic films were screened by fraternal organizations at private *stag parties* or *smokers*. In a distribution network similar to the sexploitation market, a road show operator would bring two to three hours of footage and a 16mm projector and screen the films for a price (usually between fifty and one hundred dollars).

The history of stag films reflects particular characteristics of the division of the public and private spheres and the ambivalence often found in the reception of popular culture, particularly its marginal forms. The Commission on Obscenity and Pornography found that despite an array of federal, state, and local laws that made pornography illegal, stag films, while "publicly condemned," were "shown privately not only by individual citizens, but also by civic, social, fraternal, and veterans' organizations. The National Survey conducted by the Commission revealed that 44% of the male adults acknowledged having seen one or more stag films in their lifetimes."[6] Stag films enjoyed a large, respectable, albeit clandestine, audience throughout the first decades of their existence. The composition of the audience influenced the norms codified into law. Knight and Alpert wrote in "The Stag Film" that laws meant to deter the distribution, possession, or exhibition of obscene films were rarely used to prosecute those who viewed stag films since they were "frequently such community pillars"; instead, punishment was "more often meted out to the producer, distributor or dealer than to the customer."[7] The upscale market for early pornography was also influenced by high rental costs. Historically, then, while some stag films might have aimed for working or lower class males, the smoker tradition indicates there was also an element of socioeconomic class division in the production and consumption of stag films: lower class actresses and actors performed for middle- and upper-class white male viewers.

In the 1950s, stag films shifted from the smoker market to the private home market spurred by technological developments. Film projectors and screens for home viewing became less expensive and more readily available. The production side of the market responded to the domesticated demand as road shows were replaced by an illicit distribution, sales, and rental network across the country. Hollywood acknowledged the existence of its underground competitors with a stag film screening in a private home of one of the characters in Delbert Mann's *The Bachelor Party* (1957). The audience did not get to see what was on the home-movie screen in the film. The facial expressions, reactions, and comments of the main characters, though, Charlie (Don Murray), Walter (E. G. Marshall), Eddie (Jack Warden), and Arnold (Philip Abbott), made it clear to a late-1950s audience that the film's white-collar protagonists were watching a pornographic film, a form of hidden deviance widely accepted among white middle-class male friends and acquaintances.

Throughout the 1950s and into the 1960s, production standards improved, with better casting and settings although narratives became more truncated, paving the way for the sex-only hard-core loop. The actresses were becoming younger and better looking than the women in earlier stag films. Pretty Candy Barr was only sixteen when she starred in, against her will she later claimed, *Smart Alec* (1951), one of the most popular blue movies of the decade. As pornography emerged commercially over the course of the 1960s, numerous commentators (almost invariably male) remarked upon the noticeable decrease in the age and the increase in the attractiveness of the actresses in pornographic movies as a factor that differentiated earlier stag films from contemporary pornography. By the early 1970s, William Murray remarked in the *New York Times Magazine* that "the performers themselves are a new breed," often drawn from the counterculture in San Francisco and Los Angeles.[8] Film critic Richard Corliss noted wryly that the actresses in soft- and hard-core director Radley Metzger's movies "looked as if they could communicate desire without carrying disease."[9]

Audience diversification, however small, led producers to introduce a wider variety of plots and situations for sexual encounters into their narratives. Pornographic movies lengthened, and sexual themes were embedded in narratives that often resembled those of the kinkies. There was also an increase in the variety of settings as light-weight portable equipment influenced the production of pornography just as it had Hollywood filmmakers. Sixteen millimeter films were easy to shoot and cost relatively little. Shots could be set up quickly in motel rooms, bedrooms or living rooms or kitchens, apartments, or in forests or on beaches. The quality of the movies improved at the same time that the audience for them was broadening.

EUROPEAN IMPORTS

During the 1950s, European movies developed a market with the rise of film societies such as Cinema 16 in New York City and *art houses* like the Brattle Theatre in Cambridge, Massachusetts. Such outlets could more readily screen the racier European films after the MPAA dropped the fine for exhibitioners who violated the Code in 1942. Other factors also aided the popularity of European films. In the wake of a world war, foreign cultures no longer seemed as distant or exotic as they had previously. The GI Bill financed college degrees for large numbers of veterans, leading to a steep rise in the number of Americans with post-secondary education. Mass higher education, and film courses and societies on many campuses, were changing attitudes toward movies. Opinions about film as art were embedded in larger debates fuelled by the democratization of culture, or cultural leveling, taking place. A growing number of academics, critics, and social commentators believed the cultural artifacts of mass culture—including motion pictures—could be a high art form and not just popular entertainment. Viewers who believed film could have an aesthetic value like literature or art found works that met their criteria in a number of the alternative film styles that developed in postwar Europe. Distributors and exhibitors targeted the growing audiences of highly educated Americans. Just as sexploitation and pornography had, the market for European films revealed a plurality of cultural tastes and attitudes toward sexual images. In fact, the popularity of European movies exposed at least two taste groups—those who liked sexploitation and those who enjoyed art films.

Films that had achieved high-culture status in Europe were not always marketed as art, though. Some were marketed by sexploitation filmmakers who implemented their usual salacious promotional campaigns. For example, Kroger Babb distributed Ingmar Bergman's *Summer with Monika* (1953) as *Monika, the Story of a Bad Girl* and advertised by posters of bare-shouldered Harriet Andersson with the tagline, "The Devil Controls Her by Radar!" While Babb circulated a sexploitation edition of Bergman's film in run-down theaters and drive-ins, Janus Films distributed the original in art houses in the Northeast. Whether released as trash or art, the films were frequently denied a Seal by the PCA so importers often did not seek one. While not all European films had sexual content, enough of them did so that the etiquette *European* came to connote sex for many moviegoers.

On the lighter side, the movies of Brigitte Bardot routinely played in the same theaters as European art films, contributing to the confusion. Bardot had achieved international stardom with *And God ... Created Woman* (*Et Dieu créa la femme*; 1956), which had been directed by her then husband Roger Vadim and had been a bigger success in the United States than in France. Featuring Bardot in scenes on the beach that highlighted her body as well as a famous mambo dance scene, the film became the largest grossing foreign film in American film history at that time, playing for nearly a year at one New York art house. Bardot was promoted as someone whose open sexuality was "natural," and her movies were popular, even though censors routinely edited portions of the films.

British neorealism at the end of the 1950s and beginning of the 1960s brought such films as *Room at the Top* (1958) and *Saturday Night and Sunday Morning* (1960; U.S. release 1961). *Room at the Top* challenged British censorship standards as well. Its main character, Joe Lampton (Laurence Harvey), seduced and impregnated Susan Brown (Heather Sears) while having an affair with another woman (Simone Signoret). Signaling divisions over sexuality within the industry, the film was nominated for six Oscars, including Best Actress, which Signoret won for her portrayal of Alice Aisgill, although it was denied a Seal by the MPAA. French New Wave films were particularly influential. *Hiroshima, Mon Amour* (1959) told the dark story of a nameless French woman and Japanese man, who, having survived the horrors of World War II, must now try to negotiate a sexual affair even as they try to come to grips with their pasts. *Breathless* (*À bout de souffle*; 1960; U.S. release 1961) presented the doomed love affair of a French petty criminal and an American expatriate. Both movies achieved critical acclaim and commercial success. François Truffaut's *Jules and Jim* (1962) told the story of an ill-fated love triangle in the early decades of the century. Just before the outbreak of World War I, Austrian Jules (Oskar Werner) marries French Catherine (Jeanne Moreau), and the two have a daughter, Sabine (Sabine Haudepin). Their friend Jim (Henri Serre), also French, moves in with them and becomes Catherine's lover, a relationship she instigates. From Italy, Federico Fellini chronicled the decadent experiences of a gossip columnist, Marcello Rubin (Marcello Mastroianni), in *La Dolce Vita* (1960). Michelangelo Antonioni's *L'Avventura* (1960; U.S. release 1961) enigmatically portrayed the development of a love affair between Sandro (Gabriele Ferzetti) and Claudia (Monica Vitti), when his mistress and Claudia's best friend, Anna (Lea Massari), vanishes mysteriously. *L'Avventura* (1960) troubled some critics because of its unflattering portrayal of marriage and romantic relationships, as well as the sexuality of the main characters. In an early scene in Rome, Anna shows her willingness to have sex with but not marry her lover, Sandro. After they have been separated and she expresses doubts about their getting back together, she initiates sex with him, shown famously with her in a medium profile, turning toward Sandro as she begins to unbutton her blouse. She rejects marriage. In another scene, tight framing and close-ups of Anna and Claudia changing their clothes led some critics to interpret the scene as implying Anna's bisexuality. When Anna disappears mysteriously, Sandro almost immediately expresses his sexual desire for Claudia. In keeping with many European imports, the film equated sexuality with realism and the presumption that sex is "natural." *L'Avventura* was widely praised in its successful run in art houses.

The moral skepticism of many European imports distinguished them from Hollywood films. Whereas the Production Code had suppressed marginal values and behaviors, European filmmakers were not constrained by the Code. The axiom that European filmmakers worked under no legal or cultural constraints is a myth, though. French New Wave filmmakers such as Truffaut often ran counter of government officials and public opinion in France. In adapting Henri-Pierre Roche's semiautobiographical 1953 novel *Jules et Jim*, for example, Truffaut made a number of alterations to the novel's sexual material during the production phase in order to secure release. Nonetheless, European filmmakers were often able to go further in showing their characters' sex lives than their American counterparts. Art house audiences welcomed the combination of artistic content, novel cinematic styles, and moral ambiguity of European films as a new form of cinematic realism. European filmmakers offered something new and exciting for a new generation of American filmgoers in the middle of the 1960s, regardless of whether they distinguished between the films of a Michelangelo Antonioni or a Roger Vadim. Because nudity or sex was often crucial to anchoring the films' realism and did not seem to be purely exploitive, European movies successfully challenged the vitality of the Production Code.

In 1966, Antonioni's Palme d'Or winner at the Cannes Festival, *Blow-Up*, became the first film distributed in the United States by a member of the MPAA, MGM, which showed on-screen full frontal female nudity—two teenagers at that. The two unnamed girls (played by Jane Birkin and Gillian Hills) trade sexual favors for a photo shoot with the film's main character, Thomas (David Hemmings). In the sequence, they wrestle each other out of their clothes and have sex with Thomas. Typical of 1960s films trying to capture the clichéd spontaneity and lack of inhibition of the younger generation, the three carry on with childlike abandon. Less controversial but still capable of raising eyebrows was a scene in which a woman that Thomas suspects might be involved in a crime, Jane (Vanessa Redgrave), walks around his apartment with no top on. A combination of camera work and body positioning prevents her breasts from being completely visible on-screen, but Antonioni manipulated one of the emerging methods of implying nudity within the diegetic world of the film that went well beyond use of off-screen space and glances.

In August 1966, after *Who's Afraid of Virginia Woolf?* had dealt the Code a fatal blow, the PCA review board awarded a Seal of Approval to a British import, Lewis Gilbert's *Alfie*, despite an abortion scene. An incorrigible womanizer, Alfie (Michael Caine) callously has sex with and impregnates Lily (Vivien Merchant), the wife of Harry (Alfie Bass), a man he shared a hospital room with and befriended. Alfie procures the services of a shady abortionist (Denholm Elliott) willing to perform the illegal operation in Alfie's apartment. Just before having sex with Lily, Alfie had addressed the camera, saying "What harm could it do?" A great deal, as far as Lily is concerned. She is emotionally wrecked by the experience, while Alfie simply goes to Ruby (Shelley Winters), a rich American he had taken as a lover, but finds her with a younger man. Although he expresses doubts about the worthiness of his hedonistic lifestyle, Alfie remains unreformed. Most importantly for Hollywood, abortion was loosing its status as a topic that could cost filmmakers a Seal from the PCA.

AMERICAN UNDERGROUND CINEMA

As if rivalry from abroad was not enough, American underground film-makers, whose films often included more explicit nudity and sex than European films, also challenged Hollywood. While the American underground and its audience were small, the films made an impact, not least on filmmakers' ideas about what was possible in film. The most vital underground film centers were San Francisco and New York. New York was central not least because of Jonas Mekas, who wrote for the *Village Voice* and *Film Culture* (which he also edited) and was influential in screening films that dealt subversively with sexuality, such as Jack Smith's *Flaming Creatures* (1963). The film had shots of penises, a voice-over commenting on lipstick and blow jobs, and an orgy and rape scene, which begins when one of Delicious Dolores's (Shelia Bick) breasts is exposed when a transvestite (Francis Francine) who has been chasing her throws her to the ground. The scene cuts to Dolores undoing her strap before being devoured by a group of "creatures," some completely, some partially, nude, in shots of androgynously tangled body parts, including genitalia. Not surprisingly, New York authorities found Smith's film in violation of state law, leading to a series of court cases. Indeed, transgressing aesthetic and social norms was an objective of many underground filmmakers.

Neither their sexual content nor their rebelliousness was novel, though. Earlier avant-garde filmmakers, predecessors of the 1960s underground, had turned a voyeuristic camera again and again on sexual taboos in narratives that suggested that the boundaries between dream states and daily life were as porous as those between private and public. Drawing on sources ranging from the Surrealism of such avant-garde filmmakers from the 1920s as Luis Buñuel and Man Ray to Sigmund

Freud's theories of human sexuality, the American avant-garde film-makers of the 1940s and 1950s, like Maya Deren (*Meshes of the Afternoon*; 1943), challenged social constraints. Curtis Harrington's *Fragment of Seeking* (1946), Kenneth Anger's *Fireworks* (1947) and *The Inauguration of the Pleasure Dome* (1954), and James Broughton's *Mother's Day* (1948) developed (sometimes gay) sexual themes.

In the 1960s, American avant-garde filmmakers continued to develop ideas about the interrelationship of freedom of expression and sexual freedom as integral to individual identity and self-fulfillment. *Flaming Creatures* (1963) encountered major censorship difficulties. Its depiction of men in drag (including a Marilyn Monroe look-alike) and bare female breasts sparked censure from New York authorities but praise from Susan Sontag in the *Nation*. Kenneth Anger's *Scorpio Rising* (1964) illustrated homoeroticism, transvestitism, and sadomasochism with an explicitness that went well beyond what a revised Code deemed acceptable. Barbara Rubin's *Christmas on Earth* (1963) featured a group of Rubin's friends in an orgy. In a review of *Christmas on Earth*, Jonas Mekas wrote, "A woman; a man; the black of the pubic hair; the cunt's moon mountains and canyons. As the film goes, image after image, the most private territories of the body are laid open for us.... From now on, the camera shall know no shame. Cinema has discovered all of man."[10] Mekas's remarks demonstrate how underground filmmakers often equated truthful knowledge with nudity or sex. Many underground films attempted to erase the distinction between behavior itself and the representation of behavior even as they attempted to eradicate the boundary between the private and public spheres. Nudity or sex could expand the possibilities of the film medium.

Drawing as they often did on Freudian conceptions of human sexuality, underground filmmakers believed, like Norman O. Brown and Herbert Marcuse, that filming sex was an important challenge to repressive sexual norms. Sexual indulgence was prominent in a series of underground films that emerged out of Andy Warhol's Factory. Warhol directed *My Hustler* (1965), a tableau of male hustlers and the episodic *The Chelsea Girls* (1966), in which a male prostitute and a john lie in bed together talking. Some critics equated the nudity and sex in many underground films with pornography. Yet, to the surprise of many social commentators and film critics, underground films gradually began to appeal to a wider audience. Partly through popularity, partly through notoriety, Warhol's movies, in particular, helped introduce underground perspectives on nudity and sex to new audiences. Louis Botto wrote that with *The Chelsea Girls*, a film he described as "a descent into freaksville via a double screen," Warhol "ascended to class houses."[11]

Botto's *ascension* and *descent* metaphors expressed an idea that gained currency as marginal sexualities became more readily visible and as sexual representations became more common in the public sphere: the sexual morality of the social and cultural mainstream rested upon an unstable lithosphere separating it from an aesthetic and social Hades populated with sexual and moral degenerates. The combination of anti-authoritarianism, cultural radicalism, avant-garde faith in the power of artistic expression to redeem nudity and (often gay) sex was labeled *decadent* by cultural conservatives.

By contrast, liberals accepted the end of the arc brushing against the social and cultural mainstream. They defended the right of underground filmmakers to produce, distribute, and exhibit their movies in the name of individual autonomy and freedom of expression. Conservatives, by contrast, saw decadence as overly individualistic and, as such, *decadence* was picked up by conservatives to decry the influence of underground values on liberalism. Conservatives interpreted that influence as unbridling traditional liberal individualism. Unlimited lifestyle choices and unrestrained aesthetic pluralism intersected decadently in conservative understandings of contemporary society and culture. Sex on American movie screens intersected with the increased visibility in the United States of changes in sexual morality.

SEXUAL ALIGNMENT IN POSTWAR AMERICA

Already in the 1920s, sexual pleasure had gained recognition as an important component of marital intimacy. Early sex surveys proved to at least some Americans that a woman's sexual drive was as strong and natural as a man's. The requirement for women to remain virgins until marriage and the importance of sex for a well-functioning and procreative marriage led to the concept of *marital adjustment*—the ability of women to adjust to being married and, in that context, *sexual adjustment*, women's ability to have a satisfying (and fecund) sex life with their husbands after getting married. A common "disorder" related to women's purported inability to adjust to marital sex was frigidity.

Americans' sex lives came under intensified scrutiny during the postwar era, beginning with Alfred Kinsey's research on *Sexual Behavior in the Human Male* (1948), followed by *Sexual Behavior in the Human Female* (1953). Kinsey concluded that "no American pattern of sexual behavior" existed. Rather, there were "scores of patterns, each of which is confined to a particular segment of our society," because of which "an understanding of the sexual mores of the American people as a whole is possible only through an understanding of the sexual patterns of all of the constituent groups."[12] Some patterns of male and female behavior conformed to the dominant sexual ideology established and enforced by liberals and conservatives; others did not. Kinsey's research suggested that the normative boundaries of sex were less clear in the sexual practices of individuals in their private lives. Most importantly, Kinsey found that men and women engaged in premarital sex in larger numbers than previously believed.

Socially, Kinsey's findings would exert a strong influence on public discourse about Americans' sex lives. Kinsey contributed to the shift in public discourse from justifying or repressing sexual behavior on the basis of religious edicts or medical advice to statistical distribution. If enough people engaged in any particular sexual act with sufficient frequency, then the behavior was *natural*. Such acts included acts widely held to be deviant at the time, such as masturbation, male and female homosexuality, as well as premarital sex and adultery. Kinsey basically argued that if people did something frequently enough, then the behavior more or less justified itself. Although Kinsey's results and his argument were attacked for being methodologically erroneous or morally wrong, the *naturalization* argument became a permanent fixture in public discourse on adult sexuality as Americans rethought traditional ideas about sex.[13] Lionel Trilling, among others, challenged Kinsey's conception of the naturalness of sexual behavior, which he called "the Report's strong reliance on animal behavior as a norm" in a 1948 *Partisan Review* article. Trilling saw Kinsey as being prone to "letting the idea of the Natural develop quietly into the idea of the Normal."[14] In practice, the strongest trend building upon the Kinsey reports seems to have been the idea that as private behavior, the sexual behavior of consensual adults was beyond the purview of social control. An example of Kinsey's influence was the decision of the American Law Institute "to shape its model penal code in accordance with Kinsey's scientific discoveries—by privatizing most moral questions."[15]

Film, however cautiously, was not the only medium reinterpreting how Americans' sex lives should be portrayed. As noted, novels and plays had already begun going further than Hollywood was willing or able to go in representing sexual matters. Pinups had flourished during the war, so it is no surprise that the magazine industry became one of the major forums for sex. From countless pulp magazines to Hugh Hefner's glossy *Playboy*, which featured Marilyn Monroe in its first issue in 1953 and grew with explosive subscription numbers, to women's magazines that discussed sexual matters of interest to married women, sex was increasingly covered in American media. At the same time, the nuclear family was the order of the day during the postwar era. The Baby Boom peaked in 1957, but throughout the 1950s, marriage and children were endorsed by government policies that encouraged suburbanization as well as the press that reinvested marriage, the nuclear family, and especially mothers with an elevated status. The veneration of matrimony and motherhood was accompanied by a renewed insistence on monogamy, the permanence of marriage, and the confinement of sex to marriage. Still, a sense that something was amiss in family life, not least in the suburbs where millions of families were moving, permeated the popular press nearly as much as the paeans to it. Many of the articles also expressed alarm about the status of marriage and the rise in divorce rates.

What occurred in the middle-to-late 1960s was not a *sudden* social and cultural revolution. Just as Americans started seeing sex in Hollywood movies for the first time since the early 1930s, they were acknowledging major, widespread changes in sexual morality for the first time since the 1920s. Developments during the middle-to-late 1960s and early 1970s built upon but went beyond change wrought during the first five decades of the century. An alternative to the revolution metaphor is the metaphor of *alignment*. Americans began synchronizing their perceptions about the nation's sexual morality with the sexual plurality that Kinsey had uncovered and that was becoming more visible in the media, including film.

With the increase in the privatization of experience, the public concerns of the traditional gender roles that had dominated 1950s marital public discourse and behavior seem to have become too confining for housewives and perhaps for their husbands as well. The dominant sexual ideology included the traditional Judeo-Christian conception of the bond of matrimony as sacred and permanent. Furthermore, in the public sphere, a dominant set of collective evaluations, expectations, and/or *reactions* stigmatized divorce. Sex norms related to marriage and divorce were codified in the laws of most states, and those norms ensured the difficulty of dissolving the bonds of matrimony. To that end, divorce laws in the United States originally shared the principle of *marital fault*. According to this principle, one spouse had to prove that the other spouse was guilty of adultery, desertion, or cruelty, all of which had developed as grounds for divorce following the Protestant Reformation and had influenced the development of divorce laws in the states after the American Revolution. Proof of fault was not only essential for obtaining a petition of divorce. It also influenced courts' judgments in the division of property, alimony, and child custody. Their marital lives dictated by the gender-based roles of the domestic sphere, limited access to employment, and the fault system of divorce, "few women saw divorce as a viable option even if they were deeply dissatisfied. Having invested heavily in a particular marriage, they had little ability to provide an income for themselves and their children outside marriage, and their children were a liability in finding a new marriage partner."[16] Bad marriages had been more commonly endured than terminated before the 1960s. However slowly, attitudes toward divorce did change, and in the early-to-mid-1960s, many Americans believed they were changing rather quickly.

Throughout the postwar era, the dominant sexual consensus pre-served the clearly defined gender-specific roles for men and women in their relationships, inherited from the nineteenth century. Some of the norms governing sex were codified as divorce laws, while others influ-enced the composition of the labor force. Throughout the 1950s and into the early 1960s, community leaders, including politicians, psychologists, and physicians, promoted conformity with traditional sexual values and emphasized the importance of the family to society. At the same time, transgressive sexual practices were disparaged as being in opposi-tion to matrimony. Most states had laws against sexual offenses, includ-ing *sodomy* (which varied in definition from state to state but which usually included reference to heterosexual and homosexual anal-genital contact and oral-genital contact). However defined, sexual offenses often carried stiff penalties. For example, in New York, conviction for sodomy carried a sentence of twenty years, while first degree assault carried ten years; in Pennsylvania, a conviction of pandering provided a sentence of ten years, while a conviction on the charge of assault with intent to kill meant seven years in prison. In California, sexual *perversion* carried a sentence of fifteen years, while corporal injury to one's wife or child carried two years.[17]

With the police power securing a large degree of public adherence to sexual norms, sex remained marriage-oriented, defining the roles of women and men in the public and private spheres and in their interper-sonal relationships. As a cohort, women of the GI and Depression genera-tions married earlier, had children earlier, and thus became mothers at a younger age. In 1947, the birthrate reached 3.8 million, eventually peaking in 1957, when 4.3 million baby boomers were born. The large number of families "revealed the depth of American commitment to marriage.... The state self-consciously promoted conventional nuclear family-building through massive subsidies to home ownership and to suburbanization. The 'baby boom' of the 1950s reaffirmed the institution of marriage."[18] Not surprisingly, the 1955 White House Conference on Effective Use of Womanpower concluded that the "structure and the substance of the lives of most women are fundamentally determined by their functions as wives, mothers, and homemakers."[19] Many men and women were happy to see that women's lives should be confined to those roles.

Throughout the 1950s, there had been a popular revision of the domestic sphere ideology of the nineteenth century. Based on the idea of fundamental physiological, psychological, and social differences between men and women, the ideology of the domestic sphere confined women largely to the home in the dual role of wife and mother. The toll that lack of opportunities took on some housewives had risen to the fore of cultural debates following the publication of Betty Friedan's *The Feminine Mystique* (1963). Many American women sought to escape from the private sphere, which often meant long days' confinement to empty suburban houses while their children were in school and their husbands at work.

Throughout the 1950s, suburban life had typically been portrayed either as a life of casual socializing, political conservatism, backyard grilling, and family life, or as one of alcoholism, (prescription) drug abuse, adultery, divorce, and mindless conformity. Suburban life was criticized for making life particularly difficult for women. *The Feminine Mystique* described ways in which women's confinement to the domestic sphere in suburbia was harmful to women. The suburban ideal of the housewife/mother who could alternate seamlessly between the roles of sex kitten, chauffeur mom, and homemaker was more than many women could cope with.

By the 1960s, suburbia was seen as being much more heterogeneous and diverse than earlier sociological studies had suggested. The suburbs, it turned out, did not live up to their reputations as picket-fenced Peyton Places. Although new studies dismissed findings from the 1950s, the earlier conceptions continued to influence public discourse in the 1960s. Earlier critiques were also supplemented by criticism from the New Left and the counterculture. Radicals criticized American life for being too bureaucratized, too conformist, and too technocratic. In their eyes, American society had become indifferent to the concerns of human beings. It had become cold and inhuman, highly structured on the basis of rigid rules and traditions that had come to seem hollow, and in the process had depersonalized private lives as much as civic life. Nowhere were the effects of the technocratic machine believed to have been more detrimental than in the suburbs. Few areas of life were as implicated in these critiques as human sexuality and its role in individual development and in intimate relationships.

At the same time, the 1960s witnessed the emergence of significant reversals in longstanding patterns of reproductive and marital behavior. Following the baby boom, fertility declined after the development and use of reliable contraceptives such as the birth control pill, more frequent sterilization, and legal abortion. The marriage rate, after a boom of the late 1940s and early 1950s, gradually fell while the median age of marriage rose. The divorce rate rose. These changes influenced sexual behavior. Getting married at a later age increased the odds that young people would have sex before marriage. More divorces meant there were more formerly married adults looking for new sexual partners. Their children knew their parents had sex outside of marriage. In brief, marriage was no longer the hegemonic site of sexual relationships that it had traditionally been in dominant social codes during the 1950s.

As Americans grappled in public with the new patterns of sexual behavior visible in the country, debates over sex often included references to changes in what was shown in American movies. Reactions to sexploitation, pornography, European imports, and American underground films brought strong social and cultural divisions over sex to the surface. Although pornography is an aesthetic classification of sexual representations, consumption of pornography is a form of social behavior. For liberals, ranging from Supreme Court Justice William O. Douglas and the ACLU to pornographers, individual autonomy and freedom of expression were in constant tension with the *obligations* to the community. Conservatives, such as antipornography (sometimes self-described as pro-decency) organizations like Citizens for Decent Literature (CDL; founded in 1957) and Morality in Media (established in 1962), defended social order and community standards maintained by governmental authorities. During the 1960s and 1970s, the incongruent preferences of liberals and conservatives—manifested by disparate views of sex, nudity and sex in film, individual autonomy, and community standards—created a growing cultural divide.

Ignoring the existence of sexploitation and the sexual aberrations and practices portrayed in that genre before the middle of the 1960s, numerous commentators attributed the sudden changes in nudity and sex in American cinema to corresponding sudden and extreme shifts in sexual mores in the United States—the so-called sexual revolution. In an article that appeared just before the release of *Who's Afraid of Virginia Woolf? Life* suggested that Mike Nichols's film would indicate "whether America is willing to accept contemporary change in its film as well as its life."[20]

3

Inside Out

WHO'S AFRAID OF THE CODE?

Edward Albee's Broadway play *Who's Afraid of Virginia Woolf?* debuted in 1962. A critical and popular success, it failed to win the Pulitzer Prize because some committee members objected to its profanity and sexual themes. Although the play clearly violated the Production Code and both the PCA and the National Catholic Office for Motion Pictures (NCOMP), the Legion's new name, questioned its suitability for movie theaters, Jack Warner bought the rights to it in 1964. Warner Brothers looked into ways to circumvent the inevitable resistance the film would receive from the PCA. The studio considered but rejected alternative distribution channels for the film. It also rejected resigning from the MPAA, freeing the company of the need to abide by PCA demands. Warner Brothers could have simply released the film for distribution without the PCA's Seal. Instead, Warner decided to make the film with major stars and a very large budget and to seek PCA approval.

Together with the MPAA's general counsel, Louis Nizer, Jack Valenti met with Jack Warner and Ben Kalmenson from Warner Brothers. The four discussed Warner's options in editing the script. Valenti found such discussions futile. It "seemed wrong," he thought, "that grown men should be sitting around discussing such matters."[1] They were debating what should or should not be allowed on screen within the moral framework of a Production Code that had been written and originally enforced by men who had passed away by the middle of the 1960s. It seemed to Valenti that the moral framework underlying the Code might also be dead.

The Code itself and the PCA, though, were still alive and well. Geoffrey Shurlock quickly demanded that the profanity and sexual references in the dialogue be removed, even though he admitted that such alterations would reduce the dramatic impact of the work. Jack Warner was prepared to edit Albee's script as a way of protecting the company's investment and its chances of producing a blockbuster.[2] Warner had veteran screenwriter Ernest Lehman adapt the script for the screen together with first-time director Mike Nichols, who had come to fame as part of a comedy team with Elaine May and a string of Broadway hits in quick succession. Contrary to Warner's expectations, Lehman and Nichols left the manuscript of the screenplay very close to the text of the original play. Lehman and Nichols's decision reflected the mid-1960s liberal belief that the play's revelations of a marriage's troubles had artistic value.

Conservatives countered that personal sexual revelations were not a matter of being honest or not, they were a matter of civility and decency: some things were not fit to be expressed in public. The conservative position was well represented within the film industry. Although perturbed by the film, the NCOMP recommended that Warner Brothers classify *Woolf* for "Adults Only." The NCOMP classified the film as "morally unobjectionable for adults, with reservations." The PCA's Geoffrey Shurlock refused to give the film a Seal.

To secure an exemption, Warner Brothers voluntarily classified *Woolf* for "Adults Only," a marketing technique that studios had started using in the 1950s and that Warner Brothers had used before with success with *The Bad Seed* (1956). Adults went to see the film in large numbers, making it a success at the box office. The Review Board granted the film an exemption, allowing profanity and implicit nonmarital sex without a revision of the Code. The Production Code had become a dead letter. Valenti decided the time had come to modify the Code to fit films like *Who's Afraid of Virginia Woolf?* rather than force such films to fit the Code. His first step was to revise the Code into a two-category system of general release and adults only films.

WHO'S AFRAID OF VIRGINIA WOOLF?

Who's Afraid of Virginia Woolf? takes place over the course of a single night in the life of George (Richard Burton), a middle-aged college history professor at a New England college, and his wife Martha (Elizabeth Taylor). George and Martha have George's new colleague, Nick (George Segal), and his wife, Honey (Sandy Dennis), over for drinks on a Saturday night after Martha met the younger couple at a reception for new faculty members and their spouses hosted by her father, president of the college where George and Nick teach. The visit develops into a series of confrontations between the four, particularly between George and Martha over her infidelity.

In the opening credit sequence, George and Martha stroll, or more nearly, wobble slightly, across the moonlit campus on their way home from Martha's father's party, described later by George as one of many "Saturday night orgies." They are civil with one another. Once inside the privacy of their own home, though, they attack each other verbally. George and Martha's inability to communicate is established deftly in the film's first sequence, as the couple moves about their house eating and drinking, and Martha tidies the bedroom in anticipation of its being seen by Nick. What seems to be a content couple strolling quietly together in public tranquility shrouds a private hell of failed communication in a failed relationship.

George and Martha go into their kitchen to eat. Martha explains the fate of Rosa Moline (Bette Davis), a character in *Beyond the Forest* (King Vidor, 1949): "She's a housewife ... she buys things.... She's discontent." Martha's allusion signifies her dissatisfaction with her own gender-coded role of housewife. It can also be read as a parallel indication that she is aware that her sexual desires and her plans to use sex to escape George's world for a part of the night parallel those of Rosa Moline to escape the world of her husband, Dr. Louis Moline (Joseph Cotten), whose lack of career success resembles George's, in Vidor's melodrama. George asks Martha whether the characters played by Davis and Cotton are married, and Martha responds, "Yes. They're married. To each other." The query and response make clear that being "set up in" a cottage did not necessarily mean a state of matrimony. Martha's explication also manifested how female allegiance to the division of the private and public spheres into separate gender-specific spheres for men and women was slowly beginning to wane. Sexual affairs, the film suggests, could function as a woman's way out of the traditional confinement imposed by gendered roles.

Once the guests have arrived, the couples engage in small talk made increasingly uncomfortable by the barbs George and Martha exchange before Martha takes Honey upstairs. Nick tells George he and Honey will leave when she returns because George and Martha seem to be having a spat, and he doesn't "like to ... become involved ... uh ... in other people's affairs." George assures him that he'll "get over that ... small college and all. Musical beds is the faculty sport around here." George's comment further breaks down the boundaries of décor and civility even as it announces what is really on his mind: he is worried that Nick will soon be playing "musical beds" with Martha.

When the two women return, Martha has changed into something more comfortable. George greets her with a term of endearment—"my pet"—and an ironic "your Sunday chapel dress" (it is early Sunday morning). George reacts to Martha's change of attire but tells the guests, "Martha is not changing for *me*." Verifying George's suspicions, Martha sits on the couch beside Nick and begins flirting with him. The sequence of shots begins with an extreme close-up on Nick taking a lighter and lighting Martha's cigarette after George refused to do so.

Nichols underlines the bond developing between Martha and Nick by shooting Martha and Nick in close-ups and medium close-ups and positioning them in the foreground. George and Honey are frozen out and left in the background. As Martha flirts with Nick, close-ups of her are intercut with close-ups of him, with Honey in the background saying that Nick had been "intercollegiate state middleweight champion." Martha, framed in close-up, remarks, "You still look like you have a pretty good body now, too, is that right? Have you? ... Is that right? Have you kept your body?" George's interjection from the back of the room, "Martha ... decency forbids ..." is silenced by a loud "Shut up!" from Martha framed in a close-up. When Nick says that his body is "pretty good," Honey, in a medium two shot with Nick, confirms what Martha thinks she sees: "Yes, he has a very firm body." Then in quick succession there is a cut to Martha in a close-up, then back to Nick and Honey followed by a medium shot with George behind Martha, sitting at a desk reading in a book. George breaks in again, and Martha retorts that George does not "cotton to body talk." Nichols, with the deft framing of Haskell Wexler, who won an Oscar for his camera work, visualizes the way in which sexual desire can focus the minds of two people that are attracted to one another to the detriment of those around them.

When Martha and Nick begin their bawdy dance (challenging the Code's claim that "dances which suggest or represent sexual actions ... violate decency and are wrong"), George retaliates by calling Honey "angel-tits" and "monkey-nipples." When she says that Martha and Nick are "dancing like they've danced before," George informs her, "It's a familiar dance ... they both know it...." George can see Martha and Nick's experience with seduction, but Honey, who prefers the façade of traditional sexual morality, can or will not. George does not accept what he sees. Incensed by Martha flaunting her infidelity, George tries to strangle her after she tells the guests that George had written a novel but her father had refused to let it be published. Once Nick has pulled him off Martha, George exacts revenge by changing the "game" from "Humiliate the Host" to "Get the Guests." George reveals his true motivation by surmising what games they might play. He wonders whether they should play "Hump the Hostess," but decides that game should be put off for later when he hits upon "Get the Guests."

George then concocts what he claims is the plot of a novel, but which is in fact a revelation of what he has drawn Nick into confiding to him.

Honey is devastated on learning that her husband has revealed to near-strangers that she had a false pregnancy, that she and Nick had premarital sex, that she possibly suffered from a pathological state, and that their marriage had resulted from necessity rather than love. When Nick tries to apologize, Honey screams, "You . . . told them! You told them! You couldn't have told them!" George and Martha go outside and argue ferociously in front of the roadhouse. Martha tells George that everything has "snapped." She drives off in their station wagon, picking up Nick and Honey along the way. A final shot of George smiling dissolves into a shot of George and Martha's house, with the light from their bedroom window revealing two silhouettes.

George comes home and sees the silhouettes and begins to cry. Honey, who had passed out on the backseat of the car, wakes up and babbles about the sound of bells. She has no knowledge of what's going on and keeps telling George, "I don't want to know." George's insistence that she look enacts one of the common justifications for exposure: to reveal—and thereby destroy—hypocrisy. Rather than face up to her husband having sex with another woman, Honey prattles on about the bells she heard and a dream she was having. George stands in the foreground and looks up at the window. In a point of view shot, two partial shadows can be seen moving. Muttering that he will exact revenge on Martha, George becomes exasperated and angered by Honey's desire to maintain a veil of ignorance. He drags her out into the yard so she can see the bedroom window and Nick and Martha's silhouettes. He tells her, "Listen to them! Look at them!" but she again responds, "I don't want to! I don't want to see. . . . Leave me alone!" George attempts once again to reveal something about her husband to Honey. She could not escape the thrust of George's revelations during "Get the Guests" at the roadhouse, but now she evades the knowledge George is trying to convey to her.

Once the four are together again in the living room, Martha and George trade accusations about who mistreated the son and to whom he was closest. George tells Martha that their son has been killed in a car accident and intones the Kyrie Eleison. George explains that he killed the son because Martha had broken the ultimate ground rule of their "game": she had mentioned his existence to someone else. She had revealed their deepest secret and allowed someone else into their most private space, into their darkness. Despite his revelations over the course of the night, George retains at least some sense of privacy, a line that Martha erased. When Nick has figured out that the child is fictive—he repeats to himself, "Oh my God, I think I understand this," as if shocked by such a revelation as horrible as childlessness. He asks George, "You couldn't have . . . any?" The pause conveys the gravity of the question and implies the seriousness of involuntary childlessness at the time. George replies, "*We* couldn't," and Martha echoes, "*We* couldn't." Just before leaving, Nick makes an awkward attempt at empathy and compassion. It does not seem perfunctory, but it is formal and seems to be an attempt to reestablish the private-public divide that had existed at the beginning of the evening. George cuts him short by saying, "Good night."

Fittingly, *Who's Afraid of Virginia Woolf?* ends in a private space, at the tattered heart of George and Martha's intimate association. It remains unclear whether they have arrived at a point at which they can begin to communicate. Arguing seems to have had a cathartic effect on George and Martha, bringing them to the point of listening to instead of filtering out each other. Appearances are deceiving, though. After brief overtures to one another, they sit in silence.

The allegorical setting of New Carthage and a Puritan New England college—some scenes were shot (at great expense) on the campus of Smith College in Massachusetts—established a contrast between the public image of sexual prudence and a private image of sexual promiscuity. The narrative slowly lays bare the aberrations lurking beneath the façade of sexual conformity, which Honey, Nick, and Martha have violated. Honey has faked pregnancy to get married; Nick has been promiscuous, sleeping with faculty wives to advance his career; and Martha has slept around to get revenge over George for her unhappiness in their marriage. While *Who's Afraid of Virginia Woolf?* criticizes Americans' sexual values and illusions about the sanctity of marriage, it also reestablishes the dominant patterns of postwar sexual behavior, the family, and marriage. Martha and George seem to have reconnected, and Nick and Honey seem to have reached a point where they will now move beyond their own lies and establish a family. Honest revelations, the film would have us believe, can solve marital problems.

This aesthetic of revealing even uncomfortable truths harmonized with mounting evidence that many women had become less content with their lot and men had become impotent, if not in sexual relationships, then in solving the social problems of the public sphere that men dominated. Both liberals and conservatives felt unease with the changes taking place in Americans' sex lives, not least those modifying traditional gender roles. Just as familial relationships were changing, so were the roles of women in families and in the private sphere. Women were more often lamenting, as does Martha in the film, the "hopeless darkness" of her "crushing marriage." Martha's world—the rigidly demarcated domestic sphere—was beginning to change by 1966, and Americans were beginning to acknowledge women's escape from their gender-based confinement to the domestic sphere. This world and its traditional gender roles had become too confining for Martha and perhaps for George as well.

Throughout his critique of Nick and emerging reproductive technologies, George's anxieties as a husband whose marriage is threatened by

Nick, his wife's impending adultery, and his childlessness intersect with his anxieties as a liberal historian with the troubled condition of American society and culture. George's satire of dominant American values simultaneously satirizes the difficulties liberals had in fending off cultural radicalism. George is a defeated liberal who has largely opted out of a society whose values he did not share. He embodies the dilemma of the contemporary liberal and the challenges cultural radicalism posed for liberalism. Many liberals seemed to have a natural affinity for affective, sensual, antiauthoritarian, egalitarian, and expressive sensibilities, or at least felt impelled to defend them or their advocates on grounds of individual autonomy. Many were attracted to the aesthetic works of the avant-garde and the Beats, admired the individuality of Bohemians, expressed sympathy for marginal criminal deviants, just as some incorporated the intellectual tenets of psychoanalysis, existentialism, humanistic psychology, behaviorism, feminism, or secular humanism into their liberal worldviews. At the same time, cultural radicalism threatened those elements of liberalism that cohered with conservatism to form an uneasy consensus on sexual matters.

While attempting to maintain their increasingly uneasy consensus with conservatives, liberals also had to fend off attacks from the Left. For mid-1960s cultural radicals, revealing marital conflicts or personal disgruntlement allowed individuals to get beneath the surface appearances of contentment. Cultural radicals from the Free Speech Movement at Berkeley, the student movement, and to underground newspapers to off-Broadway playwrights believed exposing problems served to save the community, not to undermine it. In their view, the individualism of liberalism had become ineffectual due to liberalism's own shortcomings and its many alliances and compromises with conservatism. For the time being, the MPAA tried to maintain the balance by distinguishing between adult content and films suitable for everyone. The distinction was unclear, since American youth often preferred movies with "adult" content. The younger generation was often at the vanguard of demands for greater sexual openness in American society and explicitness in films. Yet, the older generation was not always that far behind, at least not in Hollywood. In 1966, *Who's Afraid of Virginia Woolf?* received numerous Oscar nominations and won a few. Its critical, commercial, and industry success made it clear that sexual revelations had not only come into the mainstream: they *were* the mainstream.

THE GRADUATE AND YOUTH CULTURE

In late December 1967, Mike Nichols's second film, *The Graduate*, a sex comedy about an upper-middle-class college graduate's search for identity and self-fulfillment, opened in theaters. Part of that search involves him having an affair with the mother of a girl with whom he eventually falls in love. Once again, a Nichols film featured an adulterous housewife as a main character and became a critical and box office success. On numerous best film lists in 1968, *The Graduate* also received numerous awards and seven Academy Award nominations, including Best Director, which Nichols won.

Marketed successfully, the movie proved to be quite profitable. It broke box office records at theaters across the United States and grossed over $100 million, becoming one of the year's top-grossing films. *The Graduate* touched a nerve among viewers of all ages when it was released, but had a special appeal to younger members of the audience. It offered in its main character, Benjamin Braddock (Dustin Hoffman), an unlikely hero whose ineptness at finding meaning with his life mirrored many of America's youths' growing frustration with American society. Many saw Benjamin's inability to decide what career path to take as a lack of faith in meritocracy and upward mobility. The film's satirical portrait of the materialism of middle-class suburban life that stifled Benjamin resonated with young audiences as did its snapshot of the emerging singles culture that was bringing nonmarital sexuality into public view.

Returning home after a successful stint in college, Benjamin's parents throw a graduation party for him. Their friends congratulate him on his success at college and on his new car, the new "wop job." Mr. Carlson (uncredited) assures him, "Won't have much trouble picking up in that, will you?" Not following him, Ben asks, "Sir?" He clarifies: "The girls. The chicks. The teeny boppers." His wife (uncredited) suggests that "Ben has gotten beyond the teeny bopper stage," winking at Ben. He answers politely, "Yes, ma'am." This seemingly innocuous exchange lets assumptions about sexuality seep into the narrative and encapsulates perfectly the symbiosis of materialism and sex that the film criticizes.

When Ben attempts to seclude himself in his bedroom, Mrs. Robinson, the wife of Ben's father's business partner, begins her pursuit. When he tells her he wants to be alone, she asks, "Is it a girl? Whatever it is you're upset about." Coupled with Mr. and Mrs. Carlson's remarks, her question insinuates that concerns about sexual relationships are never far from the surface in this upper-middle-class subculture. She manipulates Ben into driving her home. Before they leave, she underscores her control of the situation by throwing his keys into his aquarium.

Once home, Mrs. Robinson manipulates Ben into coming inside with her and eventually attempts to seduce him. She offers him a drink, luring him into the jungle decor of her sunroom. Sensing what his smiling predator is doing, Ben attempts to challenge her: "For God's sake,

Mrs. Robinson, here we are, you've got me into your house. You give me a drink. You put on music, now you start opening up your personal life to me and tell me your husband won't be home for hours." Mrs. Robinson simply replies with a laconic "So?" and Ben decides to put the cards on the table: "Mrs. Robinson—you are trying to seduce me. . . . Aren't you?"

As he expresses his suspicion of her intentions, Ben is framed by her stockinged leg in the foreground while he stands in a three-quarter shot in the background in a shot that became the most famous in the movie and an icon for the film's publicity posters. Mrs. Robinson quickly denies she is attempting to seduce him, further confusing the hapless young man. She makes a second attempt upstairs in Elaine's bedroom. The sexually charged evening does not end before Mr. Robinson makes a surprise appearance and counsels Ben to "Sow a few wild oats, take things as they come, have a good time with the girls and so forth. . . . You have yourself a few flings this summer. I'll bet you're, you're quite a ladies man. . . . You look to me like the kind of guy who has to fight 'em off."

Unable to "fight 'em off," Ben calls Mrs. Robinson and asks her if she would still like to meet. They rendezvous at the Palm Room of the Taft Hotel, an elegant hotel that reflects Benjamin's ties to the social world of his parents. When he approaches the hotel clerk (Buck Henry) to get a room, Benjamin makes befuddled efforts to conceal his illicit purpose. He is there for an affair—the hypocritical approach of his parents' generation—and his affair with Mrs. Robinson begins with a door slammed to darkness and to the strains of "The Sounds of Silence."

Cinematographer Robert Surtees's expressive camerawork and lighting continually place Benjamin in the shadows or darkness when he meets with Mrs. Robinson, an apt visual allusion to his shadow deviance. Their affair is presented through a series of scenes and montage sequences that reveal that Ben and Mrs. Robinson do not have much in common other than the leisure time and money necessary to meet frequently at the lush Taft. They share so little with one another that Ben at one point asks, "do you think we could say a few words to each other first this time?"

Eventually, Elaine returns from school, and Ben is manipulated by his parents into taking her out. When he picks her up at the Robinsons, Mrs. Robinson is sitting in the jungle room, her legs covered by a leopard-skin patterned blanket as she smokes a cigarette with *The Newlywed Game* playing unwatched on the television. Ben and Mrs. Robinson have a moment alone, and she tells him that she is "very upset." He promises he will only take Elaine out this one time. Elaine and her father come in, and while the camera focuses on Mrs. Robinson's forlorn face in a close-up, her husband advises Elaine "to keep your wits about you tonight. You never know what tricks Ben picked up back there in the East." Ironically, we see Ben's real teacher while her cuckolded husband mouths the sexual platitudes heard at Benjamin's party. The scene is not completely humorous, though. By having this comment occur in the room where Mrs. Robinson first began her pursuit of Ben in earnest and by framing Mrs. Robinson's despondent face so closely, the film shifts her from a position of superiority to one of vulnerability.

Ironically, Mrs. Robinson eventually intrudes into the intimate space Ben and Elaine share when Ben comes to pick Elaine up for a date. As Mrs. Robinson forces Ben to drive around the neighborhood, she attempts to coerce him into dropping Elaine by threatening to expose their illicit relationship. In his first burst of rebellion, Ben responds by deciding to tell Elaine himself. Following his confession, the film shifts gears and locales, eventually moving to Northern California in the second half.

After a montage of parallel cutting that shows Benjamin "moping" while Elaine is seen moving back to Berkeley, Ben announces to his parents that he is getting married to Elaine although he has yet to tell her. He leaves for Berkeley to be close to Elaine and rents a room in a student boarding house run by a somewhat neurotic landlord, Mr. McCleery (Norman Fell). He confronts Elaine and is confronted by her father. He tells Ben that he "should know the consequences of what you've done. . . . my wife and I are getting a divorce soon." Reflecting the loosened grip of the institution of marriage and the sanctity of sex in the context of marriage, Benjamin asks why? Mr. Robinson is incredulous. Ben explains that "What happened between Mrs. Robinson and me was nothing. It didn't mean anything. We might just as well have been shaking hands." Mr. Robinson does not buy Benjamin's rationalization.

A liberalized sexual code clashes with a conservative one in this scene, but the film as a whole does not necessarily sanction sexual liberalism. Drawing not only on the changing sensibilities of the middle-to-late 1960s but on the relationship and sex norms of the 1950s and early 1960s as well, the film shifts in its final reel to the studio era cliché of the race to the altar, which many critics argued accounted for the film's trans-generational appeal. The race to the altar was a traditional staple of the romantic comedy and was long made memorable to American film audiences in such classics as Harold Lloyd's *Girl Shy* (1924), which served as partial inspiration for *The Graduate*'s chase scene, and George Cukor's *The Philadelphia Story* (1940).

Benjamin's pursuit begins when he discovers that Elaine is getting married, and he drives up and down the coast of California before ending up at Elaine's wedding in Santa Barbara. Arriving in the church just after she has spoken her vows of matrimony, he bangs manically on a glass partition and shouts her name. Benjamin and Elaine grapple with the adults, whom they lock in the church with a large crucifix, and make a dash for a Santa Barbara city bus. In abandoning his Alfa Romeo, Benjamin is breaking *publicly* with their values as he boards the bus and sits silently beside, again, another man's bride. The openness of the final break is significant because it is public visibility that differentiates his deviant behavior with Elaine from his earlier breach with sexual norms.

In *The Graduate*, the fluctuation between the visible adherence to norms and the surreptitious deviation from them are best represented in a European-modernist inspired montage. In a sequence inspired by François Truffaut's *Jules and Jim*, we see Benjamin's transitions, and the symbiotic relationship, between his two lives. Benjamin is seen leaving the pool and going into his parents' house only to enter a hotel room with Mrs. Robinson; he gets up from a bed and goes to shut the door of the dining room where his parents are eating dinner, lies down on his bed again, but is now in the hotel bedroom. In the hotel bedroom, Mrs. Robinson walks back and forth in the foreground, getting dressed, and then leaves, followed by Benjamin leaving his own bedroom, going past his mother (Elizabeth Wilson) to the pool for a swim and diving onto Mrs. Robinson in bed.

The narrative transgressed sexual norms during the first half of the film, during which Mrs. Robinson is sexually assertive and Benjamin is not. But, unlike Benjamin, Mrs. Robinson is ultimately punished by the loss of her lover and her daughter. Perhaps she was being punished for earlier sexual transgressions: She tells Benjamin that she had married her husband because she was pregnant with Elaine. "So old Elaine Robinson got started in a Ford" is Benjamin's less than heartfelt response to this revelation. Mrs. Robinson's out-of-wedlock pregnancy, a normative breach, intimates, as had Martha's adultery in *Who's Afraid of Virginia Woolf?* that sexual norms were—and had been—relative even while they were publicly touted as being absolute. According to a moral code not unfamiliar to Victorians, violations of the sexual code were supposed to be kept out of view.

Yet, Benjamin's affair with Mrs. Robinson is far from invisible. The hotel lobby scenes and the "recognition" of Benjamin (as "Mr. Gladstone") by people who do not know him illustrate the public nature of his seemingly covert affair. Benjamin and Mrs. Robinson's conduct may have been concealed from a mother, father, husband, and daughter. Yet, their clandestine assignations take place in front of hotel patrons and staff members when they become regular guests, since the privacy of the hotel room is accessible only through the public space of the hotel lobby and its hallways.

Benjamin and Mrs. Robinson's public trysts were in keeping with an emerging social experience. By the middle of the decade, in most cities in the United States, the sight of men and women pursuing one another in bars like the Palm Room at the Taft raised very few eyebrows. Indeed, an entire market developed to provide young urban singles with the opportunity to meet like-minded people. In Los Angeles, clubs such as the Whisky à GoGo, Chez Regine, and New Jimmy's provided a space that combined popular entertainment with public displays of affection.

The Graduate also underscored the emerging emphasis on self-fulfillment in intimate relationships. During one of their meetings, Mrs. Robinson tells Benjamin that she did not love her husband and that for the last five years they had almost never had sex. She did not hate him, though. "Well how do you feel about him, then?" Benjamin asks. She replies, "I don't." Insofar as it offers a critique of the middle-class sexual norms, *The Graduate* portrays intimate relationships insti-gated and sustained not by the desires of the individuals involved but by the demands of their middle-class social world.

The youthful desire to establish meaningful relationships meant that even the younger generation retained the romantic association of love and sex. The growing emphasis placed upon *commitment* in intimate relationships placed the institutional nature of the relationship (most importantly, marriage) in competition with the personalities and experi-ences of the individuals involved. Even though the expectation of love or marriage was not mandatory, in terms of Hollywood films, Benja-min's pursuit of Elaine had romantic appeal for the decade's youth. Benjamin represents a youth from the middle class who deviates from sexual norms (with a member of the older generation), only to reassume his parents' values in his pursuit of Elaine.

RATINGS SYSTEM

Greater sexual explicitness in popular films had not come about sud-denly, but after two years with a more or less defunct Production Code, it had become too obvious for the MPAA to ignore. Jack Valenti decided to accommodate the increased sexual liberalism of American society and filmmakers' desire to avail themselves of it. One option was to follow the trend among most Western nations and classify films by the audience age. Hollywood had been reluctant to adopt a rating system because of two main fears. First, producers and exhibitors had been afraid it would reduce box office profits. By the late 1960s, the industry recognized that the largest demographic group filling theater seats were young people in their teens and early twenties. A rating system would likely partition this group down the middle. Second, Valenti and others had been wary of having a rating system found unconstitutional.

Economic concerns had been partly allayed by the success of *Who's Afraid of Virginia Woolf?* Warner Brothers had stipulated the enforcement of an eighteen-and-over admission policy in its contract with exhibitors, and the film's box office receipts had signaled the viability of an age-based rating system. The MPAA's legal concerns dissipated after April 22, 1968, when the Supreme Court upheld a New York law that regulated exposure to sexual materials on the basis of the age of the consumer.[3] That same day, the Court overturned a Dallas, Texas, ordinance that restricted which films kids under the age of sixteen could see because of the assumed harmful influence of nudity, sex acts, and violence. The ratings board feared Dallas youth would replicate the implied "sexual promiscuity" of the two female leads (played by Brigitte Bardot and Jeanne Moreau) in the French import *Viva Maria!* (1965). Although the Court overturned the ordinance on the grounds of vagueness, it suggested that a rating system would be constitutional if it were not overly vague.[4]

Bolstered by the Court's decisions, Valenti implemented a new rating system on November 1, 1968, which the MPAA had crafted together with the National Association of Theater Owners (NATO) and the International Film Importers and Distributors of America (IFIDA). The Production Code Administration was transformed into the Code and Rating Administration (later the Classification and Rating Administration [CARA]). The rating system was voluntary, and it lacked the Code's restrictive prohibitions. The MPAA spelled out acceptable representations of nudity and sex as an absence of "[i]ndecent or undue exposure of the human body"; "[i]llicit sex relationships shall not be justified" and "[i]ntimate sex scenes violating common standards of decency shall not be portrayed"; furthermore, filmmakers were to exercise "[r]estraint and care" in representing "sex aberrations"; finally, "[o]bscene speech, gestures or movements" and "[u]ndue profanity" would not be allowed.[5] Within the ratings system, nudity, sex, theme, violence, language, and drug use were the criteria that determined the rating CARA gave a film. Furthermore, the Rating Administration would no longer control production.

Instead, filmmakers would be held in check by ratings categories that advised parents about nudity and sexual content (and violence) in movies and the suitability of the films for children and youth. Each film's rating would be decided by the ratings board, which consisted of psychiatrists, psychologists, and parents. The original ratings were "G" for *General Audiences*—all ages admitted; "M" for *Mature* audiences—parental guidance recommended; "R" for *Restricted*—those under sixteen must be accompanied by parent or guardian (the age limit was shortly raised to seventeen, but varied in some jurisdictions); and "X"—no one under seventeen admitted (the age varied in some jurisdictions).

The M rating was changed to "GP" (General audiences, Parental guidance recommended) in 1970 because the word *mature* still had sexual connotations for many parents. In 1972, GP was streamlined to "PG"—*Parental Guidance Suggested*. The MPAA registered all of their rating category symbols except X with the United States Patent and Trademark Office, which meant that no film could have an MPAA rating other than X applied to it by any organization other than CARA.

The MPAA hoped the rating system would "encourage artistic expression by expanding creative freedom," while holding filmmakers "responsible and sensitive to the standards of the larger society."[6] Reactions to the ratings system were mixed if not muted. There was little political or interest group reaction. Initially, NCOMP supported the ratings system, but in 1971 the organization withdrew its support. By then, the threat of the Catholic Church sparking boycotts no longer spelled economic peril for the industry. In the increasingly open cultural pluralism of the United States, religious conservatives were merely one group among many that would concern filmmakers.

Unfettered by the Production Code, Hollywood filmmakers represented a greater variety of sexual values—and did so more explicitly—than they had done since 1934. Already during the Code's final year, filmmakers had begun pushing the envelope. The late 1960s and early 1970s were commonly seen as "exciting Klondike days for moviemakers, young and not so young, to make (or lose) money and reputations."[7] The box office and critical success of European and underground films as well as sexploitation and pornographic films convinced many Hollywood filmmakers that there was an audience for films with more novelty in narrative and cinematic techniques, and more explicit representations of nudity and sex. The greater experimentation in film led film critics to dub the period the *Hollywood Renaissance*, the *New American Cinema*, or *New Hollywood*.

NEW HOLLYWOOD

Among the novel qualities of many American films made during the period known as the Hollywood Renaissance was the routine inclusion of sexual behavior the Production Code had forbidden. Unwed couples fornicated in *Bonnie and Clyde* (1967), *Valley of the Dolls* (1967), *Medium Cool* (1969), and *Goodbye, Columbus* (1969). Bernardo Bertolucci's *Last Tango in Paris* (1972) starred Marlon Brando as a middle-aged widower, Paul, who embarks on a purely sexual relationship with an unknown young woman, Jeanne (Maria Schneider), in a European art film set in contemporary Paris. The film includes numerous nude shots of Jeanne and an infamous scene in which Paul uses butter as a lubricant for anal sex with her. From their initial sexual encounter the first time they meet in an empty apartment they are both looking at, the film uses sex as a metaphor for their efforts to escape the loneliness of relationships that have left them unfulfilled: Jeanne's with her fiancé Tom (Jean-Pierre Léaud) and Paul's in the wake of his wife Rosa's (Veronica Lazar) suicide. Paul is in his mid-forties and Jeanne is only twenty, but the attraction between the two is immediate. They agree not to tell each other anything personal, a bargain that keeps their sexual relationship completely impersonal and devoid of emotion.

Bob & Carol & Ted & Alice (1969) explored the attractions of an open marriage, affairs, wife-swapping, and group sex for a couple, Bob (Robert Culp) and Carol (Natalie Wood), that has become involved in the human potential movement. In other films, couples lived together and had unwed pregnancies, as in *Five Easy Pieces* (1970), while spouses committed adultery in *M*A*S*H* (1970). In 1971, Cloris Leachman won an Oscar for Best Supporting Actress for her portrayal of an adulterous housewife, beating Ellen Burstyn for her portrayal of one in the same film, *The Last Picture Show* (1971). In *Night Moves* (1975), Ellen Moseby (Susan Clark), the wife of a private detective, Harry Moseby (Gene Hackman), has an affair while he has a fling of his own. At one point in *Night Moves*, Delly Grastner (Melanie Griffith), a teenage girl that Moseby is searching for, is seen topless and skinny dipping nude.

Joe Buck (Jon Voigt) was a spectacularly unsuccessful male prostitute in *Midnight Cowboy* (1969), which included a scene of implied oral sex in a movie theater as well as a fairly explicit nude romp in bed with a woman named Cass (Sylvia Miles), who Buck believes is his first customer but winds up paying instead. Even Barbara Streisand did a turn as a prostitute in *The Owl and the Pussycat* (1970). In 1971, Jane Fonda won the Academy Award for Best Actress for her portrayal of Bree Daniels, a New York City call girl, in *Klute*, beating Julie Christie for her portrayal of a brothel madam in Robert Altman's revisionist western *McCabe and Mrs. Miller*. *Guess Who's Coming to Dinner* (1967) examined the liberal response to miscegenation when Joey (Katharine Houghton) brings her African American fiancé, John Prentice (Sidney Poitier), home to meet her parents (played by Spencer Tracy and Katharine Hepburn). In Stanley Kramer's film, the importance of romantic love to identity wins out over racism. The film's portrayal of liberals' struggle to practice what they preach in race relations garnered the film ten Academy Award nominations.

Michael Wadleigh's documentary account of the three-day rock music festival in upstate New York, *Woodstock* (1970), was among the ten most successful films at the box office. There is a sequence of skinny dipping with male and female nudity. Males are shown in full-frontal nude shots (usually long shots) with clear shots of genitals. Nude females are generally shot from behind, although there are shots of female breasts. Interviewed, two of the bathers volunteer that skinny dipping is the only way to swim, the "right" way to swim. The camera lingers on a couple kissing after swimming, him naked, her wearing panties. To showcase the openness and associated innocence of late 1960s youth, there is a brief full-frontal nude shot of a young woman tossing a Frisbee. The nudity (along with drug use and occasionally vulgar language) resulted in the film being rated R by the Ratings Administration, but the Academy awarded the film an Oscar for Best Documentary Film. The industry was divided against itself, unable to decide whether the nudity in a film like *Woodstock* was a component of a film worthy of the industry's highest accolades or too racy for viewing by rock music's largest market segment.

Old Hollywood often met New Hollywood in that films often relied on implication rather than explicit representations, but with a radically changed attitude toward sex. Gone were the ambiguity and the sense of sinfulness encouraged by the Code. Most importantly, Hollywood seemed to have adopted Kinsey's notion of the "naturalness" of sex and its place in individual lives and in American society.

Given the absence of the homogenizing effects of the Production Code and the large variety of producers, directors, and actors as the studio system had declined, Hollywood film production had become less standardized than during the studio era. The innovations of New Hollywood ranged from introducing New Wave narrative and cinematic techniques to depicting graphic violence and sexuality. While not all of their films dealt specifically with sex or included overt sexuality, many of them did. Drawing inspiration from European and underground directors, and emboldened by the success of sexploitation and pornography films and the liberalness of the ratings system, filmmakers moved further from the normative boundaries that the Production Code had sustained for over a decade.

Of the two marginal sex genres, sexploitation films had by far the greater impact. The influence of sexploitation aesthetics could be seen in films like *Beyond the Valley of the Dolls* (1970), *Myra Breckinridge* (1970), and *The Magic Garden of Stanley Sweetheart* (1970). By the early 1970s, Hollywood films did not shy away from *simulated* sexual intercourse, *implied* heterosexual fellatio and cunnilingus, or masturbation, all of which had been banned by the Code but now elicited an R or an X rating from CARA. The nudity and sex in *Midnight Cowboy* or *Bob & Carol & Ted & Alice*, Brian Roberts's (Michael York) bisexuality and Sally Bowles's (Liza Minnelli) promiscuity in *Cabaret* (1972), and masturbation with a crucifix by a possessed teen, Regan (Linda Blair), in *The Exorcist* (1973), resembled sexploitation films thematically, although not in production values.

Hollywood had flirted directly with sexploitation following Russ Meyer's most successful foray into the kinkies, the X-rated *Vixen* (1968). Twentieth Century-Fox commissioned Meyer to direct the X-rated *Beyond the Valley of the Dolls*, but he quickly returned to the industry margins. Sexploitation films continued to have some success at the box office into the 1970s with films like *Ilsa, She-Wolf of the SS* (1974). By the 1970s, sexploitation filmmakers no longer needed to resort to ambivalence or subterfuge to avoid prosecution, although ambivalence remained an important genre convention. Ironically, while conservatives criticized sexploitation films for being part of a tidal wave of immorality washing over the nation, sexploitation filmmakers bemoaned pornography's commercial success. As sexploitation films lost market share to both pornography and Hollywood, sexploitation filmmakers shifted to a new version of their genre, dubbed *soft core* to distinguish the films from more explicit *hard core* pornography. Soft-core pornography generally confined its representations to nudity, including brief glimpses of female pubic hair and simulated sex while avoiding shots of male genitalia and penetration. Soft core was given a new lease on life, despite the competition from Hollywood and pornography, with the success of a French import, *Emmanuelle* (1974), and its sequels. The film's star, Sylvia Kristel, became a celebrity. Soft-core films were driven by the same narrative logic as hard-core pornography: put a man and a woman in a situation that made sex possible and then let them have sex. Both genres shared the ability to stimulate audiences sexually. Despite market growth and some box office success, the sexploitation market remained small.

Compared with sexploitation filmmakers, though, Hollywood producers had bigger budgets, better writers, directors, actors and actresses, and better production, distribution, and exhibition facilities. They were in a far better position to bring nudity and sexual content into popular culture. Like sexploitation filmmakers, Hollywood filmmakers with few exceptions confined their representations to simulated rather than explicit sexual activity, with the exception of a male caressing a female partner's breasts. By the middle-to-late 1970s, frontal female nudity was no longer uncommon (frontal male nudity appeared less frequently), but usually assured the film an R or an X rating from CARA, depending on the degree of explicitness and the length of time the nudity was shown. While Hollywood filmmakers attempted to capture a share of the marginal markets while expanding their market bases, a common practice within the industry, they showed nudity proportionately less than sexploitation films. Its centrality in sexploitation films resulted in there being on-screen nudity for 10 to 50 percent of the film's running time on average. In Hollywood films, the nudity was more peripheral, resulting in its occupying only 1 to 5 percent of the film's running time on average.[8]

While sexploitation films provided narrative strategies and cinematic techniques for representing sex, Hollywood did not adopt the diegetic world of pornography, where sex is both a beginning and an end. Hollywood saw pornography as a serious threat, though, for a brief period in the early 1970s.

The biggest box office successes were Gerard Damiano's *Deep Throat* (1972) and *The Devil in Miss Jones* (1973) and Art Mitchell and Jim Mitchell's *Behind the Green Door* (1972). All three films, rated X by the MPAA, were associated with the brief fad known as *porno chic*. *Deep Throat* was shot for $24,000 in southern Florida over the course of six days in 1972. The story of a woman (Linda Lovelace) who can only have an orgasm by performing fellatio, *Deep Throat* was released in June of that year, premiering at the New World Theater in New York City. Reviewed enthusiastically by *Screw* magazine editor Al Goldstein for its explicitness and humor, it earned decent box office receipts during its first week. As attention grew, it was reviewed by a number of leading film critics, including Judith Crist, Vincent Canby, and Andrew Sarris. Amidst the clamor in the media, the film became the center of legal battles. The owner of the New World Theater, Bob Sumner, was arrested, charged with exhibiting obscene material, and fined three million dollars. Despite censorship challenges in other parts of the country, *Deep Throat* grossed five million dollars within a year of its release.

Damiano's next pornographic feature release, *The Devil in Miss Jones*, opened at the 57th Street Playhouse in New York City in 1973. It, too, had a successful run at the box office, as did another of the movies associated with porno chic, the Mitchell brothers' *Behind the Green Door*. This film ran in the brothers' own theater, and they distributed it to theaters in major urban areas across the nation. It grossed over one million dollars. Porno chic had arrived, and the media took note, with film critics at established newspapers reviewing porn films.

Several factors converged to foster the porno chic fad during the early 1970s. Firstly, the difficulty of prosecuting for obscenity emboldened pornographers just as it had sexploitation filmmakers since the 1950s. Pornographers asserted their newly won rights to freedom of expression and refused to become invisible again, an assertiveness buoyed by the economic clout of the pornography market. Secondly, affordable home viewing technology (8mm, 16mm, and eventually video technology) allowed the middle- and upper-class segments of the audience for pornography to avoid public venues and view pornography in the privacy of their homes, a pattern of consumption established long before pornography emerged into public view, but now granted the legal protection of the right of privacy provided by the Supreme Court's ruling in *Stanley v. Georgia* (1969).[9] The Court ruled that individuals had the right to possess obscene materials in the privacy of their home.

Thirdly, pornographers also benefited from the way in which commentators in the media frequently conflated the nudity and sex in European art house movies, American underground films, sexploitation films, and Hollywood movies together with pornographic films. The benefit was twofold. Pornography benefited from being grouped with art films because pornographers could claim the same First Amendment protections for their films. After the popularity of *Deep Throat* and *Behind the Green Door* brought pornography into the media's limelight for a short period, many Americans had the impression that sex in cinema was widespread and a part of cultural diversity that would be impossible to regulate.

Fourthly, the increasing influence of the cultural radicalism on liberalism, especially liberal creeds about freedom of expression and the right of privacy, made any number of sex acts and values a matter of subjective personal "taste" rather than community standards. For example, the efforts of gays and lesbians, who fought during the late 1960s and early 1970s to remove the stigma of perversion from their sexuality, strengthened the interrelationship between individual autonomy and social tolerance, both traditional liberal values. The philosophy of "doing your own thing" was applied to watching pornography movies.

Despite the competition from explicit sex films, Hollywood generally avoided pornography's exposure of genitals because of the potential of breaking obscenity laws. Furthermore, filmmakers had a strong economic incentive not to cross the boundary between sexploitation and pornography. Many theaters refused to run films with an X rating, and many newspapers refused to run advertisements for X-rated films, so most filmmakers edited their films to avoid an X rating. Even in 1972 and 1973, the peak years of porno chic, less than 5 percent of Hollywood films received X ratings from CARA.[10] After the brief flowering of porno chic, Hollywood's greatest benefit from pornography was the latter's visibility since most Americans, especially liberals, could see that Hollywood films were not nearly as explicit as pornographic films, even if some conservatives claimed they could see little distinction.

What revolution there was in nudity and sex in Hollywood films from the middle of the 1960s to the middle of the 1970s transpired with an eye on the bottom line. The demise of the Code also meant that studios did not have to seek PCA approval during preproduction in order to secure external funding. Risks were shifted to the box office. From a marketing perspective, studios differentiated consumer segments and targeted them with suitably appealing products. Market variety was the economic response of a liberal capitalist view of providing goods according to market demand (within the limits set by the law). Much of the process consisted of the corporate ownership within the industry, through market research, trial and error, blind faith, and luck, shifting its mode of production and distribution to fit the changing demographics of the country. Anytime a film did particularly well at the box office, studios typically attempted to replicate its success with variants of imitations. When sexuality proved to draw crowds into theaters, studios jumped on the bandwagon, creating a cycle of films infused with some degree of sexual content.

By representing commercially that which the Code had repressed from general release movies, New Hollywood, sexploitation, pornography, European imports, and American underground films had the cumulative effect of sanctioning the sexual in the public sphere. Motion pictures contributed to the growing visibility and acknowledgment of a plurality of sexual norms. The banks of social acceptance had been widened as the boundaries had been pushed back to allow room in American film culture for marginal films and for what had been long been suppressed in Hollywood films. In their movie attendance patterns, audiences ratified what Kinsey had claimed: there were—and long had been—"scores of patterns" of sexual behavior in the United States.[11] The history of marginal markets provides evidence that different patterns of representations of nudity and sex in films had long existed as well. Acknowledgment was not always synonymous with acceptance, though. Despite the increased presence of nudity and sex on American movie screens, it would be misleading to say that the changes were absolute.

First, the Supreme Court established a new test for obscenity in *Miller v. California* (1973). Importantly for the film industry, the Court ruled that community standards were local.[12] Studio heads dreaded becoming entangled in a plethora of censorship cases across the nation. Their fears came true when a jury in Albany, Georgia, convicted theater manager Billy Jenkins of violating a state obscenity law when he exhibited *Carnal Knowledge* (1971). In the film, Jonathan (Jack Nicholson) has sex regularly with Susan (Candice Bergen) while they are college students and after she has started dating Sandy (Art Garfunkel), who is Jonathan's best friend. They are shown having sex once, fully clothed. Sandy and Susan's prelude to sex is also shown, in a scene that shows her emotional distance from Sandy (she has her back turned and does not look at him) more than her sexual passion for him.

Later, Jonathan has a relationship with Bobbie (Ann-Margret, who received an Oscar nomination for best supporting actress). They sleep together on their first date. Their lovemaking is first implied by a shot of Bobbie's fur coat and hers and later Jonathan's cries of passion on the soundtrack. The camera tracks into the bedroom and reveals Bobbie lying naked, on her back and side, her breasts barely visible, her buttocks very visible. The next morning, Jonathan showers while Bobbie eats in bed, naked, shot in a long shot from the side. He calls her into the shower, and she goes, her buttocks clearly visible and her breasts slightly but briefly visible. Finally, in a scene that is typical of Mike Nichols's emphasis on the importance of talking and communicating as a part of both individual personality and sexuality, the film ends with Jonathan visiting a prostitute named Louise (Rita Moreno). She is familiar with his impotence and understands his need for a well-controlled game in which she talks him to erection, which is off screen.

In *Jenkins v. Georgia* (1973), the Supreme Court overruled the Georgia courts. In rejecting the charges, the Court established that only hardcore pornography was subject to obscenity charges. The Court concluded that the film's nudity and sex was not patently offensive because the camera did not "focus on the bodies of the actors" during scenes of "ultimate sexual acts," nor were the actors' genitals exhibited during those scenes. The occasional nudity in *Carnal Knowledge* did not render it obscene.[13] Indeed, its "occasional" (and brief) nudity and sex had warranted only an R rating from CARA. The film had, though, unflinchingly presented sexual quandaries stemming from men's difficulties with intimacy and commitment. The case worried the industry anyway, since the film was Academy Award material and neither sexploitation nor pornography. Was Hollywood out of sync with the moral codes of small town America? The Supreme Court ruled it was not. Despite the Court placing stricter limits on the power of juries to define *patently offensive*, studios' fervor for sexual material cooled somewhat.

The industry's acceptance or rejection of sex in film was also affected by its acceptance of the ratings system's age groups as market segments. Even before the ratings system had been adopted, the mass audience that had made motion pictures the most important mass medium in American society during the studio era had fragmented into various age groups and taste publics. As the 1960s neared an end, audience research had made it clear to studios that a large portion of their audience was young. The children of the baby boom had come of age and their impact at the box office had been demonstrated by the tremendous success of *The Graduate* and *Bonnie and Clyde* in 1967. By the late 1960s, American youth could be divided into at least three major groups.

The smallest group, the counterculture, consisted of those who dropped out of society and pursued alternative, often collectivist and drug-infused, lifestyles in larger cities, especially San Francisco, Los Angeles, and New York. The student movement was larger than the counterculture and consisted of college students involved in the civil rights and antiwar movements. Although relatively distinct at the beginning of the decade, these two groups overlapped somewhat by the decade's end, especially culturally (long hair, clothing styles, drug use). The largest group of American youth was also the least visible in the mass media. These were the working- and middle-class youth who followed quietly in the footsteps of the silent majority. One thing all of the segments of the youth population seemed to have in common was attending movies.

Studios did not break the youth demographic into such categories as dropouts, radicals, or suburban middle class, but their film production seemed to be aimed at capturing them. In 1969, the return on investment of low-budget counterculture hits like *Alice's Restaurant* and *Easy Rider* made it clear that youth was a gold mine in waiting. *Easy Rider*, which had been produced by BBS, an independent film company, in particular was a huge success. It was the tale of two young men's cross country trip after they score big on a cocaine deal. Long-haired Wyatt (Peter Fonda) and Billy (Dennis Hopper) drive their motorcycles from Los Angeles to New Orleans and encounter counterculture hospitality and hostility along the way. They pick up a hitchhiker (Luke Askew) who takes them to his hippie commune in New Mexico. While at the commune, Wyatt and Billy go skinny dipping in hot springs with a couple of its residents, Lisa (Luana Anders) and Sarah (Sabrina Scharf). After they are in New Orleans, Wyatt and Billy, following up on a tip they got from one of their traveling companions, George Hanson (Jack Nicholson), go to a brothel and retain the services of two prostitutes, Mary (Toni Basil) and Karen (Karen Black). The four of them take LSD and during their acid trip, the couples have sex. While the sex was not central to the story, it was important for representing the two protagonists' alternative lifestyle.

Other films targeting the youth demographic included sex in their stories as well. In 1970, *The Strawberry Statement* and Michelangelo Antonioni's *Zabriskie Point* portrayed student radicals, but were much less successful. Despite ample images of young flesh in a desert orgy scene, *Zabriskie Point* in particular did very poorly. *Love Story* (1970) seemed to aim for the third demographic, young people who emulated rather than rebelled against their parents' lives. In marrying the ill-fated Jenny (Ali MacGraw) and being cut off from his father (Ray Milland), Oliver (Ryan O'Neal) does not reject his father's values, but his father's restrictions on romantic love. The film confines Jenny and Oliver's sex to kissing and implications of unsuccessful efforts at getting pregnant after they are married. The GP-rated tearjerker made in the style of Code-era Hollywood was a huge hit for Paramount.

Exhibitors accommodated shifting demographics by building smaller venues, and the studios cut their production drastically to around twenty or fewer films annually. While the appeal to younger audiences was driven by market concerns, it was at least facilitated by a new generation of studio executives—sometimes young themselves, like Robert Evans at Paramount, or middle-aged like Ted Ashley at Warner Communications—who benefited from the generational shift, as they

replaced veterans of the studio system with directors that were younger—
or at least new to Hollywood—to create films that would appeal to
America's youth. Several new names began garnering critical attention
and meeting with popular success. Over the next few years, directors as
diverse as Roman Polanski, Robert Altman, Arthur Penn, Herbert Ross,
Alan J. Pakula, Haskell Wexler, Bob Fosse, Peter Bogdanovich, William
Friedkin, Hal Ashby, Sam Pekinpah, Francis Ford Coppola, Steven
Spielberg, Martin Scorsese, and George Lucas would direct films that
injected freshness into Hollywood's output. Even veteran filmmakers such
as Stanley Kubrick, long an industry outsider, found favor with both
studios and audiences, and gained reputations for being "hip."

The emphasis on individual directors in the promotion of the films,
which roughly coincided with greater critical attention being paid to
individual directors, has led film historians to refer to the cinema of
New Hollywood as *auteur cinema*. For a few years, these mavericks were
allowed creative freedom. By the middle of the 1970s, though, changes
in tax laws that discouraged risk taking by the corporations that owned
the film production companies, the rising expense of making films,
changes in exhibition patterns with the growth of multiplex theaters in
(or near) malls, and the success of wide release distribution formats led
to the demise of experimental cinema (by Hollywood standards) and
the ascent of the blockbuster. While often credited with reinvigorating
Hollywood's creativity, the films of auteur cinema never developed the
economic clout of their successor, the *blockbuster*.

In foregrounding the clash between public virtue and private vices,
films like *Who's Afraid of Virginia Woolf?*, *The Graduate*, the experimental
films of New Hollywood, and the increased visibility of pornography,
sexploitation, and American underground films combined to create a
wave of revelation of intimate matters in popular culture. Many commentators were convinced that what appeared on American screens
reflected a broad shift concerning nonmarital sex. By the end of the
decade, *Look* magazine would conclude that "Puritan America" was
"gone forever."[14] Americans, it seemed, no longer conformed to the sex
norms codified in law.

4

Everybody's Doing It—Aren't They?

WHAT'S GOING ON?

As researchers followed in Kinsey's footsteps and uncovered Americans' sex lives, most discovered a plurality of norms. Sexologist Isadore Rubin's seven categories of sex norms are representative of the discoveries made by 1965. She found that some Americans remained very traditional—as did most state laws—and confined sex to marriage. Those with a slightly less conservative attitude stressed caution, while those with a more open attitude accepted public discussions of sex. A "humanistic liberalism" was mostly concerned with the role of sex in interpersonal relationships while a more radical humanism promoted greater sexual freedom. A "fun morality" accepted premarital intercourse without reservation while an attitude of "sexual anarchy" denigrated all sexual taboos. Rubin concluded the best Americans could hope for was to agree to disagree since there seemed to be "no possibility for our pluralistic society as a whole to reach a consensus about many aspects of sex values."[1] Other studies and the media confirmed—and repeatedly talked about—Americans' newly discovered sexual pluralism. Media attention often spotlighted fringe behaviors, giving many Americans the impression that a revolution had taken place.

In 1969, *Time* magazine surveyed changes in Americans' moral beliefs about personal honesty, drug use, and sex. *Time* simplified an array of attitudes to "Two Americas," one traditional and conservative, the other contemporary and liberal. The magazine concluded that the most obvious shifts were related to sex but rejected the notion of a sexual revolution. For example, although only one-third disliked on-screen nudity, over three-fourths of those polled had no desire to see pornography legalized. Nonetheless, one-third now believed homosexuality was a matter for consenting adults while nearly two-thirds believed decisions about abortion were best left to a woman and her physician. Just under half of those queried believed it was as acceptable for unmarried women as for unmarried men to have sex. Taking their cue from the mass media coverage of sex, respondents noted that Americans talked more about sex and over half took that to be a positive development.[2]

While the majority of Americans remained in the sexual center, enough were liberalizing to encourage entrepreneurs to accommodate sexual plurality by providing commercial outlets in a slowly sexualizing public sphere. One such response was singles bars and nightclubs that catered to young male and female singles that appeared in cities across the country. As young people began frequenting singles bars in greater numbers for the pursuit of sexual pleasure or just to meet someone, the press identified the development of a singles culture. Their sexual self-expression no longer confined to the private sphere, middle-class youth did not need the counterculture to break with their parents' sex norms. Singles bars seemed innocuous alongside other market responses to the demands of an increasingly sexualized consumer society. Topless bars, massage parlors, strip clubs, sex clubs like Plato's Retreat in New York, retreats like Sandstone in Los Angeles, and sex guides like *The Joy of Sex: A Cordon Bleu Guide to Lovemaking* (1972) were as visible in American cities as pornography theaters. Advertising filled billboards and magazines with sexual imagery. Even though more strictly regulated than film, television and popular music managed to deal with nonmarital sex. The overt commercialization of sex coincided with greater openness among Americans about sex as well as fierce debates between conservatives and liberals about changing sexual values and behaviors.

At the center of the debates were increases in the rates of nonmarital intercourse. Both males and females had increased their nonmarital sexual activity steadily since 1965, but the most novel changes occurred among young women. The double standard, which proscribed premarital sex for women but often tolerated it for men, had weakened by the middle of the 1970s. Marriage, or the promise of marriage, was no longer a necessary precondition for sex for many middle-class Americans. The increase in premarital sex among young women was nearly three times that of young men, to some extent because the increase involved a leveling of the sexual playing field. As a result, differences in the views and behavior of young men and women were less distinct by the end of the 1970s.[3]

Of all of the social developments that influenced changes in men's and especially women's attitudes toward nonmarital sex and cohabitation, the most significant was, directly and indirectly, second-wave feminism. Second-wave feminism had become visible with the founding of the National Organization for Women (NOW) in 1966 to fight against gender discrimination in the workplace and to advance the cause of women's civil and political rights. Organizations like NOW were largely reformist and liberal, seeking to change the laws that governed women's behavior. Alongside liberal feminist organizations, radical feminist groups were formed in the late 1960s by women who had abandoned student movements because of gender discrimination. Often called *women's liberation* groups, they sought alternatives to, rather than modifications of, mainstream sexual norms. While liberal and radical feminist groups often disagreed over goals and strategies, they were united in their denunciation of the roles women were traditionally forced into. Radical feminists, in particular, fought for women's right to greater control over their bodies, including greater sexual freedom.

Over a relatively short period of time, women began to assert their right to the same sexual standards as men. In 1971, fewer than 40 percent of never-married women living in metropolitan areas had experienced sexual intercourse by the age of eighteen compared to nearly 57 percent in 1979. For nineteen-year-olds, the figure increased from just under 47 percent to nearly 70 percent during the same period.[4] No longer did America's youth automatically deem premarital sex immoral or avoid it. Sex may have lost its conjugal moorings, but it remained central to intimate relationships. Most singles accepted sex as crucial to self-fulfillment and satisfying intimate relationships. *Commitment* and *meaningful relationships* became the buzzwords associated with sex.

As assumptions about what constituted a committed, meaningful relationship changed in the 1970s, the rate of cohabitation tripled, becoming more common among the middle class.[5] Research revealed, however, that cohabitation did not replace marriage. Cohabitation was less a substitute for than a prelude to marriage, although not necessarily to the same person. Serial monogamy became common. The increase in premarital sex accompanied a fall in the age of sexual debut and a rise in the age of first marriage. As more and more men and women chose to live together without exchanging marriage vows, Americans simply acknowledged nonmarital sex, and adherence to the double standard declined. Conservatives still encouraged and supported marriage and disapproved of what had once been dubbed "living in sin," not least because of cohabitation's sexual implications. For liberals, couples living together without legal sanction represented no more than a life-stage choice for couples who preferred the benefits of pursuing self-fulfillment and greater sexual equality over those of a permanent marital relationship. Men and women themselves differed slightly in their attitudes toward living together out of wedlock. Even though more women than men chose cohabitation in hope of marrying the person they lived with, a majority of neither women nor men lived with someone of the opposite sex with the sole intention of marrying them. Women were becoming more independent and attaining greater sexual equality.[6] Serial monogamy crossed gender lines.

In American films, the absence of ambiguity or explicit conservative attitudes toward nonmarital sex suggests that filmmakers assumed that nonmarital sex had become commonplace, unremarkable, or inoffensive. The race to the altar was replaced with a race to intimacy, and sex became a familiar symbol of intimacy in a relationship. Sometimes, the road to intimacy was hectic and strewn with obstacles, as in *Shampoo* (1975).

SHAMPOO

Shampoo bridged the experimentalism of New Hollywood with the industry's growing faith in blockbusters. It was directed by Hal Ashby, a prototypical New Hollywood director, but produced by Warren Beatty, who also starred in it. Typical of many Hollywood films during the middle-to-late 1970s, *Shampoo* represented sex with little ambiguity, even though it remained acceptable to CARA, which gave it an R. The decline in Hollywood's cinematic double entendres pointed to conservatives' diminished influence on the boundaries of nudity and sexual content in Hollywood films. Characters were free to have sex.

In *Shampoo*, the characters' sex is curbed, it seems, only by interruptions, a motif established in the credits sequence when Beverly Hills hairdresser and rake George Roundy (Warren Beatty) and Felicia (Lee Grant), one of his customers who he is having an affair with, have their lovemaking broken off by the ringing telephone. The call comes from another woman, whom George asks to come by the salon. In a later scene, Felicia's husband, Lester (Jack Warden), from whom George is trying to secure money to start his own beauty salon, interrupts his own mistress, Jackie (Julie Christie) and George making love on two different occasions.

First, Lester walks in on the two in Jackie's bathroom, although they manage to conceal what they were doing and convince Lester that George is only setting her hair—and that George is gay. The second time, Lester finds George and Jackie in the pool house at a party and catches them in the act. Initially, Lester is simply being a voyeur until the light in the pool house comes on and he discovers who the couple is. As in the beginning of the film, lovemaking concealed from the screen is accompanied by the sounds of lovemaking on the soundtrack before light reveals who is illicitly making love. In the beginning of the film, the audience is made privy to a couple's infidelities and the narrative is set in motion; with Lester's discovery, a similar revelation moves the film toward its conclusion.

Despite characters that have sex more frequently than in most Hollywood films because of its Don Juan theme, *Shampoo* was typical of Hollywood films that received R ratings for their nudity, dialogue, and "adult" situations. While the sex in *Shampoo* is uninhibited, the on-screen sex and nudity are not. On-screen sex is presumably simulated, and there are no shots of male or female genitals. Nudity in the film is almost always implied or off-screen although there are a few exceptions. The most visible exceptions occur in a Jacuzzi sequence at the same party at which Lester and George's girlfriend, Jill (Goldie Hawn), discover Jackie and George making love. The party is held in a swank house but reflects the degree to which countercultural values were being adopted by all social classes. Besides the open pot smoking, groups of men and women get into a hot tub together, and in the scene, the breasts of one of the young women are seen in a medium shot. There is also a brief long shot of a young woman standing totally nude in profile (her arms conceal her breasts) in the same sequence.

Despite competition from sexploitation, pornography, European, or underground films, Hollywood filmmakers had not embraced, nor had CARA allowed them to embrace, the nudity or sex found in marginal films. Yet *Shampoo*, while not graphic, does occasionally borrow narrative cues from sexploitation and pornography. For example, in one comic scene, after George has cut Jackie's hair in her bathroom, she examines the haircut in the mirror, likes what she sees, calls George a genius, and gives him a kiss. As in pornography, a single kiss suffices to unleash uncontrollable sexual urges in George and Jackie, and they react to physical stimuli like sexual automatons. The film's narrative also resembles pornography in the interchangeability of sexual partners. Whether inspired by sex films or William Wycherley's Restoration comedy *The Country Wife* (1675), which screenwriter Robert Towne said inspired the initial premise of the film, the narrative is driven forward by George's bustling from one sexual liaison to the next, with futile efforts to finance his own salon wedged in between.[7]

Despite its surface comfort with showing sex, the film expresses a critique, chiefly conservative but also voiced by liberals, of sexual promiscuity consistently levied at the time: it was depersonalized, or in the parlance of the period, *hedonistic* and *narcissistic*. George's inattention results from his self-centeredness. His obsessive self-interest leads him to ignore or interrupt Jill whenever she attempts to communicate with him and achieve greater intimacy. In an early scene, Jill talks about their relationship with him, but George pays no attention to her as she walks around in a baby doll nightgown (echoing sexploitation). At one point, she sits facing the camera, in a medium close up, opening and closing her legs, revealing and concealing her panties, in a shot that could be interpreted as a parody of the Production Code. Because George is absorbed with his financial difficulties, and presumably sexually spent, he pays little attention to Jill and makes no firm commitments when she discusses their future.

For the upper class and their sexual lackeys like George and Jackie in *Shampoo*, sex is intricately related to, or dependent upon, economics. None of the characters see themselves caught up in a sexual economy, though. George says to Jackie after they have an argument that he does not have sex with "anybody for money. I do it for fun." George's barb is aimed at Jackie, who he insinuates prostitutes herself by being Lester's "kept woman." Yet, Jackie is not the only character unable to separate sex from commercial demands. Sex motivates George's career choice to be a hairdresser in order to meet women, Jill's decision to invite Johnny Pope (Tony Bill) to a party after it becomes clear that she has a chance of landing a part in a commercial he is directing, Felicia's acceptance of her role as a pampered housewife, and Lester's ability to juggle a marriage and a mistress.

Each of the characters behaves hypocritically. In Warren Beatty's view, *Shampoo*'s main theme was the hypocrisy of Americans who attempted to conceal their conflicting desires. Beatty's point was that support for the dominant sexual ideology, especially that of conservatives, had become hypocritical, a point stressed repeatedly by youth during the 1960s. The highlight of the film, in Beatty's view, is a scene during the Republican election-night banquet sequence at which Jackie, who is intoxicated, responds to overtures from a man, Sid Roth (William Castle), sitting next to her. Roth tells her, "I can get you anything you'd like. What would you like?" She replies, casting a glance at George, who is also sitting next to her, "Well, first of all, I'd like to suck his cock." She proceeds to get on her knees at the table, and the film represents fellatio, presumably simulated since the mise-en-scène is composed so that the table and the other guests largely obscure what Jackie is doing. David Begelman, the president of Columbia Pictures, which coproduced and distributed the film, found the scene offensive and requested it cut, but Beatty, who coproduced the film, refused, reasoning that it was "the best line of the movie ... the very point of the movie," according to Peter Biskind.[8]

Juxtaposed with Lester's blatant personal hypocrisy, Jackie's answer and her subsequent sex act shatter the carefully orchestrated façade. According to Beatty, the "reason Julie's line made for such an explosive moment was because it shredded that hypocrisy."[9] In trying simultaneously to stop Jackie and pretend nothing is happening, Lester represents the conservative preference for preserving a façade even if others know what it conceals. By contrast, the liberal infatuation with revelation drives Jill to demand that George confess his infidelities. She wants to know, she says, because then she would know that he had lied to her throughout their relationship and that he was incapable of love. He confesses he had slept with "them all. That's what I do." He appends an unsolicited confession: that he has no regrets. She thanks him for telling her. With their advocacy of communication, liberals preferred painful truths to dishonest façades. This point is underscored by the scene following Jackie's exploits at the banquet. When Felicia asks Lester to confess his infidelity, she implores him to "be straight with me for once in your life."

In *Shampoo*, the narrative makes no comment on the legal status of George and Jill's relationship or their living arrangements other than her expression of a desire to make the relationship permanent through marriage. By this time, American films depicted cohabitation as a viable housing arrangement for an intimate relationship. By the end of the 1970s, Hollywood represented cohabitation nonchalantly in romantic comedies like *The Goodbye Girl* (1977), in which the main character, Paula McFadden (Marsha Mason), lives with a series of boyfriends before falling in love—and living—with Elliott Garfield (Richard Dreyfuss). Narratives cued viewers to care about the quality of the intimate relationship as experienced by each individual in it rather than the relationship's legal status. Cohabitation was acknowledged and, by liberals at least, accepted by the middle of the decade. Hollywood filmmakers for their part, allowing for variations deriving from the restrictions of the various ratings categories, represented cohabitation regularly and without condemnation, in films rated PG or R.

Feminists often took filmmakers to task. They found the changes in the way Hollywood studios handled nudity (usually female) and sex wanting. Despite significant erosion in the double standard, feminists argued that women were still too often represented as maternal figures for the sustenance of or as sexual objects for the pleasure of men. Even a self-sufficient character, such as Bree Daniels, played by Jane Fonda, who won an Academy Award for Best Actress for the part, was represented in terms of a deviant sexual role, the prostitute, in *Klute* (1971). In *Thunderbolt and Lightfoot* (1974), a suburban housewife (Luanne Roberts) stands nude at her glass patio door for the viewing pleasure of Lightfoot (Jeff Bridges), who is doing yard work. Women were not just sex objects, though. In *Alice Doesn't Live Here Anymore* (1974), there were more than glimmers of independence in the title character, Alice Hyatt. Women's roles in Hollywood films were changing, but women were still often represented in traditional gender roles and too rarely as the main protagonists in Hollywood films, feminists justifiably argued. While not a feminist film, Woody Allen's *Annie Hall* (1977) portrayed a young woman's struggles to become independent and maintain her own identity while in an intimate relationship. Even though she is shy and awkward the first time she meets stand-up comedian Alvy Singer (Woody Allen), Annie Hall (Diane Keaton) already has the independence and willingness to meet new people that eventually lead her to take greater control of her life.

ANNIE HALL

Woody Allen's *Annie Hall* portrayed changing attitudes toward intimacy by emphasizing the impermanence of intimate relationships. Allen did this partly through the nonlinear episodic structuring of the film so the viewer asks the question: Why did the relationship deteriorate and fall apart? A linear approach more typical of the traditional romantic comedy would have led audiences to speculate over the genre's usual question: Will the two become a couple? The nonlinear structure also makes the outcome seem to be almost predetermined, not so much because of Annie and Alvy's personalities but because, Allen suggests, contemporary society is no longer conducive to permanent relationships.

Annie and Alvy seemed fated to always be searching for a love that will last but never finding it. They are trapped in a cycle of relationship beginnings and endings (with often unsuccessful sexual middles), which are exactly what many of the film's small vignettes present. The growing disenchantment some Americans felt at the prospect of any relationship lasting longer than a given phase of one's life emerges through flashbacks of Annie and Alvy's earlier relationships.

In one vignette, Alvy is backstage at a political rally for 1960 Democratic presidential candidate Adlai Stevenson. He is talking to, and flirting with, Allison Portchnik (Carol Kane). In the next scene, Alvy and Allison are shown together in bed sometime after the release of the Warren Commission Report in 1964. Alvy, Allison points out, is using his obsession with a conspiracy (President John F. Kennedy's assassination) to avoid having sex with her. Addressing the camera, Alvy confesses he has no idea why he is no longer attracted to Allison. The viewer has no idea, either, since the narrative elides over their life together. Alvy's pattern of making sure that his relationships fail, though, is clearly established.

Alvy's inability to remain in a relationship is underscored by a flashback to his marriage with Robin (Janet Margolin), a New York writer. Alvy encourages the cerebral Robin to be more physical, exhorting her to make love in a bedroom at a cocktail party while the other guests socialize. She rejects his entreaties, telling him that he uses "sex to express hostility." Interestingly, both Robin and Allison are intellectually and culturally the polar opposites of small-town, Midwestern Annie.

Between the flashbacks sketching Alvy's failed marriages, flashbacks show Annie with her first "love," Dennis (uncredited), a boy she dated in high school in Chippewa Falls, Wisconsin. Next, Annie stands with her back against a wall as she listens intently to the babble of a hippie actor (John Glover) she is dating. In a very revealing shot, the actor caresses the top of her bare arm. Annie glances very briefly at his hand, indicating that she is taken aback by the intimate, physical contact. She allows him to caress her arm, though. The scene subtly embodies the transition many young Americans made from conservative small-town backgrounds to the more experimental lifestyles available in urban America.

Los Angeles is the apex of experimental hedonism, personified by Alvy's friend since childhood, Rob, who moves to California where he has a hit sitcom drenched in canned laughter and applause. Alvy is thrown in jail while in L.A., after wrecking a rental car and ripping up his driver's license. Rob bails him out. As they are leaving, Rob tells Alvy—whom he inexplicably calls "Max"—that he had interrupted him having sex with "Twins, Max. Sixteen-year-olds. Can you imagine the mathematical possibilities?" To conservatives, tolerance was becoming synonymous with indulgence and decadence, creating a social climate not conducive to permanent relationships. For liberals, tolerance stemmed from recognizing and accepting the existence of sexual diversity and the importance of sex for intimate relationships, a concern in *Annie Hall*.

Well into the film, there is a flashback of Annie and Alvy's initial meeting. After playing tennis together with Rob and his girlfriend at the time, Annie and Alvy go to her place. She is wearing the Chaplinesque outfit that sparked a fashion trend in the late 1970s: a large black floppy hat, a matching vest, man's chinos, white dress shirt, and tie. He compliments her appearance. They go out onto her balcony for what became one of the most famous scenes in the film. As they make small talk and discuss Annie's photography, their thoughts are placed in titles at the top of the screen. While Annie worries about making a good impression, Alvy wonders "what she looks like naked." Basic gender stereotypes enable Allen to parody the way in which couples initiate relationships.

At one point in their on again/off again relationship, Alvy and Annie break up as she gets into a cab, so he walks down the sidewalk asking strangers for their opinion on relationships and what makes them work. One of the film's central messages, that relationships are doomed, is confirmed by an older woman who passes by on the sidewalk just as Annie breaks off her relationship with Alvy. The woman assures Alvy that it is not his responsibility, but rather it is relationships that are destined to fail: "Never something you do. That's how people are. Love fades."

The film ends with Alvy concluding pessimistically that people keep entering into relationships even though they are "totally irrational, and crazy, and absurd." The absurdity is not that people do not have strong feelings for one another. At one point, Alvy tells Annie, "Love is, is too weak a word for the way I feel—I lurve you, you know, I loave you, I luff you." The conundrum was the fleeting intensity of the passion that accompanies the beginning of an intimate relationship. Once the intensity has died down, the relationship no longer seems sufficient, and each of the partners begins to look anew for that ephemeral passion. Fittingly, the film's working title had been *A Roller Coaster Named Desire*. Ever the comedian, Alvy draws a parallel between an old joke and the desire to stay on desire's rollercoaster as it goes up and down and around and around despite the apparent impossibility of his generation maintaining relationships like an older generation had. Throughout the film, Allen satirizes individuals' newfound freedom to fluctuate in their relationship commitments because of their narcissism, a narcissism tied to sexual pleasure.

The centrality of sex in *Annie Hall* can be seen in Allen's use of Freudian psychology in the film in jokes, in dialogue as explanations of sexual desire, in having the characters be in analysis, and so forth. Allen foregrounds the school of psychological thought that was instrumental in placing sex at the forefront of Americans' concerns throughout the postwar era. In one scene, Alvy compliments Annie by telling her that she is "polymorphously perverse," because, he elaborates, "you're exceptional in bed because you get pleasure in every part of your body when I touch you."

Allen satirizes the "talking cure" of Freudian therapy in a split-screen sequence in which Annie and Alvy are in session with their respective analysts. Annie and Alvy's problem is that they do not talk to each other so their divergent perceptions and experiences of their life together cannot be reconciled. The inanity of trying to salvage an intimate relationship through dialogue with a third party—the analyst—is underlined by the disparity in Annie and Alvy's perceptions of their sex life, which they agree is important. Each of them tells their analyst that they have sex three times a week. Annie believes they have sex constantly while Alvy thinks they almost never make love anymore, playing on the role of sex in enhancing or wrecking intimacy.

Annie Hall also makes fun of the loosening up of middle-class sexual mores. At one point, Alvy buys Annie sexy lingerie and at another replaces a regular light bulb with a red one to give the bedroom "a little Old New Orleans essence," an allusion to that city's famous Storyville red-light district. The emergence of sex talk into public is treated hilariously in the film. When Annie and Alvy are bickering while waiting in line at a movie theater, he interprets her having overslept as being "a hostile gesture." She retorts rather loudly, "I know—because of our sexual problem, right?" Alvy quickly tries to cover up her indiscreetness, by asking loudly, "Wasn't that a novel by Henry James? A sequel to *The Turn of the Screw*?" The scene nicely encapsulates the variety of perspectives on making private matters public.

It is not the sexual as such that bothers Alvy, since he was seen earlier making a joke based on sexual innuendo during a period of greater sexual reticence. In the scene in which he meets Allison, he tells the audience that he had little luck with a woman he had been dating: "I was trying to do to her what Eisenhower has been doing to the country for the last eight years." What upset Alvy is having his private life aired in public. He asks Annie if "everybody in line at the New Yorker has to know our rate of intercourse?" His dilemma is precisely that in a sense everybody already knows: sex had gone public. Fewer and fewer eyebrows were raised by pronouncements such as Annie's.

Annie Hall satirized the prevalent notion that sex is the foundation on which contemporary relationships rests. The importance placed on sex was not surprising after decades of having psychologists, sex therapists, and even religious leaders emphasize the importance sex in the companionate marriage and as the main concern of marital adjustment. Sexual desire and performance, Americans had been taught, were essential to keeping intimate relationships whole because when desire and performance no longer meshed, then one or both of the individuals in the relationship became unsatisfied. *Annie Hall* was far from the only film made in the new climate.

NO TURNING BACK

Taken for granted in many Hollywood films was the widespread notion that self-expression, personality, and sexuality were intertwined. As Robert Bellah noted, "the expressive aspect of our culture exists for the liberation and fulfillment of the individual. Its genius is that it enables the individual to think of commitments—from marriage and work to political and religious involvement—as enhancements of the sense of individual well-being rather than as moral imperatives."[10] Even as the liberal 1970s were ending and a more conservative era dawning, sex remained significant in American life and in American cinema.

Sex in film had been mainstreamed. Not all films had sexual content, obviously, and not all films with sexual content had explicit or a great deal of sex. But sexual themes and brief shots of nudity or brief sex scenes had become much more accepted and frequent in films rated R. The surprise mega-success *Saturday Night Fever* (1977) included several scenes with sexual content. For example, in an early scene the film's hero, king of the disco dance floor Tony Manero (John Travolta), agrees to dance with a fawning Annette (Donna Pescow) in an upcoming dance contest. They discuss the upcoming contest while sitting in a side bar in the 2001 Odyssey, a disco club where much of the film's story plays out. While they talk, a woman does a striptease on a small stage behind the bar. Tony leaves Annette at the bar. The stripper bares her top, and Annette looks nonchalantly at the dancer's bare breasts. She then looks down and smiles at her own cleavage. A stripper does not offend the young working-class women who hang out with Tony and his friends—they are light years from Elaine Robinson.

Outside the Odyssey, Tony helps one of those friends, Joey (Joseph Cali), get Double J (Paul Pape) out of the car they share for scoring with girls on the side of a busy sidewalk outside the club. Double J is on the back seat of the car, his bare buttocks visible, having sexual intercourse with a young woman. He brings her to orgasm while the other friend and his date look on, smiling. To underscore the Club 54-style hedonism and the impersonal pick-ups of the disco scene, Double J first asks the woman what her name was when they get out of the car. Despite his and his friends' sexual freewheeling, Tony has a conservative view of women's sexuality based on the traditional double standard. He later condescendingly asks Annette whether she is "a nice girl or a cunt." She answers, "Both." Tony, though, does not think it is possible for an unmarried young woman to be sexually active and remain "nice." In his chauvinistic worldview, there are women you pick up and take out to the car and those you might marry. He eventually ends up in the back seat of the car with Annette. Unable to have sex, he crudely orders her to give him a blow job. Later, he tries to force himself on his new dance partner, Stephanie (Karen Lynn Gorney), but she rejects him.

In the film's murkiest sequence, Tony's friends come outside and announce "Annette is going to give everybody snatch pie." Tony tries to stop them, but they drive around while first Joey and then Double J have sex with her. She obviously (and audibly) does not want to have sex with the second guy, but he does not stop. After they park on the bridge, Tony tells Annette she is now a "cunt." She runs from the car hysterical. He chases her down and apologizes. The sequence culminates when the youngest of the group, Bobby C. (Barry Miller), falls to his death.

Even tamer films such as Paramount's adaptation of the smash Broadway musical *Grease* (1978), with its sentimental portrait of the 1950s, hinted strongly at premarital sex even though it was aimed at a teen audience. Rizzo (Stockard Channing) initially rejects Sandy (Olivia Newton-John) as a member of her girl gang, the Pinks, because she is "too pure to be Pink." Even more pointedly, Rizzo herself fears she is pregnant. Also starring John Travolta, *Grease* was the highest grossing film of the year. *National Lampoon's Animal House* (1978) parodied—but included—ample doses of sex and on-screen nudity. Major hits of the final years of the 1970s, *Superman—The Movie* (1978) and *Every Which Way But Loose* (1978), *The Deer Hunter* (1978), *Rocky II* (1979), *Alien* (1979), *Breaking Away* (1979), *The Amityville Horror* (1979), and *Star Trek: The Motion Picture* (1979) were by no stretch of the imagination lurid pot-boilers—not even those that received an R rating from CARA. Neither were Oscar winners like *Being There* or *Kramer vs. Kramer*, both of which were rated PG when they were released in 1979. Yet, such successful fare was not necessarily void of nudity or implied (or simulated) sex acts. In *Being There*, one of the main characters, Eve Rand (Shirley MacLaine) masturbates to orgasm, although there is no on-screen nudity.

Kramer vs. Kramer tells the story of the pangs of divorce and child custody from the perspective of a single father. The movie traces the struggle of a divorced man, Ted Kramer (Dustin Hoffman), to become a competent parent after learning parenting skills he obviously had not acquired while married. Besides learning how to raise a son, Ted also has to learn to date again. Phyllis Bernard (JoBeth Williams), a legal secretary/paralegal at the advertising agency where Ted works, asks him out. The scene cuts to them lying in bed together asleep, implying they have had sex that night. Phyllis wakes up first, sees how late it is and says she has to go. She gets out of bed, shot from behind in a three-quarter full nude. She walks into the hall and runs into Ted's young son, Billy (Justin Henry), who is nonchalant about running into a naked woman in his hall. She is embarrassed but faces him. Phyllis is shot in full body shot, but her body is blocked by his. She is then shot in a medium close-up with her breasts visible as she talks with the boy. Phyllis tells him her name and explains she is a business associate of his dad's. The shot cuts to Ted throwing his head down on his pillow and pulling the blanket over his head. Phyllis backs into the bedroom, with one arm covering her breasts and the other hand covering her pubic hair. The boy goes into the bathroom. The encounter is humorous, the only moral insinuation being that a single father should be more discreet.

Throughout the 1970s and 1980s, films rated PG, which was expanded to include PG-13 in 1984, and R repeatedly used filmic conventions to imply sex had taken place: a couple waking in bed, women with bare shoulders covered by bed sheets, morning-after shots of a woman wearing the man's shirt. Echoing the old ploys of sexploitation films,

Hollywood narratives relied on the convention of context to justify nudity, having characters skinny dip, take baths, or change clothes, even if the nudity added nothing to the story, for example, in *An Unmarried Woman* (1978), a film praised on its release for representing the experience of divorce from the point of view of its female protagonist, Erica Benton (Jill Clayburgh). In an early scene before she and her husband split up, Erica changes her clothes to get ready for bed and walks around the bedroom topless while talking with her husband, Martin (Michael Murphy).

By the late 1970s, Hollywood's flirt with greater experimentation in film content and style eventually took a backseat to commercial concerns since many of the New Hollywood films had less than stellar box office returns. One of the reasons auteur directors had found doors open to them had been the financial catastrophes of a number of Hollywood's major productions in the 1960s. Although there had been a few spectacular successes like *The Sound of Music*, many mega-productions flopped and contributed to the industry's declining fortunes. By the late 1960s, Hollywood was in financial crisis because of dwindling audiences, inflated production costs, and misfires such as *Mutiny on the Bounty* (1962), which nearly tanked MGM. *Cleopatra* (1963), with Elizabeth Taylor in the title role, nearly ruined Twentieth Century Fox, as did Julie Andrews's vehicle *Star!* (1968). Paramount's musicals *Paint Your Wagon* (1969) and *Darling Lili* (1970; again starring Julie Andrews) nearly drained that studio's coffers. Studios accrued enormous debts and were forced by the banks that held their loans to stop sinking money into production bonanzas.

After the brief flowering of New Hollywood, though, studios returned to their traditional focus on profits and made crucial changes to ensure that their films remained commercially viable. For example, the committee system developed in film production, with each concept and script being market-tested before being approved. Furthermore, greater emphasis was placed on targeting the youth market (which meant more films rated G or PG) and family-oriented blockbusters. Because film production and distribution had become exorbitantly expensive, production companies bet on blockbusters to meet costs and turn profits.

Universal set the pattern with *Jaws* (1975) followed by Columbia's *Close Encounters of the Third Kind* (1977), both directed by Steven Spielberg and rated PG. Twentieth Century-Fox had a tremendous hit with George Lucas's *Star Wars* (1977). Under the industry's conglomerate structure, films became entrenched in a broader concept of entertainment, produced to have their theatrical runs, to have their cable release, to be broadcast on network or syndicated television, and to be tied-in with ancillary products such as toys, games, and clothes.

The conglomerates that dominated the industry often looked at the presence or absence of sex or nudity to be no more than one of several considerations in marketing a film. The MPAA claimed that ratings did not influence box office receipts, but film executives believed that a film's rating shaped the audience it might attract. From their perspective, including or excluding nudity or sex was a sword's edge, since how they were represented, and the resulting rating, could influence distribution, exhibition, and word-of-mouth buzz positively or negatively. At the same time, the PG-13 and R ratings given to films that treated nudity or sex subtly indicate that both CARA and Hollywood studios assumed brief nudity, brief heterosexual sex scenes with mild or no visible nudity, or implications of sex between consenting adults or even older teenagers were not only inoffensive to many viewers but taken for granted or in stride. Neither sex nor nudity had become ubiquitous in Hollywood films, but both were now treated in a matter-of-fact-like manner in the movies that included them.

AN OFFICER AND A GENTLEMAN

An Officer and a Gentleman (1982) exemplifies the degree to which Hollywood and CARA had come to terms with brief nudity and sex scenes by the early 1980s. Taylor Hackford's romantic drama about two lower-class Americans succeeding through the power of love was the year's third largest box office success.

The story begins early one morning, as Zack Mayo (Richard Gere) stands in the dimness of a room where his father (Robert Loggia) can be seen lying naked in bed with a naked woman. Zack, looking disconsolate as he stares at them, has a series of flashbacks intercut with him looking at and talking to his father. In one flashback, his father introduces young Zack (Tommy Petersen) to a couple of women who are presumably prostitutes. Zack, the audience can anticipate, will have sexual issues. His attitude toward women as sexual objects is revealed later at a dance for naval candidates. He watches a fellow candidate who is hitting on young women while his new friend, Sid Worley (David Keith), notices another of their fellow candidates dancing with a wife of five years. "Still in love," he says, "that's what it's all about."

While at the dance, Zack and Sid meet two young working-class women, Paula Pokrifki (Debra Winger) and Lynette Pomeroy (Lisa Blount). Zack and Paula pair off. A medium-close-up two shot hints at their growing intimacy as they make small talk and inquiries into each other's background. She asks him, smiling prettily and coyly, whether he has a girlfriend. The camera shifts to a close-up of Zack, shot over Paula's shoulder, as he replies "Ain't looking for one either." Although he is dismissive and asks whether she is one of the women who come to the dances to meet a potential husband, the film language sends another message. Close-ups, the downward glances of his eyes, and his shifting smile indicate Zack is actually more attracted to her than he admits. Paula picks up on this, as we can see when the shot cuts to her and she laughs. Very soon they are dancing and kissing. Paula's actions blend traditional concerns with fidelity and monogamy with a contemporary young woman's lack of need for long-term commitment as a necessary precedent for sexual intimacy.

The two couples leave the dance. "Something tells me you girls have been here before," Sid says to Lynette on the soundtrack as the shot cuts to his hands trying to open her shirt. He fumbles with it and she tells him to let her do it. They are making out on the back seat of a car, her joking she will "respect him in the morning," to which he replies she is crazy. Quickly, the film has established that she is experienced while Sid, no virgin, is naïve. The shot cuts to Paula and Zack on the beach in a shoulder two-shot shot from the side as they tenderly caress one another, the film's romantic center. After a passionate kiss, they vanish from the frame. The camera lingers, framing a house in the distance before cutting to the candidates training the next day. The film typifies Hollywood's treatment of sex after nearly a decade and a half with the ratings system. Although it is possible to infer that Zack and Paula sat and watched the waves, the film does not expect viewers to make that inference, as it would have been required to do under the Code. The film is equally unambiguous about Lynette and Sid having sex. Importantly, though, it is also clear that Paula and Zack's mutual attraction will blossom into romance.

On their next date, Paula and Zack go to a motel. They arrive there after Zack has beaten up an obnoxious drunk who provoked him. Upset, he behaves very rudely to Paula, expressed through sexual slurs. She tells him she is not "some whore" he picked up. Again, the film emphasizes that she is not "just" having sex with him but is romantically attracted to him. She even tells him she is trying to be a friend and when he insists that she leave, she accuses him of "treat[ing] women like whores" and sobs as she fumbles with the lock on the door. He stops her. They are shown in a close up in semidarkness before the scene cuts to the next morning.

Zack lies in bed naked as Paula scrambles eggs for breakfast. Although they have already slipped into the gendered roles of traditional marriages, Zack is not ready to slip into the commitment demanded by that institution. He again makes sure she does not expect anything from him, and she again assures him that she only wants to have a good time until he leaves, a line that reflects the screenwriter's confidence that audiences would accept sexual pleasure as part of casual fun in a romantic context. Besides revealing that the promise of marriage is no longer necessary for sex, Zack's reluctance and Paula's willingness to go along on his terms work as a delaying device, which is central to romantic drama. He then pulls her too him, telling her that "Last night was incredible" and she agrees.

By the early 1980s, the sexual compatibility that psychologists in the 1950s and 1960s had promoted as crucial to a successful marriage was now generally accepted as vital for nonmarital relationships as well. As seen in *Annie Hall*, sexual adjustment, as it had been called, had migrated from the marital bed to dating. Rather than waiting until marriage to find out if they were sexually compatible, couples could try each other before marriage. Paula mixes her sexual attractiveness with other facets of her personality to create a sense of romance, daring Zack not to fall in love with her. It will be difficult, she assures him, because she is "like candy."

After a long series of Zack's candidate experiences, mostly his being punished for insubordination, there is a fade to an overexposed image of Paula and Zack making love. It begins with the two of them in a two-shot with her kissing him repeatedly and the two of them staring into one another's eyes. Hackford combines traditional Hollywood's swooning, romantic stares with New Hollywood's naked bodies, compromising by making sure no explicit sex acts have been shown. Very soon, after shallow focus kissing and embracing, the camera is repositioned lower in the next shot and Paula's right breast is visible from the side for just a moment. The camera pans back up to Paula's head as she gently goes up and down, which, combined with Zack's gasping, indicates that they are making love. In the next shot, the camera is further away, so that we see them from Paula's back, both of them from the waist up, Zack's hand covering Paula's breast.

This cinematic tactic is one often employed by soft core to conceal genitalia. In *An Officer and a Gentleman*, the technique served a dual function. First, Richard Gere's hand obscures Deborah Winger's breast, preventing CARA from giving the film a rating higher than R. Second, Zack's hand on Paula's breast can be read as a sexual caress. Zack also seems to lick her breasts, although shadows and her arm obscure this. The scene cuts to the other side of the couple, revealing Paula's other breast, this time on-screen for a much longer period.

When Paula's breast is briefly visible, the camera focuses attention on their faces as they (again) stare lovingly into one another's eyes. They lie in bed talking for a long time. As with many films from the 1970s forward, the bed serves as a location for intimate dialogue and functions to make that dialogue even more intimate. The scene ends as bed scenes often do, with a two shot close-up of the couple snuggling contentedly. For now, in the romantic drama, all is well in romantic relationships.

The film highlights the influence of socioeconomic class on the sex lives of its characters. With three weeks left in his officer training, Zack eats lunch with Paula's family. Afterwards, she queries him about his future and his thoughts about marriage and reveals that her real father (who had refused to marry her mother) had been an officer candidate like Zack. The film is quite harsh in dialogical implications that the candidates simply use local women for sexual gratification while in camp and then abandon them thoughtlessly. At the same time, it does not show any of the candidates in the film behaving that way except implicitly in the background at the dance or in the local bar.

An Officer and a Gentleman was a traditional Hollywood melodrama despite breaching the Code in spirit and letter. The extent to which nudity and sex were taken for granted in Hollywood can best be appreciated by their appearance on-screen in another genre that flowered in the 1980s and 1990s and catered to audiences that might identify with protagonists who lacked sexual experience and often fumbled in relationships: teen films.

TEEN FILMS

Teen films were nothing new when they enjoyed a renaissance in the 1980s. During the 1930s, Hollywood had promoted teenage stars like Deanna Durbin, Judy Garland, and Mickey Rooney. Aware of the Americans' concern with juvenile delinquency during the 1950s, Hollywood produced a number of youth films, all of which had sexual under- or overtones. At one end of the spectrum was *Rebel Without a Cause* (1955). Starring James Dean, Natalie Wood, and Sal Mineo as discontented middle-class suburban teenagers, the film clearly implicated the youths' repressed sexuality in their rebelliousness. At the other end of the spectrum were pseudo-exposés such as the B movie *High School Confidential* (1958), featuring Mamie van Doren. The 1960s saw a number of beach party movies such as *Beach Blanket Bingo* (1965) from American International Pictures, and films like *Easy Rider* aimed at the counterculture. After teen films declined in the 1970s, they revived in the 1980s, driven by the success of directors like John Hughes and the industry's efforts to draw suburban mall-cruising teens into multiplex theaters.

Hughes's films were not overtly sexual in the manner of *Porky's* (1981), but neither were they devoid of sex. *Sixteen Candles* (1984), *The Breakfast Club* (1985), and *Ferris Bueller's Day Off* (1986) keep sex to a minimum but it is present. Hughes's films explored emotional growth and the development of relationships during a phase of life in which the outcomes of decisions in novel intimate situations are a grand mystery. Other teen films from the 1980s were more forthright in tying their sexual concerns to coming of age and often included sexual initiation as a crucial step in maturation and self-discovery. That step was often treated as a positive experience even if it was morally dubious, as when Lana (Rebecca De Mornay), a prostitute, has sex with teenaged Joel Goodson (Tom Cruise) in *Risky Business* (1983). Sexual awakening would remain common in teen films over the next two decades. How filmmakers handled that theme ranged from delicately, or at least relatively subtly, as in Hughes's films, to bluntly, and quite often, crudely.

A variety of sex-related themes were pursued in teen films through the 1980s and beyond. Stories often center on the antics of heroes who rebel against parental authority, including defying prohibitions against sex. Even during the Code era, parental prohibitions against sex were examined in films like *Splendor in the Grass* (1961). Parents' reasons for prohibiting sex or relationships vary from well-intentioned, as the single father (David Morse) in *Down in the Valley* (2005), to near-pathological religious obsessions with gendered presumptions about sexuality, as with the main character's mother (Piper Laurie) in *Carrie* (1976) or father (Richard Kiley) in *Looking for Mr. Goodbar* (1978). Sometimes the parents are right, as in *Endless Love* (1981), when fifteen-year-old Jade (Brooke Shields) is forbidden by her father (Don Murray) to see the slightly older and, it turns out, dangerous, David (Martin Hewitt).

Not all parents attempted hard-fisted suppression of their adolescent children's sexual urges. The role of parents fluctuated, from complete or near total absence as in *Halloween* (1978), *Porky's* (1981) or *Fast Times at Ridgemont High* (1982) to playing supportive roles as Jim Levinstein's dad (Eugene Levy) in *American Pie* (1999). The era of crude teen films that has continued nearly unabated up to the recent *American Pie* series—*American Pie, American Pie 2* (2001), *American Wedding* (2003), and *American Pie Presents: Band Camp* (2005)—can be traced back to a low-budget 1980s teen comedy that succeeded wildly at the box office and ushered in a wave of similar films.

Porky's begins with a high school student named Pee Wee (Dan Monahan) lying in his bed, half asleep listening to the morning weather forecast on the radio in southern Florida in the 1950s. The camera pulls back to reveal his tent-shaped underwear, held up by his very erect penis. He sits up and measures his penis, which is apparently getting shorter. Typical of the cruder teen sex films, the visual emphasis is on readily discernible physical reactions. The film's dialogue is just as crude. Had the film been produced during the Code era, nearly every line of the kids' exchange would have been quickly excised. By the start of the 1980s, screenwriters, in this case the film's director, Bob Clark, did not hesitate to put words of sexual experience and wisdom into the mouths of adolescents, even if that experience or wisdom was feigned. Sex permeates the campus in the form of incessant talk and boys and men ogling girls and women.

Because the boys are obsessed with sex, they are easy prey for a practical joke played on them one night by Tommy (Wyatt Knight), Billy (Mark Herrier), and Mickey (Roger Wilson). Pee Wee and several other guys believe they are being readied for sex with an exotic dancer named Miss Cherry Forever (Susan Clark), who, they have been warned, has an African American boyfriend. Once inside a small shack out in the swamp, the victims strip naked for an "inspection" by Cherry. She sashays out in red underwear, eliciting excited catcalls from the teenagers. Afterwards, Tommy and Billy sneak Cherry's "boyfriend," played by a man named John Conklin (John Henry Redwood), in through the bedroom window. Tommy, Billy, and John prepare a "blood-soaked" machete and then make sexual sounds and catcalls. Cherry enthuses "keep pumpin', baby." Billy sits on the bed and makes the springs squeak as Cherry fakes orgasmic sounds, playing on cinema's ability to simulate sex on the soundtrack.

In the adjacent room, the naked teens are beside themselves with anticipation. When they are fooled into believing Tommy has been stabbed and they are going to be killed by a machete-swinging madman, all of the boys run out the door or hop out the window, frightened out of their wits.

The American sexual underbelly comes into full bloom in the next scene when the teens go to Porky's and watch a strip show, part of which is shot through the dancers' legs down toward the expectant faces. Porky (Chuck Mitchell) tricks them into giving him money to spend half an hour with prostitutes and then opens a trap door and drops them into the brackish water around the club. They are further humiliated when the sheriff (Alex Karras) arrives and turns out to be not only in cahoots with Porky, but his brother as well.

At the end of a gym class, Billy, Tommy, and Pee Wee scamper into a secret crawl space and finally realize their wildest voyeuristic fantasies as they watch a group of six to seven girls showering. The frame is matted to resemble an old silent movie peephole. The shot is a medium long shot, but the girls are clearly nude and there are ample full frontal shots. The boys comment crudely on the girls' pubic areas, beside themselves with excitement: "the mother lode," enough "wool" to "knit a sweater," and in an allusion to Florida's role as a setting of choice in a number of sexploitation films, "This has gotta be the biggest beaver shoot in the history of Florida." The girls discover the boys when Pee Wee blows their cover by yelling through his hole for one of the girls to move so he can see. Some of the girls run from the shower, while the others wrap towels around themselves but otherwise react good-naturedly to being spied on. While critics have rightfully pointed out the film's sexist treatment of females, they overlook the implication of how comfortable these girls are with their bodies and their sexuality.

The attribution is perhaps anachronistic and no doubt objectifying, but a woman's being comfortable with her body would later become a staple of debates on women's growing sexual freedom.

The final third of the film is given over to the boys' revenge, which is exacted by destroying Porky's nightclub. As the credits roll, one last sexual situation is depicted: Wendy lives up to her side of a losing bet and has sex with Pee Wee on an empty school bus while the others mill around outside it. The humor is crude, the depiction of the female characters at times misogynist and often ridiculous. The characters are poorly developed and uninteresting, but the film was a huge success. In comedies from *Shampoo* to *Porky's*, sexual desire is raunchy, lewd, vulgar, or carnal, depending on one's taste. To be sure, sexual desire in comedies can lead to serious complications and conflict, but widespread audience acceptance of sexual conflicts as humorous predicaments rather than moral quandaries demonstrated the width of the spectrum of American sexual moralities.

Even more influential than *Porky's* was Amy Heckerling's feature-film debut, *Fast Times at Ridgemont High* (1982). The film begins with details of the lives of teens in a Southern California suburban mall. Importantly, for most of the characters, their time at the Ridgemont Mall revolves around working, with the exception of Mike Damone (Robert Romanus), whose "job" involves scalping concert tickets. For the others, jobs create a social world in which teen girls like Stacy Hamilton (Jennifer Jason Leigh) and Linda Barrett (Phoebe Cates) can discuss sex with each other, a social network outside of traditional areas of authority such as the family, schools, or churches. A job enables Stacy to meet older guys, such as Ron Johnson (D. W. Brown), the twenty-six-year-old who works in the mall. More importantly, working allows the kids to replicate the responsibilities of adult life, making the transition to sex part of a larger period of maturation.

The importance of a steady income is made clear when Stacy accidentally becomes pregnant after having sex with Mike and decides to have an abortion. All she asks of Mike is that he split the cost and drive her to the clinic. When he lets her down because he is unable to raise the money, she apparently has enough saved to pay for the abortion herself. Able to navigate the adult world because of her work experience, she makes an appointment and goes through with the abortion on her own.

Stacy ends up in her predicament through a combination of curiosity about sex, naivete, and bad advice. Following Linda's guidance, she flirts with the older Ron, who asks her out after she tells him she is nineteen (she is actually fifteen). On their one date, he takes her to the Point, a baseball field, and they have sex in the dugout. Stacy is passive but willing, apparently eager to lose her virginity after being goaded on to do so by the sexually verbose Linda, who claims to have a fiancé in Chicago and to have lost her virginity at the age of thirteen. Stacy follows Linda's advice and has sex with Mike, who has a premature orgasm and gets her pregnant. Stacy is topless in both of her lovemaking scenes and completely nude (in profile with no shot of her pubic hair) after having intercourse with Mike. Shots of nude fifteen-year-old characters would not become a norm in Hollywood, but Heckerling presents Stacy's nudity as if her age were no big deal. The film is equally casual about the teen girls' repeated conversations about sex.

Linda's sex life is confined to her incessant talk of sex, her demonstrating to Stacy how to perform fellatio with a carrot in the school lunch room, and her role in a fantasy of Stacy's brother, Brad (Judge Reinhold). She opens her bikini top after she comes out of the pool and approaches Brad, visualizing a fantasy Brad masturbates to in the bathroom. To his great embarrassment, Linda accidentally walks in on him. Suggesting the degree to which sex was a part of these kids' lives, neither Brad nor Linda react to the situation in any way other than expressing their mutual embarrassment.

After she figures out that Linda's advice is less than stellar, Stacy decides to get together with the nerdy but sincere Mark Ratner (Brian Backer), whose relationship with Mike mirrors Stacy's relationship with Linda. While Linda coaches with a vegetable, Mike teaches with a cardboard replica of Debbie Harry, the lead singer of Blondie, as a prop. *Fast Times at Ridgemont High* implicates the media in the sexualization of teen culture through the use of centerfolds as well, both on locker doors and bedroom walls. Despite being bombarded with sexual images and myths, Heckerling assures the viewer, these teens will survive.

By the early 1980s, sexual intimacy had become a conventional narrative cue for viewers that two characters had cemented their relationship. Either they were a couple and they were in love, or they were intensely attracted to one another physically, which could lead to either love or disaster, depending on the story. The correlation of nudity and sex with frankness and cinematic realism that had once been associated with European films and independent American films in the 1950s and 1960s had become a Hollywood convention in PG-13- or R-rated films by the end of the 1980s. Studios, critics, and audiences seemed to agree through their production, favorable reviews, and attendance, respectively, that brief nudity and delicately portrayed sex lent a realist authenticity to narratives. Filmmakers no longer needed to resort to the ambiguity that had characterized the Production Code era.

Throughout the 1980s, Hollywood films consistently revealed a plurality of sexual attitudes and quite a bit of naked (especially female) flesh. Nudity or nonmarital sex featured in films ranging from comedies like *Stripes* (1981), *S.O.B.* (1981), *Trading Places* (1983), and *Something Wild* (1986); thrillers like *Dressed to Kill* (1980) and *Body Double* (1984) from Brian de Palma, *Angel Heart* (1987), and *Fatal Attraction* (1987); or dramas like *Body Heat* (1981), *Witness* (1985), *About Last Night. . . .* (1986), *The Accused* (1988), and *The Grifters* (1990). The substantial number of Americans who saw these films reveals that a lot of Americans had or were comfortable with a liberal attitude toward representations of nudity and sex, even the sexual antics of teens. While Hollywood films could arguably be said to reflect the liberalization of attitudes towards sex in American society since the 1960s, the complexity of such a claim becomes clear when a specific form of nonnormative sex—adultery—is an element of a film's narrative. While a majority of Americans have never expressed approval for adultery, they have not shied away from films with adulterous main characters.

.

5

To Have or
Not to Have Sex

By the middle of the 1970s, the postwar liberalization trend had leveled off.[1] Yet, the liberalization in sexual behavior that had occurred between the 1950s and 1970s remained ingrained in American society. Sex among unmarried adults as well as cohabitation became a fixture on the American sexual landscape. With sexuality uncoupled from marriage, most Americans believed consenting adults had a right to make decisions about their sexual lives. Greater sexual freedom and a continual decline in the double standard were also well established. At the same time, conservatives launched a backlash against what they considered the excesses of the sexual revolution and their detrimental impact on marriage and the family. The Moral Majority emerged in the late 1970s and together with other factions of the Religious Right promoted social policies intended to revert the influences of liberalism on sexual behavior and representations of nudity and sex in film.

During the 1980s and 1990s, religious conservatives like Moral Majority leader Jerry Falwell condemned all nonmarital sex, sexual promiscuity, pornography, abortion rights and birth control, and gay rights, which they perceived to be an "avalanche of corruption ... threatening the moral stability of our nation."[2] Religious conservatives equated their own values with "traditional morals" and "family values," and they believed the family was endangered by sexual liberalism and diversity. The open circulation of pornography infuriated the Religious Right, and they assailed what they believed were sexual excesses in Hollywood films. While highly vocal and exerting some influence on sex-related government policies, the Religious Right had limited influence on film distribution, as seen in the fate of Martin Scorsese's *The Last Temptation of Christ* (1988). The film's portrayal of Jesus Christ as having a sex life angered many conservative Christians, who protested its release.[3] Although Universal ran into problems distributing and exhibiting Scorsese's film, it had a successful opening. Protesters thronged outside movie theaters, but as at other times in the history of American film, audiences headed right past them and into the theaters. The threats of religious conservatives' boycotts were not dismissed out of hand, but conservatives did not hold unlimited sway. National surveys of Americans' sexual behavior and their attitudes confirmed the persistence of sexual pluralism.[4] Conservative and liberal sexual pluralism extended to tastes in film as well, manifested by the tightening of the ratings system on the one hand and the increasing vitality of independent filmmakers on the other.

Partly in recognition of sexual plurality among audiences' cinematic tastes and partly as a mechanism to rein in filmmakers who might push the envelope of sexual representations, the MPAA modified the rating system by changing the more or less dormant X rating to "NC-17" in 1990, which excluded anyone seventeen and under. The rating was copyrighted so the MPAA could distinguish mainstream films with adult sexual content from X-rated pornographic films. The first film to be rated NC-17 was *Henry & June* (1990). In 1995, CARA gave Paul Verhoeven's *Showgirls* an NC-17 rating. The film bombed at the box office, not only because it was a bad film, but also because the distribution difficulties facing any film rated NC-17 abetted its failure. The rise of multiplex theaters in malls constrained filmmakers because multiplex owners often were forbidden to exhibit NC-17 films by their rental contracts. Rather than usher in a category of adult-oriented mainstream films, NC-17 quickly became stigmatized as the new X and was assiduously avoided.

More often, rather than risk an NC-17 rating, mainstream filmmakers relied on more subtle ways to represent sexuality. One way was narrative implication through cohabitation. Typical of this would be the casual way PG-rated *You've Got Mail* (1998) and countless other films treated cohabitation, indicating it was simply one option among many living arrangements. This was a safe method since by 2006, the *New York Times* could report on census data showing cohabiting couples outnumbered married couples.[5] It also meant that sexual behavior itself could be kept completely off-screen, often reduced to nothing more than the assumption that a couple living together had an active sex life. This tactic seemed useful since almost nine out of ten of the top twenty films in 2005 were rated PG or PG-13. Furthermore, there was a decline in the number of R-rated films, with PG films bringing in a higher box office gross than films rated R, a shift some attributed to a change in the cultural climate with regard to sex in film.[6] The shift more likely reflects the size of the teen audience for films as well as government and industry pressure on filmmakers. Thus, a widespread liberal acceptance of sexual pluralism on-screen and off-screen was curbed by the significant presence of conservatives on the cultural landscape. While shrinking, the market for R-rated films remained commercially significant.[7]

Most filmmakers who wanted to represent sexual themes grudgingly edited their films to secure an R rather than an NC-17, just as an earlier generation of filmmakers had done to avoid an X. Stanley Kubrick's last film, *Eyes Wide Shut* (1999), a controversial examination of the impact of adulterous cravings on an ostensibly happily married couple, William (Tom Cruise) and Alice Harford (Nicole Kidman), posited the safety of procreation and parenthood against the danger of desire. The film garnered attention because of its stars and an orgy attended by William, which was digitally censored by Warner Brothers after Kubrick died, to assure an R rating. Kubrick was no stranger to editing to placate CARA. After CARA gave *A Clockwork Orange* (1971) an X rating, Kubrick delayed its release in the United States and successfully reedited the film to get an R rating.[8]

Because of the threat of the NC-17 rating, mainstream films rarely depict sex explicitly or deal with controversial sexual issues, although there have been some exceptions among independent films and imports whose distributors release sexually graphic films without submitting them to CARA, although doing so limits the number of theaters that will exhibit a film. Good Machine distributed Todd Solondz's *Happiness* (1998), a narrative driven by sexual obsessions, including those of a same-sex pedophile, without a rating. In the ending of *Requiem for a Dream* (2000), released by Artisan without a rating to avoid CARA's NC-17, one of the film's main characters, Marion Silver (Jennifer Connelly), performs a graphic anal lesbian sex act with a dildo in front of a large audience of chanting males in business suits. The sequence cross-cuts Marion's performance with brief images of the downward spiral of the other main characters. Wellspring Films distributed *The Brown Bunny* (2003) without a rating since the scene in which Daisy Lemon (Chloë Sevigny) explicitly performs fellatio on Bud Clay (Vincent Gallo) would have guaranteed an NC-17.

The late 1980s and early 1990s saw the rise of independent cinema and its annexation by the mainstream, exemplified by the success of New Line Cinema, which became part of Time Warner in the mid-1990s. New Line Cinema's R-rated *Boogie Nights* (1997) portrayed the adult film industry with considerable nudity and some sex scenes, including scenes of sex being recorded on camera. The film's director, Paul Thomas Anderson, agreed to cuts to avoid an NC-17. A number of independent filmmakers dealt with a variety of sexual issues, often portraying greater racial and ethnic diversity than Hollywood. Spike Lee's R-rated *Do the Right Thing* (1989) includes a sex scene with ice cubes involving African American Mookie (Spike Lee) and his Hispanic girlfriend Tina (Rosie Perez), representatives of two cultural groups whose sex lives are rarely shown in mainstream cinema. In John Singleton's R-rated *Boyz 'N the Hood* (1991), an African American teen couple, Tre (Cuba Gooding Jr.) and Brandi (Nia Long), have their sexual debut, consummating their relationship. John Sayles's *Lone Star* (1996), also rated R, includes a subplot about the romantic relationship between an Anglo-American sheriff in a small Texan border town, Sam Deeds (Chris Cooper), and a first-generation Mexican American, Pilar Cruz (Elizabeth Peña). While a number of independent filmmakers were grouped together in terms of their race or ethnicity (New African American Cinema, Asian American Cinema, and so forth), numerous gay and lesbian independent filmmakers were grouped in terms of their sexual orientation, and their output was labeled New Queer Cinema. Regardless of which "new cinema" independent filmmakers were associated with, independent films tend to have more audacious sexual content than their mainstream counterparts, a quality they frequently share with imports.

As they have done since the 1950s, and adding to the diversity in sexual representations that has characterized American cinema since the 1990s, imports have also included fair amounts of sexuality and nudity, often more extensive than in domestic productions. For example, CARA rated the English-language French import *Swimming Pool* (2003) R for its strong sexual content and nudity. *Swimming Pool* is an erotic psychological thriller about the strained relationship between a reticent English mystery writer, Sarah Morton (Charlotte Rampling), and a lustful young English-French woman, Julie (Ludivine Sagnier). Julie is often nude or topless and there is a great deal of implicit sex. The film in part concerns Sarah's opening up from her severe demeanor, emphasized by the dark interiors of her home in London. Her approach to all things sexual is more traditional, less direct. There are vague hints that she might have a sexual relationship of sorts with her publisher, and her flirting with Franck (Jean-Marie Lamour) borders on the imperceptible. By contrast, Julie is very direct, and she ends up sleeping with Franck as well as a number of other men.

Other imports went much further than *Swimming Pool*. French director Catherine Breillat gained renown with her semipornographic *Romance* (1999), which was distributed in the United States by Trimark without a CARA rating. The Spanish erotic drama *Sex and Lucia* (2001) included fairly graphic sex scenes and frontal nudity. Bernardo Bertolucci returned to a sex-driven narrative with *The Dreamers* (2003). Two young French twins and an American living in Paris engage in a weekend of sexual adventures, with hints of incest. There is a considerable amount of male and female frontal nudity as well as simulated sexual intercourse. An MPAA member, Fox Searchlight Pictures, released Bertolucci's film with an NC-17 rating, the first film with that rating since the independent film *Orgazmo* (1997) from the creator of the television series *South Park*.[9] The British film *9 Songs* (2004; Michael Winterbottom) included numerous representations of graphic and explicit sex acts, including penetration in sexual intercourse, fellatio, and male ejaculation. Tartan Films distributed the film without a CARA rating.

By and large, though, in contrast to the more graphic fare in independent films and imports, mainstream American films have opted for representations of sex like that in the R-rated *Wedding Crashers* (2005, David Dobkin). A long introductory sequence encapsulates the way in which Jeremy Klein (Vince Vaughn) and John Beckwith (Owen Wilson), the two wedding crashers of the film's title, successfully seduce women they meet at wedding receptions. The sequence ends with a montage of each of the men collapsing into bed with a series of dates in quick succession. The women are topless and in their underwear and resemble Victoria's Secrets models. Jeremy and John's blatant pursuit of casual serial sex is treated lightheartedly.

Implied in the *Wedding Crashers* montage is an important, indeed necessary, component of nudity and sex in film: actors and actresses are willing to do nude and/or sex scenes. Throughout the 1990s and into the 2000s, there has been no shortage of well-known performers, some stars, who have been willing to remove their clothes and simulate lovemaking for the camera. Although many actors and actresses refuse to do nude or sex scenes and often include no-nudity clauses in their contracts, actresses such as Melanie Griffith, Kim Basinger, Demi Moore, Jennifer Connelly, Nicole Kidman, Angelina Jolie, Heather Graham, Halle Berry, Ashley Judd, Charlize Theron, and even Meg Ryan have been vital to sex in American films, since, whatever inequalities female actresses experience with regard to salaries, role choices, or star billing, they have dominated the exposure of flesh on-screen. Male stars that have done fully nude or sex scenes include Richard Gere, Robert De Niro, Kevin Bacon, and Peter Sarsgaard.

Given the belief that there is an audience for sexual themes and the willingness of performers, writers, directors, and producers both in and out of the mainstream to include sex in film, American films have come to include sexuality as a prominent element. The NC-17 rating remains widely perceived within the industry as a box office kiss of death, with *Henry & June* and *Showgirls* being the only films to gross over ten million dollars.[10] The norm in the industry is closer to the sexuality in the R-rated *Pretty Woman* (1990), in which the sex between a prostitute (Julia Roberts) and her client (Richard Gere) does not make it to the screen. *Jerry Maguire* (1996) has soft-core nudity and simulated sex scenes typical of R-rated films, as well as implied sex scenes typical of films rated PG-13. The title character (Tom Cruise) has sex with his fiancée, Avery Bishop (Kelly Preston), who is also shown nude. Later, after he is single, Jerry goes to bed and wakes up with love interest Dorothy Boyd (Renee Zellweger), a single mother, but their sex is implied.

Numerous teen films resemble the PG-13-rated *10 Things I Hate About You* (1999) in keeping desire onstage and humorous but downplaying its physical manifestations. Although typically played for humor, sex is a significant component of the narratives of PG-13 films.[11] Even films targeting one of the most significant age groups, like the PG-rated *The Sisterhood of the Traveling Pants* (2005), might imply teen sex. One of the members of the sisterhood, Bridget (Blake Lively), seduces Eric (Mike Vogel), one of the coaches at her summer soccer camp in Mexico. The consummation of their fling occurs off-screen. By contrast, the R-rated *American Pie* (1998–2006) franchise placed sexual lust, teen nudity, as well as implied fellatio and cunnilingus at the center of high school students' lives, updating *Porky*'s take on adolescent sexuality.

One final development needs to be considered: the success of VHS in the 1980s and DVD in the 1990s, two formats that significantly changed distribution and exhibition with the tremendous growth in home viewing. These formats not only opened up new markets for rentals and sales, they also paved the way for greater sexual explicitness even though Video Software Dealers Association members applied CARA's ratings to their products and some outlets refused to stock films rated NC-17. While the latter may have nudged the industry toward reticence, similar to the influence of ratings on theater distribution, filmmakers nonetheless found substantial VHS and DVD markets for more graphic sexual content. On the margins of the industry, the pornography industry discovered a gold mine in the two formats. Mainstream companies re-released films in *uncut* or *unrated* editions that included nudity or sex scenes excised from theatrical releases, a variation of the studios' dual releases for the European and American markets in the 1950s. This policy applied to both current releases and older films. For example, the DVD of the Director's Cut of *The Last Picture Show* includes a scene in which a teen girl, Jacy Farrow (Cybill Shepherd), is about to have sex with a much older man, Abilene (Clu Gulager), at a pool hall. The theatrical release only implied that Jacy had sex with her mother's former lover. The unrated edition of *Wild Things* (1998) included more skin of Kelly Van Ryan (Denise Richards) and a lengthier lesbian scene between Kelly and fellow high school student Suzie Toller (Neve Campbell) in a swimming pool, two duplicitous teens in the erotic thriller.

While some filmmakers take advantage of the array of outlets available to them, others do not need multiple versions for various degrees of sexual explicitness. The romantic comedy genre often provided films that subtly incorporated the changes in sexual morality over the previous decades while attenuating or eschewing overtly sexual representations. By doing so, the genre proved successful at the box office while splitting the difference between liberal and conservative positions in popular debates over sex.

ABSTINENCE MAKES THE HEART GROW FONDER

Characters in romantic comedies since the 1980s are sometimes *pseudo-abstinent*. Two Meg Ryan and Tom Hanks box office smashes deal with finding true compatibility and, indirectly, abstinence, since, in contrast to numerous romance films since the 1970s, sex plays no role in the characters' race to intimacy. Nonetheless, *Sleepless in Seattle* (1993) and *You've Got Mail* wove a number of contemporary assumptions about sex into their narratives. In each film, the Meg Ryan character is either engaged, as Annie Reed is in *Sleepless in Seattle*, or "practically lives with" another man, as Kathleen Kelly describes her situation in *You've Got Mail*. Annie pursues the possibility of a relationship with Sam Baldwin (Tom Hanks) after hearing him on the radio one night even though she has a fiancé, Walter (Bill Pullman). Kathleen Kelly breaks up with her live-in boyfriend, newspaper columnist Frank Navasky (Greg Kinnear) before she begins falling in love with Joe Fox (Tom Hanks), although some sort of spark between them has been established. Joe breaks with his live-in girlfriend, Patricia Eden (Parker Posey), as well.

While *Sleepless in Seattle* partially replicates the tension raised by alluding vaguely to a race to the alter, *You've Got Mail* removes competing love interests and lets audiences follow Kathleen and Joe as they gradually discover their identities as cyber "soul mates" who anonymously communicate with one another via e-mail. Joe and Kathleen have a relationship based on their self-expression in writing about their likes and dislikes, cares and worries. Their e-mails are never erotic, yet Joe and Kathleen seem to realize that the cyber attraction is more than platonic, although neither wants to admit it. Kathleen is the more forthright of the two. Kathleen discusses her growing attraction to "NY152," the moniker of the person she met in an over-thirty chat room, with one of her employees, Christina (Heather Burns), who asks whether Kathleen has had cybersex yet.

Just as Christina's question suggests, the film makes clear that Joe and Kathleen are on shaky moral ground because of their current relationships. They both realize this, as the parallel opening morning scenes show. In bed or pajamas and with their lovers, each of them waits impatiently for their intimate other to leave for work so they can go online and check their e-mail. The narrative cues the viewer to understand that their actions are duplicitous when Kathleen looks out the window to make sure Frank is leaving. Jaunty music on the soundtrack briefly modulates to a tone associated with thrillers, indicating Kathleen does not want to get caught. A similar routine plays out in Joe's apartment as he waits for his live-in girlfriend to head off to work. The "infidelity" is sexless, even though it involves the pursuit of a deeper love.

Even when sexless, the pursuit can be challenging. Kathleen tells Christina she is "definitely thinking of stopping because it's getting ... confusing." The narrative cues viewers to sympathize with the two main characters and to accept what they are doing. It portrays their partners in less than flattering light but also primes the viewer to understand that Kathleen and Joe each have unfulfilled needs that online chatting and e-mailing have partially helped them meet. Typical of the romantic comedy, it is the characters' goodness and attractiveness that drive them toward one another, not sexual lust. In romantic comedies, narratives often achieve this by hinting the two characters have insights into each another that other characters just do not get. Because the protagonists share common interests, the two *ought* to be attracted to one another and what is more, they ought to *be* together. In both romantic comedies and romantic dramas, emotional and spiritual and intellectual compatibility often plays as large a role as sexual attraction or compatibility. While sex can be used on-screen to express an array of emotions—attraction, affection, or love—other actions can as well. In *You've Got Mail*, the beginning of the film has Joe take over the narration of his e-mail from Kathleen on the soundtrack, making concrete the way that the two *think* alike.

With their emphasis on intellectual and personal compatibility, *Sleepless in Seattle* and *You've Got Mail* are exemplars of sexless love, possibly symbolizing a latent anxiety about AIDS or a return to traditional values. Sexless relationships and platonic races to intimacy can be categorized either as Hollywood's contribution to the conservative backlash or as an expansion of cinema's relationship palette. Meg Ryan's characters in her romantic comedies with Tom Hanks seemed to glide around the boundary between the spiritual and the carnal. By contrast, *When Harry Met Sally...* (1989), in which Ryan starred with Billy Crystal, offered sexual intercourse as the distinction between friendship and an intimate relationship. Sex typically played this role in dramas. Alternatively, sexual intercourse is used in dramas to indicate the sheer strength of the physical attraction of a couple on the path to an intimate relationship. For example, sexual attraction fuels the relationships between Leticia Musgrove (Halle Berry) and Hank Grotowski (Billy Bob Thornton) in *Monster's Ball* (2001), and Alice Loudon (Heather Graham) and Adam

Tallis (Joseph Fiennes) in *Killing Me Softly* (2002). In erotic thrillers such as *Killing Me Softly*, sexual allure merges with danger. In contrast to the romantic comedy protagonist looking for a soul mate, the protagonist in erotic thrillers is sexually captivated by a suspicious character that might end his or her life.

EROTIC NEO-NOIR THRILLS

After knowledge of the dangers and risks associated with HIV and AIDS had become widespread in the middle 1980s, critics often interpreted neo-noir erotic thrillers as embodying the premise that sexual attraction was potentially fatal because certain sexual acts were risky. At the practical level, safe sex referred to wearing a condom or remaining abstinent to prevent the transmission of the HIV virus. At the figurative cinematic level, protection meant the need for vigilance and self-preservation in bed. Sex had become complicated since the erotic thrill was the association of sex with risk. The theme of the lover or spouse as potential or suspected murderer underscored the genre's basic anxiety about the instability and impermanence of the contemporary relationship: not only might your lover break your heart, he or she might thrust an ice pick into it.

The theme of the suspicious lover was not new to the late 1980s. Alfred Hitchcock examined it in *Dial M for Murder* (1954), remade with Michael Douglas and Gwyneth Paltrow as *A Perfect Murder* (1998). Furthermore, film noirs from the early 1940s to the late 1950s made the dangerous, seductive female—the femme fatale—a central icon. Sexual allure was precisely what made the femme fatale dangerous. In *Double Indemnity* (1944), unhappily married Phyllis Dietrichson (Barbara Stanwyck) manipulates an insurance agent, Walter Neff (Fred MacMurray), into murdering her husband (Tom Powers). She betrays Neff when he no longer appeals to her. Always after something other than what she seemed to pursue, the femme fatale trapped the male protagonist through his sexual desires.

This also seems to be the fate of Frank Keller (Al Pacino) in the neo-noir erotic thriller *Sea of Love* (1989). Frank embarks on a highly physical and strongly passionate relationship with Helen Cruger (Ellen Barkin) even though he, unknown to her, is an undercover cop who believes she might be the serial murderer he is trying to apprehend. Frank is a divorced NYPD detective with a drinking problem, and Helen is a single mother working in a Manhattan shoe store. The film begins with a camera panning up the side of an apartment building to an open window from which the 1959 hit by Phil Phillips with the Twilights, "Sea of Love," can be heard playing. The camera pans from a record player and the spinning 45 across an apartment to the bedroom, along a man's (Brian Paul) naked body shot from the side who appears to be making love (implied) to an unseen partner. He moans and says, "I can't," before asking desperately, "Is this ok?" As he turns his head and looks behind him, the camera follows his glance, panning to a close-up of a pistol fired by an unseen assailant, killing him.

Frank discovers that the victim placed contact ads in a singles magazine, the *New York Weekly*. The singles world is portrayed as one populated by the lonely and sexually frustrated, and at least one psychopathic individual. It turns out that a colleague, Sherman (John Goodman) is also investigating the death of another man who had placed an ad in the *Weekly*. The two are assigned the case, and they place a personal in the *Weekly* to lure the killer, whom they assume is "some psycho woman killing guys," as Sherman puts it. Frank meets Helen when she answers the phony ad. He runs into her again at a green market one evening, and they go out. Frank is about to follow Sherman's advice and blow Helen off, but the scene cuts to the two sitting in a bar telling each other why they got married. The next scene opens with a medium two-shot of the couple making out passionately in a darkened room in Frank's apartment, with Frank backed up against a wall. The quick cut from the bar to the sexually charged bedroom scene contributes to the feeling that Frank is out of control, consumed by sexual passion. Helen borrows Frank's bathroom, and while she is in there, he discovers a pistol in her purse. As she closes the door, Helen tells him to "get in bed," but he goes into a panic instead. When she comes out (wearing his bathrobe), he attacks her, frisks her, and locks her in a closet. When he realizes it is only a starter's pistol, he lets her out. She is furious but calms down and accepts his apologies.

The film then has a truly *noir* moment: the rain can be seen through the Venetian blinds pouring down. Frank—with the camera almost solely on him so that we see little of her facial expression—tells her, "You don't know. This city—what it does to people." She has calmed down and begins to kiss him; a jazz-inflected saxophone wails on the soundtrack, and Frank and Helen kiss more fervently. She breaks away suddenly, then swings Frank around and pushes him against the wall, frisking him and asking, "What are you looking for?" Her frisking turns into caressing and becomes more and more sensual. By having Helen behave at the border of erotic and threatening, the film can remain ambiguous about her guilt.

She pulls his shirt up and her robe open, revealing a breast in medium close-up. The camera cuts to a plain American shot, revealing her nude body in profile. She mounts him from behind and then swings around in front of him and leans against the wall, the shot cutting as she moves and the camera moving back to a long shot of the couple.

They are in the far left of the frame with the rest of Frank's bedroom and the rain outside the windows filling out the frame.

The next morning when Helen gets dressed, she removes Frank's shirt and her breasts are partially visible from the side and she is wearing panties. The shot cuts to Frank for a moment, then back to Helen who has managed to put on a t-shirt and a pair of jeans. This speed with which she has managed to finish dressing points up the gratuitous nature of the previous shot of her topless and in panties. Before she leaves, they express their affection for one another and she adds, "You've no idea how many creeps are out there." The genre maintains the tension of possible victimization and potential rage that could imply Helen is indeed the killer. This reading is buttressed when Frank queries her about what she meant. "Guys who wait till you're in deep before you find out who they really are. Then you're fighting for your life." She leaves and Frank bags her coffee mug to lift her prints but then decides against it.

In typical erotic thriller fashion, the film plants clues that give Frank every reason to suspect Helen while it deepens his attraction to her. Eventually, he becomes convinced she is the murderer, so he confronts her with his suspicions and offers her his gun so she can shoot him. She has no idea what he is talking about and leaves. The doorbell rings, Frank answers it and is attacked by Helen's ex-husband, Terry (Michael Rooker). Terry forces Frank onto the bed in the missionary position and mounts him, demanding that he tell him what it was like to have sex with Helen. After a protracted fight, Frank kills him. Frank and Sherman meet some months later at the bar and discuss the case. Sherman wonders what Helen ever saw in Terry, and Frank responds, "I don't know. What does anybody see in anybody? People are work, brother." Despite his cynicism about relationships, Frank approaches Helen again, and the film ends with them going for a cup of coffee together, walking down a Manhattan street devoid of *noir* ambiance.

Paul Verhoeven's successful erotic thriller, *Basic Instinct* (1992), opened with a much more graphic sex scene than *Sea of Love*. Beginning with a shot of a couple, the woman clearly nude, in a ceiling mirror, the camera pans down to a shot of the couple having sexual intercourse, the woman from behind as she sits on the man, later identified as a rock star named Johnny Boz (Bill Cable). The woman's face remains obscured throughout the scene, since her identity will be a missing piece in the film's puzzle. There are lengthy takes of her buttocks and breasts, which Boz kisses. She lashes him to the bed posts with a white Hermes scarf, and as the music becomes more intense, she stabs him to death with an ice pick. Detective Nick Curran (Michael Douglas) and his partner Gus (George Dzundza) quickly suspect crime fiction author Catherine Tramell (Sharon Stone). Despite his suspicions—or perhaps because of them, the film at times darkly hints—Nick becomes sexually attracted to Catherine. The film follows the same trajectory as *Sea of Love*, but ends with a twist that suggests Catherine may indeed be the killer. Before Nick and Catherine end in bed together in the final scene, the film depicts Catherine's bisexuality by having her dance seductively with her lover, Roxy (Leilani Sarelle). Nick also finds Catherine and Roxy with a man in a toilet stall in a nightclub restroom. Nick is a voyeur in one scene in which Catherine disrobes and can be seen in total frontal nude in a long shot from Nick's point of view. Finally, in *Basic Instinct*'s most famous scene, Catherine taunts a room full of police officers by wearing a very short dress and no underwear and uncrossing her legs after asking Nick if he "ever fucked on cocaine." Despite its depictions of sex and nudity, CARA gave *Basic Instinct* an R rating.

Jane Campion's *In the Cut* (2003), with its tagline, "Everything you know about desire is dead wrong," inverts the erotic thriller pattern when Franny Avery (Meg Ryan) a schoolteacher, becomes sexually attracted to Detective James Malloy (Mark Ruffalo), a police officer who might kill her. Franny is an English teacher living in New York City. In an early scene, she meets one of her students, Cornelius Webb (Sharrieff Pugh), in a pool hall and bar called the Red Turtle. Franny goes downstairs to the bar's basement restroom. She comes around a corner in the darkened basement and gasps, but keeps her eyes on what she sees. The shot cuts to a medium long take through a doorway of a woman kneeling in front of a seated man whose identity is concealed in the darkness. The woman's back is turned to the camera and her head is moving open and down, implying that she is performing oral sex on the man. The narrative crosscuts between Franny and the woman fellating the man, which can be heard on the soundtrack. The camera pans up to the man's head. He seems to have noticed Franny, but does not care.

In the next shot, from a medium distance, we see the man, with a cigarette in one hand, take the other and pull the woman's hair to one side—away from the camera, a move taken straight from pornography. The next shot is a close up of the man's penis being massaged by the woman's hand as it goes in and out of her mouth. Champion includes an explicit sex act—fellatio—with a shot of male genitals, supposedly a prosthetic. The woman can be heard gulping as the man presumably comes to orgasm, but there is no "money shot." Franny watches as if mesmerized until the man takes a drag on his cigarette. As she runs back up the stairs, she pauses to take her glasses off and collect herself. She seems slightly shaken, which is odd given that she engages in casual sex.

In a later scene, Franny masturbates to orgasm while her new lover, Malloy, who is investigating the gruesome murder of a woman, watches. Franny lies topless in her underwear on her stomach, the masturbation implied by her body movements, the placement of her hands, and the sounds she makes. Cinematographer Dion Beebe's handheld camera pans her body and there are cuts to her feet and shoulder shots of her face, her eyes closed as she fantasizes that Malloy was the man getting the blow job in the basement. She imagines, that is, performing sexually for a man who might have murdered a woman. When the camera cuts to Malloy, he is smoking and there is a red neon sign shining through the window behind him. In a later scene, Franny and Malloy make love. Franny's breasts are visible several times, and Malloy (presumably) simulates cunnilingus or anilingus. In an after the lovemaking shot, Franny walks from the kitchen with a glass in a brief full frontal nude. Mark Ruffalo's penis is visible briefly before he covers himself with a bed sheet. In the erotic thriller, nudity, sex, and violence thrill. *In the Cut (Unrated Director's Cut)*, released on DVD, included extended, more explicit, versions of the basement scene and Franny and Malloy's lovemaking.

GROWING UP IS HARD TO DO

Throughout the 1980s and 1990s, religious conservatives joined school boards and lobbied state legislatures to challenge abortion rights, sex education in schools, and contraceptive use among teenagers. The influence that religious conservatives wielded on sex-related policies often belied their minority status and contradicted the support most Americans expressed for abortion rights and sexual education in schools in polls. Furthermore, the liberalization trend in sexual attitudes continued largely unabated during the period as teenagers continued having their sexual debuts at increasingly younger ages. The increased time span between sexual debut and marriage meant teenage girls had sex more often and with more partners than earlier generations. One result of the increase in sexual intercourse was an increase in teen pregnancies, which were perpetually considered a national social problem by both liberals and conservatives, although the former promoted contraception while the latter promoted abstinence to bring down pregnancy rates.

While many commentators saw teen sexuality as a focal point in the culture wars, the marketers at Shining Excalibur Pictures, a company Bob and Harvey Weinstein created to distribute *Kids* since their contract with Disney would not allow them to distribute it through Miramax, used it as fuel for publicity.[12] The publicity campaign for *Kids* succeeded in stirring up controversy, which helped it at the box office. Production company Shining Excalibur Pictures promoted Clark's film as a documentary-like portrayal of teen sexual behavior in contemporary America. *Kids* was not a descendant of the teen films of the 1980s.

Reviewers speculated over whether the sex in *Kids* qualified as *kiddie porn*, with most concluding it fell well short of that sobriquet. Director Larry Clark carefully remained within the confines of the law, but his film would have received an NC-17 rating from CARA. Instead, the film was released without a rating. Clark, who was well-known as a photographer, had long specialized in erotic images of teens. His debut film, praised by some critics for its documentary-style gritty realism, picked up where sexploitation had long ago left off in blending sexual images with a moralizing story line. Harmony Korine wrote the film's screenplay at nineteen, giving it an added veneer of authenticity, as did Clark's casting nonprofessionals, with the exception of Chloë Sevigny.

The film opens with a black screen cutting to a close-up of Telly (Leo Fitzpatrick) French kissing a girl around twelve years old (Sarah Henderson). The girl remains anonymous, indicative of the impersonality of Telly's sexual conquest. Calming her fears about pregnancy, Telly makes his conquest, neither of them ostensibly concerned about becoming infected with HIV. He opens her bra. The camera shows her body from the side, her teddy bears in the background. *Kids* borrows staging devices and attitude from sexploitation: the young girl's breasts remained covered, but the staging and the camera that shifts and hovers above her suggest that it is only fortuitous that the breast is covered. Clark's film is clearly a descendent of the sexploitation genre in its promotional claims of concern about excessive and risky teen sexual behavior that contradicts its on-screen treatment of that sexuality. Typically, the camera pans slightly and quickly in a close-up on the girl's bare stomach and her chest and bra. In a voice-over, Telly quickly confirms what the narrative has hinted at: that his tender promises are no more than a ploy to have sex with a virgin. Ironically, one of the reasons he prefers virgins is their lack of "disease." His indifference to the girl is highlighted when he fails to slow down when she tells him she is in pain. Clark establishes a sexist motif: boys manipulate girls into having sex; girls naively let themselves be manipulated.

Kids follows two teens whose paths will cross by the end of the film. Telly meets a fellow skateboarder, Casper (Justin Pierce), and the two walk the streets of New York while Telly brags about his experience, calling himself the "virgin surgeon." They go to a party at Paul's (Sajan Bhagat) and smoke pot with a group of kids. Telly will soon embark on his next sexual campaign. Jennie (Chloë Sevigny) is one of Telly's conquests. She tests HIV-positive and decides to contact Telly and inform him since he is the only sex partner she has had, an anomalous narrative point for a film about excess. *Kids* does not concern itself with whom Telly contracted HIV from but perhaps the "virgin surgeon" was himself duped. As a sexploitation film, *Kids* is more interested in exploiting teen sex than understanding it.

Clarks lets the teens' sexual energy bubble to the surface in a scene at a city swimming pool. Together with a group of peers, Telly and his new quarry, Darcy (Yakira Peguero), break into the pool and proceed to strip to their underwear. The guys compliment the girls' bodies. A naked African American named Harold (Harold Hunter) asks the other boys and girls, "You ever seen a black man's lasso?" and swings his penis back and forth by rotating his body. He remains framed from the waist up, but there is the sound of his penis hitting his thighs on the soundtrack. The boys and girls play and splash, and the boys try to cop feels of the girls' breasts. The girls' nipples are visible through their wet bras. Clark's vision of easily manipulated teen girls is repeated when the guys talk two girls into kissing each other. They then recommend skinny dipping as the scene cuts to Telly doing his snow job on Darcy, who is not allowed to date because her older sister got pregnant at fifteen.

The sequence crosscuts several times between Jennie searching for Telly before she arrives at the party and Telly and Darcy sitting naked on a bed, Darcy's breasts obscured by her and Telly's arms. Eventually, the couple starts having sex. Jennie opens the door and watches dumbly until Telly yells, "Shut the fucking door," which she does. She fails to intercede. The next morning, Casper wakes up and wanders through the apartment strewn with the debris of the party, shirtless boys, and girls in bras. Seeing Telly sleeping on the bed totally nude with an equally nude Darcy, shot in a medium shot from a slightly oblique angle so no genitals are visible, Casper mutters, "Lucky bastard." Casper finds Jennie asleep on the couch and rapes her. The protagonists are clueless, and as a result they either assault others or are the assaulted. Ironically, *Kids* was released just as the HIV-related risk behaviors depicted in the film—unprotected sex and multiple sex partners—began to decline in the United States, a trajectory that has continued since.[13] *Kids* provides an example of the shortcomings of film criticism that looks for too neat a fit between diegetic worlds and the real world they are purported to reflect. It is important not to be lured too easily by the ability of film to look like social or personal reality. It is easy enough to recognize images and stories of American life on-screen, but recognition can be as deceiving as it is powerful. Even if film is granted the ability to represent some sort of "social truth," as French film critic and theorist André Bazin wrote of *Picnic* (1955) and *Bus Stop* (1956), which "is integrated into a style of cinematic narration," it is a truth of a certain kind.[14] Film critics, theorists, and some members of the audience interpret a film (or something in its narrative) as a *representation* of something in reality rather being *representative* of something in reality. In other words, the sex a character like Telly has in *Kids* does not represent teen sexuality as such (an overgeneralization proffered by the film's promoters and its detractors alike); at most it represents the sexuality of clueless, urban teens *like* Telly.[15] If *Kids* reflects anything, it is more nearly Clark's obsessive interest in adolescent sexuality, which resurfaced even more explicitly in *Bully* (2001) and *Ken Park* (2002).

A film that deals with teen sexual development and the deadly consequences of violent homophobia is *Boys Don't Cry* (1999), which made a big impression at the film festivals in Venice, Toronto, and New York. The Academy's willingness to promote a film about the tragic fate of a gender-bending teenager was light years from the moral universe of Will Hays or Joseph Breen. Hillary Swank won an Oscar for Best Actress for her transgender portrayal of Teena Brandon, a young girl who changes her name to Brandon Teena and begins dressing and acting like a boy. *Boy's Don't Cry* begins in Nebraska in 1993, with Teena sitting in a mobile home getting her hair cut by her cousin Lonny (Matt McGrath). "So," he tells her, "you're a boy," asking, "Now what?" Lonny wonders what Teena has in mind for the evening, but the question resonates much larger. Brandon/Teena has a longer term strategy of having a sex change operation so she no longer has to disguise her gender by hiding her breasts or stuffing her pants.

The narrative embeds the threat of impending doom in the initial sequence. After pretending to be a boy at the local skating rink and going on a date with a young girl named Nicole (Cheyenne Rushing), Brandon/Teena is chased back to Lonny's trailer by a group of infuriated men, one of whom is Nicole's older brother. (S)he barely escapes into the trailer. Unable to cope with his cousin's lifestyle and the risks that accompany it, Lonny asks Brandon/Teena to move out. Brandon/Teena hooks up with Candace (Alicia Goranson) and her crowd, led by roughnecks John (Peter Sarsgaard) and Tom (Brendan Sexton).

Brandon/Teena moves to rural Falls City, Nebraska, and gains the guys' acceptance. Believed by those who know her to be a boy, she eventually enters into a romance with the chronically despondent Lana (Chloë Sevigny). The clock is ticking, though, because there is obviously not room in the moral universe of an ex-con like John for Brandon/Teena's transgression of gender norms. John and the other males are shown in situations that emphasize their rough and tumble masculinity. John has a violent temper, and Tom, who once burned his family's house down, now slices himself with a knife to keep his inner demons at bay. "Welcome," says Kate (Alison Folland) to Brandon at one point, "to the psycho ward."

Teena is arrested, and while she is in jail Candace discovers her secret. Candace tells Lana, who promptly visits Teena in the women's section of the jail. Teena tells her that she is a "hermaphrodite," but assures her that it "sounds a lot more complicated than it is." Lana says she does not care if Teena is "half monkey or half ape" and gets Teena out of jail. She makes love to Teena in the front seat of a car that night. The sex is on-screen, with nudity and Brandon sucking briefly on Lana's breast. The scene was shortened to get CARA to change its initial NC-17 rating to an R.

When John discovers Brandon's gender identity, he barges into Lana's house and tells her mother that Brandon has "got her brain-washed. That's what they do." He finds a pamphlet in Lana's bedroom entitled "Cross-Dressers and Transsexuals: The Uninvited Dilemma" and reads out loud "Sexual identity crisis." From a section shown on-screen called "Genital Reconstruction," he reads, "The grafted skin will mimic the loose skin of the natural male penis" before exploding, "Get this sick shit away from me!" Lana's mother's (Jeanetta Arnette) reacts as violently emotionally as John and Tom do physically. John and Tom find Teena and drive to a deserted area and rape her. The rape scene is graphic, and the purely abusive, vindictive nature of their crime is made clear. In the end, John and Tom go on a senseless, murderous rampage, killing not only Teena but also Candace. In their ignorance, they have assumed that Candace is lesbian, and she, too, needs to die. Tom tries to kill Lana as well, but John prevents him from doing so.

The film captures the irrationality of homophobic rage and the way in which hostility to gays, lesbians, and in Teena/Brandon's case, the transgendered, morphs quickly into violence. Another film that depicted the violent consequences of homophobic rage was *American Beauty* (1999), which also looked at teen sex through the pedophiliac eyes of its main character, Lester Burnham (Kevin Spacey).

AMERICAN BEAUTY

British stage director Sam Mendes's debut for the big screen, like Mike Nichols's earlier transition, wears its sexual themes on its sleeve. Like *Who's Afraid of Virginia Woolf?* Mendes's film, given an R by CARA because of its sexual content, introduces the viewer quickly to the dys-functional side of a family's life that each member at first would prefer to keep from public view. In a voice-over, Lester introduces himself; his wife, Caroline (Annette Bening); and their sixteen-year-old daughter, Jane (Thora Birch). He is dissatisfied with his life. He tells us, in voice-over, that he will be dead in less than a year, but that he is spiritually dead already, symbolized by his "jerking off in the shower," which he sardonically notes, "will be the high point of my day." He presents his wife as a cold perfectionist who has lost the ability to be happy. He tells us his daughter is "insecure" and "confused" as we see her checking out a Web site for information on breast implants. Jane wants to change herself, the trope for all of the major characters. That she looks to change her sexual appearance is not a coincidence: in *American Beauty*, sex and personal identity are closely interwoven.

There are several parallel journeys toward self-discovery. Lester's journey is at the center of the narrative. His quest is to reconquer the past, to erase the last twenty years, during which he now feels he has been unconscious, a state embodied in an early scene when he slouches nearly asleep on the back seat of Caroline's Mercedes-Benz. He begins as an ineffectual protagonist who over the course of a journey motivated by sexual desire becomes a new man. The importance of the sexual for Lester is underlined when he queries Caroline: "Whatever happened to that girl ... who used to run up to the roof of our first apartment building to flash the traffic helicopters? Have you totally forgotten about her? Because I haven't."

Lester spends much of the film attempting to remember and to return to his early twenties, physically, mentally, and sexually. He begins jogging and lifting weights. He quits his job as a self-described "whore for the advertising industry." Given that the film places sexuality at the center of identity, it is no surprise that the chief motivation for his attempted rejuvenation is his pursuit of a high school cheerleader, Angela Hayes (Mena Suvari), Jane's sixteen-year-old friend. He eavesdrops and hears Angela tell Jane, "If he built up his chest and arms, I would totally fuck him." Lester is spurred by his desire for Angela to refurbish his body, to "look good naked," as he tells his neighbors. Lester's desire is played out in a series of fantasies.

The first occurs the first time he sees Angela cheering at a basketball game. She dances seductively for him in an empty gym, opening her shirt to reveal a sea of rose petals. The motif of red rose petals covering her body recurs in his other fantasies as well. Ironically, the American Beauty rose that connotes his desire for Angela symbolizes his disdain for Caroline. When associated with Caroline, the roses become a facade of suburban success; they have been cut to be put on display in vases and are therefore dying. When associated with Angela in Lester's fantasies, the roses are fragmented into petals as we also see in the scene in which she is in a bath filled with petals and after she kisses Lester, who pulls a single petal from his mouth.

Perhaps in his mind, he is only six years older than Angela, since he is regressing to twenty-two. Yet, his metamorphosis into a more assertive person is matched by Angela's shift in demeanor from brass sex kitten (a precociousness that turns out to be braggadocio) to inexperienced and frightened young girl. Early in the film, Angela goes to the kitchen to flirt with him; she is the aggressor and her flattery leaves him speechless, triggering another sex fantasy. In a later scene, when she repeats her flattery, a change is signaled by her voice, facial expression, and quick retreat. When Lester asks, "You like muscles?" "I—I should probably go see what Jane's up to," she stammers as she leaves. Throughout the remainder of her relationship with Lester, Angela becomes more childlike. On discovering she is still a virgin despite the sexual bravado he overheard when he eavesdropped at Jane's bedroom door, Lester becomes more fatherly. He drops his efforts to seduce her although she has opened her shirt to reveal her breasts and indicated that she wants to have sex with him. The scene brings Lester's development full circle—he stops trying to be young again and begins to act his age.

Lester's interest for the younger girl is established as problematic early on. In a sequence repeated in the film, Jane tells her boyfriend, Ricky (Wes Bentley), "I need a father who's a role model, not some horny geek-boy who's gonna spray his shorts whenever I bring a girlfriend home from school." She wishes, she says, someone would "put him out of his misery." The particular girlfriend in question is, of course, Angela, who appreciates being the object of and encourages Lester's lust. Angela's coyness makes clear that Lester is not the only character for whom sexuality is central to identity.

The teen girls talk about sex constantly, usually prompted by Angela. She calls Jane a "total slut" when she figures out that Jane likes Ricky. Another school girl (Chelsea Hertford) calls Angela a "total prostitute" when Angela claims to have slept with a fashion photographer, babbling that it would have been "majorly stupid of [her] to turn him down." Angela also believes she has attracted males' sexual attention since she was twelve years old, an attention she enjoys. Angela fabricates tales of sex and graphically describes for Jane what she would do sexually with Lester. Although Jane does not notice it, the viewer can see that Angela is only kidding around, denoted by the way that she laughs at what she is saying.

Besides being central to identity, sex is also crucial for relationships. The fault line in Lester and Caroline's marriage goes straight through their bed, which is no longer a site of sexual activity. When she wakens and catches him masturbating later in the film, he is angered by her attention. He mockingly belittles masturbation, calling it by slang terms—"whacking off," "choking the bishop," "shaving the carrot," "saying hi to my monster"—but defends the practice. Caroline calls it "disgusting," but Lester tells her "I've changed. And the new me whacks off when he feels horny." Again, sex is made crucial to Lester's rediscovery of his "true" or better self: masturbation now signifies the new, assertive Lester, while in the beginning of the film it signified how desolate his life had become. They argue, with Caroline asking Lester if he thinks he is "the only one who's sexually frustrated"? She comes close to asking for a divorce, but he argues, somewhat anachronistically given no-fault divorce laws in the United States, that she does not have grounds for divorcing him, threatening to take half of her real estate agency.

Caroline, too, uses sex to find relief from her failed marriage. She has an affair with a competitor she admires, Buddy Kane (Peter Gallagher), the self-crowned Real Estate King. Their affair begins over lunch in a fine restaurant, Celine's, and proceeds to the room of a ratty hotel with Caroline's SUV parked outside beside a Jaguar, the film economically implying that the well-off frequent motels for sexual rendezvous. After Caroline has sex with Buddy, she jokes with him, "That was exactly what I needed. The royal treatment, so to speak. I was so stressed out." For his part, Buddy tells her that he goes to a firing range to relax and that "nothing makes you feel more powerful. Well, almost nothing." Caroline gets his sexual prowess joke and they make love again. More than a temporary relaxation, the event spurs changes in Caroline, who no longer bothers to put her trademark roses on the dining table and is soon seen singing happily along with Bobby Darin while driving in her car.

Lester's journey, while seemingly on the verge of success for a brief moment, ends tragically when his quest intersects with the failed attempt by Ricky's father, Colonel Fitts (Chris Cooper), to come to terms with his own repressed homosexuality. What appears to be a strictly homophobic reaction to the welcome given him by the Burnham's other next door neighbors, a gay couple, turns out in retrospect to have been an anguished self-interrogation. Driving Ricky to school, Fitts asks his son, "How come these faggots always have to rub it in your face? How can they be so shameless?" Ricky replies, "That's the whole thing, Dad. They don't feel like it's anything to be ashamed of." As it turns out, it shames Colonel Fitts psychopathically. Having mistakenly concluded that Lester is gay, Fitts comes on to Lester but, after Lester gently rebuffs him, returns to murder him. The repressed homosexual career military soldier was not new to Hollywood. The territory had already been explored in *Reflections in a Golden Eye* (1967, John Huston), with Marlon Brando playing a repressed major, and in *The Sergeant* (1968, John Flynn), with Rod Steiger playing a repressed master sergeant. There were also shades of *Psycho* in *American Beauty*'s suggestion that the only cathartic release for repressed homosexuality is murder, a cliché reworked in *The Talented Mr. Ripley* (1999, Anthony Minghella).

American Beauty rehashes the theme that if private lives are at odds with and less admirable than public lives, then sexual deviance must be factored into the equation. To do so, it foregrounds invasions of privacy and the exposure of unfortunate relationships. It draws on the cinema's unique power to establish and then invade private space through the viewer's and the characters' voyeurism. Nearly all of the characters steal looks at each other through windows at one point in the film (or through the viewfinder of Ricky's digicam or his recordings).

Sometimes what the voyeur sees is sexual: Jane removes her shirt and bra when she knows that Ricky is looking at her. Sometimes what the voyeur sees is pseudo-sexual: Angela moves her body seductively for Ricky's camera when he films through Jane's bedroom window. Unknown to Angela, Ricky zooms in on Jane's reflection in her mirror, signaling his ability to see beyond surface beauty. Sometimes what the voyeur sees only appears to be sexual: Colonel Fitts mistakenly believes he sees his son perform oral sex on Lester in Lester's garage.

Playing on the long tradition within American film of concealing behavior in order to reveal it, Mendes composes the shot so Fitts gets the wrong impression. The garage wall conceals what the Colonel believes is a sexual act (Ricky is actually rolling a joint), while the two windows reveal actions that *could* imply sex. In one window, Lester reclines with a somewhat blissful expression on his face while in the other, Ricky's head and shoulders seem to move downward toward Lester's crotch, a standard filmic device used in sexploitation, soft core, and Hollywood films to imply oral sex. Revelations—what is seen on-screen, or through windows—can be misinterpreted. Lester tells Colonel Fitts that his and Caroline's marriage "is just for show. A commercial, for how normal we are. When we are anything but." Colonel Fitts inter-prets this off-hand confession to confirm his suspicion that Lester is gay. The film ends with Lester's preordained death, the changed man shot in the back of the head by a sexually confused Fitts, with each of the surviving characters' lives changed by the blend of violence and sex in its various permutations.

As in *American Beauty*, films typically weave different sexual themes throughout their narratives. For a better understanding of the way in which American films have dealt with sex in its myriad of guises, the following section examines in detail how American cinema has repre-sented the specific sexual themes—homosexuality, adultery, and pedo-philia. First, though, it will look at the cinematic rewriting of the sexual past.

The Production Code was eventually unable to keep adultery from being portrayed in a positive light. Burt Lancaster and Deborah Kerr in *From Here to Eternity* (1953). (Courtesy of Photofest)

By the late 1960s, American motion pictures targeted youthful audiences with tales of the sexual peccadilloes of the younger and older generations. Dustin Hoffman and Anne Bancroft in *The Graduate* (1967). (Courtesy of Photofest)

By the early 1970s, divisions within American society over sexual behavior on-screen and off had become clear, not least during the period known as "porno chic." From *Inside Deep Throat* (2005). (Courtesy of Photofest)

New Hollywood examined the darker aspects of sexuality. Faye Dunaway and Jack Nicholson in *Chinatown* (1974). (Courtesy of Photofest)

American cinema gradually began to include representations of African Americans' sex lives. Whoopi Goldberg and Margaret Avery in *The Color Purple* (1985). (Courtesy of Photofest)

By the late 1980s, adultery in cinema had become more commonplace but no less perilous. Glenn Close and Michael Douglas in *Fatal Attraction* (1987). (Courtesy of Photofest)

Throughout the 1990s, Hollywood seemed uncertain whether sex signaled the beginning of a relationship or the end of one. Sharon Stone and Michael Douglas in *Basic Instinct* (1992). (Courtesy of Photofest)

Jake Gyllenhaal and Heath Ledger in *Brokeback Mountain* (2005). (Courtesy of Photofest)

6

Puritanical Past in a Pornographic Light

Because historians have extensively documented the sex lives of earlier generations only over the last few decades, works of art and popular culture have been a major source of knowledge about sex.[1] At the time the Code was written, there was a paucity of empirical sexual research, which Kinsey would note a few years later.[2] "Mostly all we know is what society has thought about sex," sex historian Vern L. Bullough could still write in the mid-1970s. "We know what activities were against the law, the sexual mores that religion sanctioned or philosophy attempted to establish, and the assumptions medical or scientific writers made, but only rarely what people actually did."[3] Bullough's observation points up the importance of the Production Code: its restrictions did not deny sexual diversity; they repressed it, and in so doing asked audiences to deny it. Americans were not completely ignorant of sexual diversity, but their knowledge was limited by restrictions such as the Code, censorship laws, and public notions of propriety that kept sex in the media within the dominant moral framework. While numerous media gradually presented accounts of America's sexual diversity, American cinema distorted sexual realism to conform to censorship laws and the Production Code.

With the demise of the Production Code, Hollywood had its own "Kinsey Report moment." Of course, it would be an exaggeration to claim that Hollywood first discovered the nation's history of sexual diversity in the late 1960s. The conflicts between filmmakers and the PCA over the content of their films throughout the Code years testify to both sides' realization that Americans engaged in a wider array of sexual practices than the characters in the films produced under the terms of the Code. Already in the mid-1950s, the MPAA acknowledged that the sexual morality in its members' films did not approximate the sexual diversity that existed in the United States. The organization celebrated the movies' sexual conservatism while rejecting popular magazines' "reports of social behavior that is greatly at variance with previously accepted standards.... It must be said as emphatically as possible that the U.S. motion-picture industry has strongly resisted the trend to break down accepted standards. We are not at the head of this parade, nor indeed in the middle of it. We are, in fact, far behind and are proud of it."[4] Despite its proclamation, the PCA revised the Code within a year to permit other formerly taboo topics: prostitution, abortion, miscegenation, and profanity.

As Hollywood incorporated sex into the lives of characters set in the past, films represented the sexual diversity that preceded the sexual revolution of the 1960s. *The Last Picture Show* presents life in a small Southern town as an inversion of the sexual morality enshrined by the Code. Marriages are hollow and painful, wives commit adultery, and teen girls pursue sex with teenage boys and grown men. Roman Polanski seemed to mock the Code in the opening scene of *Chinatown*. After nostalgic Art Deco opening credits recalling the cinema of the late 1920s, a close-up of a black-and-white photograph of a man and a woman (Elizabeth Harding) engaged in sex in a wooded area fills the screen. The shots of the fully clothed man having sex with the fully clothed woman hint at the pornographic postcards that could be readily—if illegally—purchased in 1937 in a city the size of Los Angeles. After a couple of other shots of the couple, including one of the man having intercourse with the woman from behind, the camera pulls back to reveal private detective Jake Gittes (Jack Nicholson) and the cuckolded husband of the woman in the pictures, Curley (Burt Young). Curley is visibly upset, Gittes cynical and detached. The year is 1937, when enforcement of the Code was well underway, but this is not Will Hays's Hollywood. The images in the photographs violated the Code and were not a part of the image of American life films projected at the time. They also establish a theme of the film, the pursuit of truth through knowledge of sexual behavior, beginning with adultery and moving toward acts harder to fathom—incest.

Through the 1970s, Hollywood's sexual revisionism also mocked the PCA's last gasp at a cinema dominated by the sexual morality bracketed by *Pillow Talk* (1959) and *That Touch of Mink* (1962). In a diegetic world shaped by the Code, Doris Day could play a virgin in her late thirties working in New York City in *That Touch of Mink*, the year Helen Gurley Brown's *Sex and the Single Girl* was published. By contrast, Hollywood in the late 1970s assumed college students were less chaste than Day's character. By contrast, in *National Lampoon's Animal House* (1978), which parodied the sex life of college students during the early 1960s, college co-eds had sex. Katy (Karen Allen) cheats on her boyfriend Hoover (James Widdoes), sleeping with her college professor, Dave Jennings (Donald Sutherland). Mandy Pepperidge (Mary Louise Weller), a conservative sorority girl, masturbates her equally upstanding fraternity boyfriend, Greg Marmalard (James Daughton), while they are parked in a car. One of the main characters, Eric Stratton, or "Otter" (Tim Matheson), seduces the college dean's wife, Marion Wormer (Verna Bloom).

Milos Forman's 1981 adaptation of D. L. Doctorow's 1975 historical novel *Ragtime* takes place from 1900 to 1913, and includes as part of its subplots the tale of a murder that played a role in the development of film censorship in the United States. Millionaire Harry K. Thaw murdered architect Stanford White in 1906 in a jealous rage that developed because Thaw's wife, the model Evelyn Nesbitt, had been White's mistress a few years before Thaw married her. Thaw attempted to avoid prosecution by appealing to the "unwritten law" of the cuckold that justified his vengeance. That Thaw's ploy failed was perhaps indicative of the transitional nature of American society and culture at this time. Chicago's censorship ordinance had followed on the heels of a *Chicago Tribune* crusade against nickelodeons. The *Tribune* had singled out films like Siegmund Lubin's highly popular *The Unwritten Law: A Thrilling Drama Based on the Thaw White Case* (1907). *The Unwritten Law* told the story of White's murder. The story that helped spark censorship in 1907 drew a PG rating in 1981. In *Ragtime*, an early scene depicts a party that architect Stanford White (Norman Mailer) is holding with town dignitaries, including the city police commissioner, Rheinlander Waldo (James Cagney). Chorus girls serve the guests dessert and sit in their laps.

In a later scene, after Thaw (Robert Joy) has been found insane, Evelyn Nesbit (Elizabeth McGovern) is in a hotel room with a character known as the Younger Brother (Brad Dourif). Evelyn leaves the room for a moment and then returns, standing in the shadows wearing nothing but her black stockings. "All my clothes slipped away," she giggles as she walks toward Younger Brother, one hand covering her pubic hair. The shot cuts to Younger Brother's reaction and then to her falling over him, her buttocks briefly visible, typical of the coy, sexploitation-like use of nudity in the early 1980s. Hollywood had not so much abandoned the use of sexual implication as upped its ante. Instead of panning away or cutting the scene prior to a view of the naked body or sexual act, the camera panned or the scene was cut just *after* showing carefully composed glimpses of fragments of flesh.

Martin Scorsese's controversial *The Last Temptation of Christ* (1988) is perhaps the ultimate revision of the Catholic theology that underlay the Production Code's strictures. In Scorsese's adaptation of Nikos Kazantzakis's novel, Jesus Christ (Willem Dafoe) goes to a brothel and watches the prostitute make love with a black man behind a thin, gauze-like curtain. He sits with a group of men who patiently wait their turn to have sex with Mary Magdalene (Barbara Hershey). The film allots a considerable amount of time to the first customer and shows fragments of Mary's bare breasts and buttocks. Long shots of the sex from the men's point of view are interspersed with brief close-ups. After the last man leaves, Christ goes to her. She is lying on her side, her buttocks visible. After arguing, he leaves her. At the end of the film, while being crucified, Jesus fantasizes that he is not the Messiah, but instead lives a traditional family life. During the fantasy, there is a shot of Jesus and Mary making love, medium close-ups and long shots.

Another topic that points to Hollywood's relative comfort with topics once considered taboo for film—and still highly controversial and divisive in the United States—is abortion prior to its legalization in the late 1960s and early 1970s. *The Cider House Rules* (1999) portrayed, in somewhat saccharine terms many critics felt, the experience of teens and young women who sought abortions to end unwanted pregnancies. Obstetrician Dr. Wilbur Larch (Michael Caine) spends his professional life dealing with what he calls "unhappy pregnancies" as he delivers the babies of unwed, often very young, mothers at St. Cloud's orphanage in Maine during the 1930s and 1940s. One of the children, Homer Wells (Tobey Maguire), grows up at the orphanage, and learns to assist the doctor with births but refuses to help with abortions.

The film's treatment of abortion as a valid choice for women angered pro-life groups in the United States. Indeed, from Larch's perspective, abortion is often the only sensible choice unmarried girls or young women have. The film supports Larch's point of view when Homer finally drops his opposition to abortion. He performs an abortion on a young girl named Rose (Erykah Badu), who has been sexually abused by her father (Delroy Lindo). Before Homer performed the abortion on Rose, the film depicts his affair with Candy (Charlize Theron), a young woman engaged to be married. Homer met Candy when she got an abortion from Larch.

Under the ratings system, Hollywood films take the sex lives of their characters in films set in the present more or less for granted. Historical films likewise assume that characters had marital or nonmarital sex in the past, with the sexual attitudes of the protagonists familiar to contemporary audiences. For example, Anthony Minghella's *Cold Mountain* (2003) begins with a series of long flashbacks detailing how Inman (Jude Law), a Confederate soldier, and Ada Monroe (Nicole Kidman), a woman who lives near Cold Mountain, North Carolina, fall in love just before he goes to war. The narrative shifts to the parallel stories of his desertion and journey back to Ada and her trials and tribulations and longings for him during the war. Finally reunited near the end of the film, they make love in a scene meant to be a sublime image of love expressed through tenderness and sharing sexual pleasure. *Cold Mountain*'s melodramatic love story wraps much of the Code's morality in a contemporary package. It blends the sexual morality of the Code era—marriage is important to the couple—with contemporary morality—marriage is not immediately attainable—which allows it to combine a semblance of the traditional sexual morality of the nineteenth century with sexual images expected by audiences at the start of the twenty-first century.

MODERNITY, THE CODE, AND NEW HOLLYWOOD'S 1930s

The conservative Christian morality encoded in the Production Code had dominated American society and culture throughout the nineteenth and much of the twentieth century. Its Victorian incarnation had been particularly strict, with sexual morality in many ways made the measure of bourgeois respectability. Although the Victorians' seamier indulgences have been documented, Victorian elites invested considerable effort into keeping sex out of the public sphere.[5] Modernity in the first three decades of the twentieth century displaced Victorian public sensibilities socially and culturally. With urbanization and the emergence of the "new woman" symbolized by the flapper, Americans' public and private sexual behavior was gradually changing. Censorship laws and the Code were part of elite efforts to stem the visibility of the tide of change.

Some of the challenges to censorship came from the modernist avant-garde. These modernists attempted through their aesthetic works, and in the case of bohemians, their lives, to provoke cultural shock through novelty. They found a great deal of shock value in sexual matters. Thus, they attempted to shatter literary, musical, art, and social expectations and conventions as they pushed aesthetic and social boundaries in their exploration of the new. Modernism was trans-Atlantic, with numerous Americans flocking to cities such as Berlin and Paris, where they sought out new experiences and ways of expressing themselves. From exiled authors to American émigrés seeking sexual escapades in Continental cities, Americans abroad were a staple of the modernist cultural landscape. One such city was Berlin, Germany, during the final years of the Weimar Republic, infamous for its wild nightlife, which catered to an array of sexual tastes.[6]

New Hollywood filmmakers found the early 1930s, the period of the birth of the Production Code, ripe for revision. Bob Fosse's *Cabaret* (1972) takes place in Weimar Berlin during the rise of the Nazi Party. The film was the latest in a string of works loosely based on Christopher Isherwood's collection of sketches and vignettes entitled *The Berlin Stories* (1939). First, John Van Druten's play *I Am a Camera* (1951) ran on Broadway in the early 1950s. Julie Harris won a Tony for her portrayal of Sally Bowles in the play, which she reprised in a British film of the same name in 1955. Joe Masteroff then reworked Isherwood's stories into a musical called *Cabaret*, which debuted on Broadway in 1966 for a three-year run. Any conception of the relationship between film and reality has to take into consideration the gap between the creation of a film's source material, in the case of an adaptation, and its release. Fosse's revisionism was possible because both film regulation and Americans' sexual attitudes relaxed. Similar institutional and social changes would make it possible to make sexual abuse the center of a Hollywood blockbuster by the mid-1980s.

Already during the early years of the sound era, films were set in cabarets. Josef von Sternberg's *The Blue Angel* (1930) made a star of Marlene Dietrich. Throughout the Code era, movies often included scenes in nightclubs and hazy implications of sexual misbehavior. Yet, as with any setting that included sexual implications during the Code era, the implications were either vague or ambiguous. Even though it largely confined sex to dialogue and narrative implication and included no nudity or explicit sex, *Cabaret* retained none of the ambiguity or vagueness of Code era films. Fosse's representation of promiscuity and homosexuality is much more explicit than the PCA would have allowed during the Code era.

The cabaret of the film's title is the Kit Kat Klub, where, the Master of Ceremonies (Joel Grey) assures the crowd, "life is beautiful" and "the girls are beautiful." In classic sexploitation style, the Master of Ceremonies entices the crowd by announcing that it had been a battle to keep the women in their clothes the night before, but tonight that battle may be lost. Throughout the film, the Master of Ceremonies functions as a one-man Greek chorus commenting on life inside and outside the Kit Kat Klub.

An American dancer at the cabaret, Sally Bowles (Liza Minnelli) meets and befriends an English graduate student, Brian Roberts (Michael York), when he seeks a room in the boarding house where she lives. Sally describes its residents, including Fräulein Maura (Sigrid von Richtofen) "a masseuse—for ladies only," gesturing quotation marks for "masseuse" with her fingers, and Fräulein Kost (Helen Vita) "a terribly sweet streetwalker." The characters' nonchalance about sexual deviance or perversions distinguished the film's morality from the Code's. Rather than the PCA's strained sexual hints, the film invites viewers to share Sally's "divine decadence." Passing by Fräulein Kost's room, Sally jokes to Brian, "You can just imagine," as once required by the Code. She shows him her own room, blustering that she occasionally brings men home but prefers going home with them. In later scenes, Sally entertains older male patrons between stage performances.

Sally's casual attitude toward her own and her fellow boarders' promiscuity illustrate her bohemian rejection of bourgeois sexual morality. She rebels against her father, whom she describes as "practically" an American ambassador. Likewise, Brian seeks experiences unavailable to him as a philosophy major from Cambridge, and he is willing to subside by earning fifty marks translating a pornographic novel. Although the wayward children of the social elite indulge in the hedonism that made the Weimar Republic infamous, Sally attempts to maintain a double life when she goes to meet her father. She wears a black, Victorian-style dress with a high and tightly buttoned collar. Her father fails to show, sending his regrets by telegram instead. Sally's absent father symbolizes the correlation between the lack of parental authority and the breakdown of sexual morality.

In its treatment of the rise of Nazism, *Cabaret* suggests the German nation went too far in its search for a father figure. Brown shirts appear periodically at the Kit Kat Klub as well as a countryside restaurant. The culture's tolerance for sexual variation did not extend to ethnic variation. Anti-Semitism simmers beneath the surface, most poignantly in the fate that viewers realize awaits Brian and Sally's Jewish friends, Fritz Wendel (Fritz Wepper) and Natalia Landauer (Marisa Berenson), the daughter of a wealthy department store owner. Fritz and Natalia get married, but the future does not bode well for the film's one successful intimate relationship.

Cabaret obliquely portrays the strange coexistence between the Weimar Republic's sexual decadence and the rise of an intolerant totalitarian regime. The film does not establish a causal relationship between the two; instead, it underscores the futility of decadent entertainment in the face of brutal repression. The Kit Kat Klub's patrons, symbolizing a populace diverted from political reality by sexual diversions, were not blinded by political ignorance but an indifference fomented by sexual excess. Sally and the other performers at the cabaret, by contrast, draw on the sexual excesses of the decadent demimonde that thrived in early 1930s Berlin to mock the society around them. In one stage act, a man plays a saw on the stage while behind a translucent curtain, a woman in silhouette, whose breasts appear to be bare, whips another woman, who is chained to a frame that resembles the end of a bed. At the other end of the stage, a nude woman plays a violin while a man, clothed and wearing a hat, sits in a chair watching the S&M scene and smoking a cigar.

In another act, mud-wrestling women symbolize the ineffectualness of sexual decadence as entertainment when confronted with totalitarianism. The inanity is accentuated through a brief montage of close-ups of people in the cabaret laughing hysterically at the antics of the emcee and the mud wrestlers. The cabaret is dark and crowded, the film is grainy, the camera kinetic. Faces are intercut with action shots of wrestling and long shots of Brian contemplating the scene in ascetic repose. A concerned maître d' pushes a Nazi through the crowd and out of the club. In a later scene, the Nazi and a group of his brown-shirted henchmen hit and stomp on the maître d' until he falls unconscious to the ground, their abuse intercut with scenes of the dancers performing a parody of Tyrol folk dancers wearing lederhosen. The film's circus-and-bread message is that the crowd at the Kit Kat Klub ignored or was unable to conceive the imminent threat gathering around them until it was too late.[7]

Cabaret does not confine its sex to onstage parodies or Sally's innuendoes about the boarding house residents. It traces Sally's relationship with Brian. The first time Sally tries to seduce Brian, she fails. Confused at being rejected, she taunts, with a touch of disdain in her voice, "Maybe you don't sleep with girls." Brian explains that after three failed attempts at having sex with women, his sex life is nonexistent. Brian becomes Sally's lover after her father's canceled date. Sally's promiscuity, the film imputes, results from low self-esteem: "Maybe he's right," she breaks down and sobs to Brian. "Maybe I'm not worth caring about. Maybe I am just … nothing." Brian comforts her, and their embrace leads to a kiss and smiles. The camera pans toward the ceiling. A montage of the friends turned lovers follows, all dissolving back and forth between Sally singing "Maybe this time he'll stay" in a nearly deserted Kit Kat Klub. Ironically, when Sally attempts to express genuine feelings, no one is there to pay attention.

The couple morphs into a threesome after Sally meets Maximilian von Heune (Helmut Griem). Sally sees the baron as her ticket to stardom, while Brian sees him as a threat. It turns out that Max is married. He and his wife have, he informs Brian, "a very special understanding," which Brian admits "must be useful." The film hints at Brian and Max's attraction to one another when Sally, Brian, and Max dance together, their faces tightly framed and their faces circling in front of the camera. The following day the three go for a drive in the country. While sitting outside a country inn, Brian gives Max a cigarette and a light. Max holds Brian's hand as he puts his cigarette to the flame, pauses slightly, and looks at Brian. Both men react ever so slightly to the physical contact and exchange a sustained glance. They exchange a toast and continue staring into one another's eyes.

The narrative confirms its hints. Some days later, Brian and Sally begin arguing. When Sally tells Brian that Max is "divinely sexy," Brian angrily explodes, "Screw Max." Sally says she has, and to her great surprise, Brian says that he has, too. Her tolerance evaporates suddenly, and she calls Brian and Max bastards. She has a change of heart, though, and comforts Brian after he is beaten up by two Nazis. *Cabaret*'s sympathetic portrayal of Brian's bisexuality was a milestone for a major Hollywood film.

The film has one final sex-related event: an abortion of an unplanned pregnancy. Although Sally is not sure who the father is, Brian is willing to marry her. Sally agrees, but then has an abortion without telling him. After walking Brian to his train to Cambridge, Sally ends where she began, apparently none the wiser for her ordeals, taking to the stage to sing the title song. Sally, the drag queens, the women dancers and wrestlers, and the audience all remain captivated by and captive to their decadence. Urbanization's loosening of sexual morality provides Sally and Brian with little freedom beyond promiscuity, which they find unfulfilling. Sally and Brian experience one side of modernity's break with the past: the attraction of disorder. The characters in *Cabaret* seem destined to end like the images in the pornographic postcards and pornography films circulating in modernist cities. Sally's experience of modernity's break with the sexual vestiges of Victorianism remains carnal.

Another response to modernity's assault on tradition was intellectual and aesthetic, which were combined in the life and work of French writer Anais Nin and her lover, the American author Henry Miller, in Paris, France, at the beginning of the 1930s. With sex passages that many considered obscene, Miller's *Tropic of Cancer* (1934) would be involved in an important landmark in an obscenity case in 1962 just as his ideas about sexual liberation would gain a following among counterculture youth during the 1960s.[8] *Henry & June* (1990) retells the story of a love affair in 1931 and 1932, the years of the Production Code's infancy. Philip Kaufman's film captures not only the characters' sex acts, but also their ultimately futile exertions to burst through what they felt were the limits bourgeois sexual morality placed on individual identity. Their efforts were both literary and physical.

Henry & June begins by playing on the modernist conceit of the interpenetrability of fiction and reality for budding Parisian author Anais Nin (Maria de Medeiros). Impressed by the "authority" with which Anais writes about sex, a book editor (Juan-Louis Buñuel) of the Black Manikin Press assumes she "must've led a rather free life." He associates sexual expressiveness with sexual experience and freedom. Anais is puzzled, though. "Free?" she asks. The editor wants to know the source of her "insights into the erotic."

Anais explains her "real awakening" resulted not from affairs but from chancing upon some pornographic postcards and photographs, which are shown briefly in a flashback. Anais says in a voice-over that the images revealed "the endless varieties of erotic experience." The underground images and her description of their effect convey both her budding wantonness and her entrapment by the sexual decorum required of women. Soon, her creative imagination leads her into sexual risk-taking. By the early 1930s, pornographic postcards had long been a staple of the underground commerce in erotic images.[9] Anais's enjoyment of the postcards is doubly transgressive, since the market for sexually explicit images was overwhelmingly male.

Richard Osborn (Kevin Spacey), a friend of Anais and her husband, Hugo Guiler (Richard E. Grant), introduces the couple to Henry Miller (Fred Ward), an unpublished American writer living in Paris. Henry soon explains his view of sexuality, marginal in the early 1930s, but one that would gain momentum through the postwar era, strengthened by the success of the Kinsey reports. "To my way of thinking," Henry tells Anais and the others, "sex is natural like birth or death." After dinner, Henry and Anais are alone discussing writing. Henry picks up one of Anais's postcards, which pictures a couple making love. Anais is slightly embarrassed, but Henry just says "huh" and smiles, an exchange of shots that contrasts her (public) sexual uptightness with his sexual casualness.

The two sequences with brief shots of pornographic postcards introduce a crucial element of Hollywood's revision of the sexual past: the acknowledgement of pornography and its role in documenting the existence of sexual subcultures to those who consumed it. Pornography is particularly powerful in this regard since the acts photographed were actually performed, faked passion and orgasms notwithstanding. The images provide traces of sexual deviance, both when posed, as in Anais's postcards, or recorded surreptitiously by a private detective, as in *Chinatown*. Sexual imagery, whether in pornography or erotic fiction, a line Miller blurred in his work, is established as sexually edifying. For Miller, what Osborne understands to be writing about "fucking" is actually, he tells Anais and the others, "about self-liberation."

The conflation of individual freedom, personal growth, sexual experimentation, and moral purity was a common motif on the bohemian fringe. In bohemian circles from Greenwich Village to Berlin to Paris, taboo sexual experiences were touted as a key to esoteric knowledge. Many bohemians believed that sexual experimentation was a path to individual growth, a modernist trope that would make its way into mainstream sexual attitudes by the late 1960s. Thus, when Anais acts on her sexual desire for Henry, at a nightclub while her husband plays "Haitian drums" on stage with the band, in a hectically edited scene, she writes in her diary afterwards that she feels "innocent." Another bohemian conceit was that sexual abandon could lead to spiritual exaltedness, exemplified when Anais and Henry make love in a tunnel. The scene emphasizes the relationship between sexual experience and self-knowledge. As they make love, their talk is not only erotic; for Henry, the carnality of sex is always inseparable from knowledge, experience, personal identity, and sincerity. Henry expresses the connections succinctly as they make love in the tunnel when he tells Anais, "I want to fuck you, teach you things." Anais responds to Henry's remarks by saying, "I feel so pure. So strong. So new, Henry." Henry fluctuates between the spiritual and carnal, telling Anais, "Maybe I should get down on my knees and worship you. I'm gonna undress you. Vulgarize you a bit." The camera cuts from close-ups and medium close-ups to long shot, shifting emphasis from the private intimacy of their exchange to the public space.

The film threads together a number of scenes evoking the sexuality pulsing through the characters' lives. In one brief scene, Anais enters Osborne's apartment without knocking and opens his bedroom door, interrupting him in bed with three naked young women. Anais and Osborne apologize to one another, but neither seems perturbed. The women in Osborne's bed are completely indifferent. In a café with Anais, Henry recounts how he met and married June (Uma Thurman), a fancy talking "taxi dancer." In flashbacks, June dances with an artist named Jean (Liz Hasse), who is dressed like a man and whom June brings home to live in a ménage à trois with Henry. Henry also tells Anais that June lived off money she got from Pop (Maurice Escargot), a man she slept with. In another scene, Anais follows Henry into a brothel where women walk around naked or scantily clad, one of the women in sheer lingerie (Brigitte Lahaie) heading up the stairs with Henry. Anais revisits that same brothel with her husband, and they pay to have two prostitutes perform a lesbian act together.

Anais's desire to see two women make love emerges after she becomes attracted to June. She fantasizes she is June one night, demanding that Hugo pretend she is June. Anais's fantasies lead her to experiment. She and June go to see *Mädchen in Uniform* (1931), a German lesbian film. In another scene, June takes Anais to a lesbian bar, where they dance. Near the end of the film, they are on the cusp of making love when Anais accidentally reveals that she has been sleeping with Henry. Incensed, June storms off. Even bohemians, it seems, set limits to free love.

The film thus aligns itself with the limits on the sexual freedom that Henry and Anais believe they want but have difficulty achieving. Despite such hypocrisy, the bohemian fringe influenced mainstream sexual attitudes in the postwar era. Ideas about sexuality from writers such as Nin and Miller or avant-garde films such as Luis Buñuel and painter Salvador Dali's surrealist film *Un Chien Andalou* (1928), which the characters in *Henry & June* watch in an art house cinema, challenged the dominant limits on expression in literature and film. The intermingling of freedom of expression and sexual liberation gained a popular audience in the writing of authors like Jack Kerouac in the 1950s and a film audience in the underground films of the 1960s. One of the more influential of the once marginal ideas about sexuality that moved from the bohemian fringe to the mainstream was the belief in sexual self-determination.

There were numerous other factors influencing the popular understanding of sexual self-determination during the 1960s and 1970s, not least the demand by second wave feminists for greater gender equality, sexual or otherwise. Feminists challenged gender inequalities within and outside of marriage because laws had long institutionalized male dominance over the female. In the realm of sexual relationships, one of the darker chapters in American history was the conjugal right of husbands that allowed them to have sex with their wives whether their wives wanted to or not. Second wave feminists moved to the forefront of efforts that had taken place in state legislatures since the nineteenth century to have nonconsensual marital sex classified as marital rape. The Production Code required that rape only be "suggested" and not shown directly. Although Hollywood represented rape in numerous films, marital rape did not make it past the PCA since it would have constituted a negative portrayal of marriage.[10] Furthermore, marital rape did not gain widespread legal recognition before the demise of the Code. Although still a taboo topic in the 1980s, a major Hollywood production included marital rape.

THE COLOR PURPLE, THE COLOR OF RACE, THE COLOR OF SEX

Steven Spielberg's 1985 adaptation of Alice Walker's bestselling novel *The Color Purple* (1982) focuses, as Hollywood films had rarely done, not only on the experiences of African Americans in the segregated South, but on the lives, including the sexual experiences, of African American women. It follows Celie (Whoopi Goldberg), a poor African American woman living in rural Georgia, as she struggles to survive sexual and physical abuse between 1909 and 1947. In the larger community, Celie is the victim of the racial discrimination that characterized the Jim Crow South; at home, she is the victim of sexual abuse as a child, and marital rape and adultery as an adult.

The film portrays several other strong women who befriend and eventually embolden Celie. Shug (Margaret Avery), a singer with a degree of regional renown on the "Chitlin' Circuit," is occasionally the mistress of Celie's common-law husband, Albert (Danny Glover), so their lives intersect occasionally. Another woman with tremendous will-power and no fear of men is Sofia (Oprah Winfrey), who is married to Albert's son, Harpo (Willard E. Pugh). Each woman survives her ordeals, often empowering other women in the process. In Celie's case, abuse began in early childhood.

The film establishes the psychological cruelty Celie must endure during the credit sequence. Two young African American girls are playing in an idyllic field of purple flowers, shot in shallow focus. They are only children, but one of them is pregnant, a jarring image set against the pastoral landscape. Their father (Leonard Jackson) calls them to supper, telling Celie (played by Desreta Jackson as a child) she has "the ugliest smile this side of creation." Celie starts to cover her mouth but her sister stops her. Tragically, insults are the least of Celie's problems. The man she calls "Pa" is the father of her unborn child. The next scene portrays one of the darker consequences of child sexual abuse as Celie gives birth during the winter of 1909. Her father comes in and asks gruffly, "ain't you done yet?" After Pa warns her not to "tell nobody but God," Celie begins writing letters to God. Her babies disappear, so Celie speculates that Pa killed the girl and may have sold the boy. She discovers much later in her life that Pa was actually her stepfather and that her children are alive.

By the time Celie is fourteen, Pa sleeps with her younger sister, Nettie (Akosua Busia). Rather than suffer Pa's sexual abuse, Nettie eventually comes to Celie and Albert, or "Mister," as Celie calls him. When Albert openly flirts with Nettie, Celie tells her to leave before he "make his move on you," or, as Nettie mockingly puts it, "do his business." Their premonitions prove right. Albert stalks Nettie on horseback as she walks to school one morning. On the soundtrack, the amplified sound of the horse's hooves pounding and its breathing accentuates the difference in physical power on which male abuse of females, especially underage, is based. Nettie manages to escape, though, by hitting him in his scrotum with her school bag. Enraged, Albert forces Nettie to leave.

As Albert's attempted rape of Nettie demonstrates, Celie had escaped her stepfather only to suffer abuse at Albert's hands. Pa had "given" her to Albert, although Albert had preferred Nettie. Albert, a widower, had sex with Celie their first night together. She lay passively thinking, her voice-over accompanied by the sound of the squeaking bed banging into the wall. Albert finished, looked at Celie, exclaimed "Jesus." Spent, he rolled over to fall asleep. She is no more than a receptacle for his sexual outlet.

In his relationship with Celie, Albert believes that his own sexual satisfaction is his prerogative and that she should be subservient. By contrast, Albert's vaulted gender roles are reversed in his relationship with Shug. Shug tells Albert she needs a *man*, with the clear implication that he is less than masculine in her eyes. Albert even cooks for Shug, much to Celie's surprise. Power structures in the film are complex and depend on psychological as well as physical strength, although the latter is the more fearsome of the two. The kaleidoscope of individuals and heterosexual relationships variously exposes the men in these women's lives as cold, vicious, or ineffectual.

Not surprisingly, given the rarity of portrayals of African Americans in Hollywood cinema by the mid-1980s, Spielberg's film rekindled debates originally ignited by Walker's novel. A number of (mostly male) literary critics had condemned Walker's portrayal of African American males as abusive tyrants in their relationships with women.[11] With the film's release, some African American critics argued that the lack of positive portrayals of African American male characters throughout American film history exacerbated the problems with Walker's depictions. Not only did Spielberg's characterization of Albert, Harpo, and other African American male figures draw the same fire, but many white critics' interpretations of the film also drew heat. Novelist and essayist Ishmael Reed summarized what he believed was a racist overgeneralization on the part of many white critics, the tendency to interpret the "heinous crimes" committed "against women and children ... as excuses to indict all Black men."[12]

Reed's point does not hinge on whether there was a statistical or historical basis for the inclusion of African American male spousal abuse or rape in *The Color Purple*. Reed critiques the tradition in American popular culture of representing African American males as violent and sexually threatening. Reed also targets the tendency of white critics to ignore race when white male characters beat or rape their wives. Historically, the question of whether the incidence of spousal abuse was higher among African Americans than white Americans tends to obscure historical realities such as common law granting husbands the right until the 1870s to "chastise" their wives as long as they did not cause physical harm. Courts continued to exempt men from prosecution for marital rape until the 1980s, but today courts generally rule that spousal exemptions violate the Constitution's equal protection clause.[13]

Reed is not debating demographic realism, but rather the role played by film in the creation and maintenance of social memory. Even if some recent sociological studies have found a higher prevalence of spousal violence perpetrated by African American males against their wives,[14] others have found the evidence contradictory and inconclusive.[15] What Reed's insight reveals is how (usually white) critics read African American characters as stereotypical representatives of all members of a group. Thus, white critics interpreted Albert not as an individual, but as representative of all African American males. Such overgeneralizations usually require recounting film history selectively and ignoring Hollywood's representation of battered white wives. Stanley Kowalski (Marlon Brando) beats his wife, Stella (Kim Hunter), in *A Streetcar Named Desire* (1951). Don Vito Corleone's (Marlon Brando) daughter, Connie (Talia Shire), is beaten by her husband, Carlo Rizzi (Gianni Russo) in *The Godfather* (1972). Jake LaMotta (Robert De Niro) batters his wife in *Raging Bull* (1980). In *Fried Green Tomatoes* (1991), Ruth (Mary-Louise Parker) is beaten by her husband, Frank Bennett (Nick Searcy).

More subtle debates over *The Color Purple* moved beyond racial stereotypes to gender concerns. African American male and feminist critics debated the historical accuracy of sexual violence and general abuse of African American women by their husbands and other males. Feminist critics often praised Walker's book as a major breakthrough because it represented sexual oppression from a woman's point of view.[16] The same praise resurfaced with the release of Spielberg's film, which not only represented marital rape, but child abuse and adultery as well. In the melee, numerous critics seemed to forget that Pa and Albert are not the only males in the film. Albert can be contrasted with both Harpo, who has a much more egalitarian relationship with Sofia, and his father (Adolph Caesar), who berates him for letting his mistress, Shug, live in his house. Albert's father tells Celie she has his sympathy since not "many women's let they man's whore lay up in they house." Celie does get one thing out of Shug "laying up" in Albert's house. While Shug lives with Albert, her relationship with Celie deepens.

To express her feelings for and admiration of Celie, Shug writes and performs a song called "Miss Celie's Blues." As their intimacy grows, Shug dresses Celie up in her stage outfit, and the two women discuss their relationship with Albert. Shug admits she really enjoys having sex with him while Celie says, "Most of the time I just pretend like I ain't even there." Celie complains that Albert never asks her how she feels, that he only "climb on top of me and do his business." Shug points out that the expression also refers to the act of excreting. That, Celie replies, is what "it feels like." The possibility of Celie experiencing sexual (or any other) pleasure in her relationship with Albert is eliminated by his utter indifference to her. Whereas Shug knows she is the object of Albert's desire, Celie knows she is simply sexually at hand.

The difference in their relationships to Albert results partly from their physical appearance. Shug is an attractive woman while Celie is

homely, of which both Shug and Albert remind her. After Shug and
Celie bond, though, Shug tells Celie that she thinks she is beautiful. In a
scene parallel to Nettie's actions at the beginning of the film, Shug pulls
Celie's hands away from her face when she covers her smile. Shug's
kindness leads to the women kissing. Framed in a two-shot from a
medium close-up, she leans over and gives Celie a kiss on the cheek. A
close up of Shug from over Celie's shoulder to register the reaction in
her eyes cuts to Celie to register hers. The sex is driven as much by
emotional as sexual desire. Shug then kisses her on the forehead, causing Celie to look around somewhat sheepishly. Shug kisses Celie's face
a few more times and then her lips. Reluctant at first, Celie smiles
broadly (in a close-up) and returns Shug's kisses. The two women then
begin a long kiss, the camera slowly panning to Shug's hand on Celie's
shoulder, then down to Celie's hand which moves up to Shug's shoulder.
The camera pans over to wind chimes, and the shot fades to black.

Numerous critics derided Spielberg for watering down Shug and
Celie's lesbian relationship. By traditional Hollywood editing conventions, the scene clearly implies that the two women continue kissing
and make love. Head over heels after someone has finally seen her
inner beauty, Celie describes Shug in a voice-over in the next scene as
"honey" and herself as a bee that followed her everywhere. Shug soon
leaves, though, devastating Celie.

Shug returns in the spring of 1936 with a husband, Grady (Bennet
Guillory). Shug and Celie discover the letters Nettie has mailed from
Africa, where she is a missionary. Emboldened, Celie finally stands up
to Albert, threatening to kill him. After Shug restrains Celie, Albert
sums up Celie's socioeconomic predicament: "Look at you. You're poor.
You're black. You're ugly. You're a woman. You're nothing at all."
Albert's words have more resonance than the simplistic effort to kow-
tow Celie through ridicule. They also echo the racial discrimination that
suppresses him and limits his own opportunities. Both African American men and women had little chance of enjoying dignity, respect, or
success outside the segregated world they lived in. They were rendered
invisible unless they attempted to make themselves seen, which could
have dire consequences.

The ferocious violence that secured racial discrimination in the Jim
Crow South breaks Sofia, one of the film's most indomitable characters.
Sofia is able to overcome the double standard of the sexes, but she is
rendered powerless by the racist taboos that govern her life. After turning down an "offer" from the mayor's wife, Miss Millie (Dana Ivey), to
be her maid, Sofia gets into an argument with and pushes the mayor
(Phillip Strong) to the ground. In the ensuing melee, Sofia is blinded in
one eye, hobbled, and sentenced to jail. A broken spirit after serving
time, Sofia ends up working for Miss Millie, who separates Sofia from

her family. As an act of condescending charity, Miss Millie takes Sofia to see her kids one Christmas.

The visit goes terribly awry when Miss Millie cannot drive her car on the icy ground. She misinterprets friendly offers of assistance from a group of African American men as an impending sexual attack. The film mocks the dual myths of the African American sexual predator who threatens the pure white woman on a pedestal of Southern virtue. It conveys the frightening madness of a society as frozen in time as the frosted landscape, a society in which men risk being lynched because a silly woman's racism blinds her to acts of kindness.

Despite Albert's dire warning, Celie does succeed after she leaves him. Albert goes to seed without the pillar of support that Celie's un-rewarded labor had provided. At the end of the film, Celie is reunited with Nettie, who returns with Celie's two children, whom she had raised in Africa. Albert, passing by through a nearby field, seems reconciled with his fate and Celie's happiness. Albert's demeanor changes in some measure because of the modernization of the South. *The Color Purple* brings its characters into a world less isolated than the one that provided Albert with the opportunity to beat and rape his wife with impunity. The isolation was diminished by technological developments that reduced the social and cultural estrangement of the hinterland, symbolized by Nettie's return from Africa, a world immeasurably distant from rural Georgia early in the film's narrative.

More importantly, African Americans were also isolated because of racial segregation, which had existed outside the South, including Hollywood, California. Because of structural racism in the American film industry through most of the twentieth century, African Americans were largely absent from mainstream American cinema, confined to supporting roles. The title of Donald Bogle's landmark history of African Americans in American films, *Toms, Coons, Mulattoes, Mammies, and Bucks*, denotes the effect of discrimination.[17] The last category in Bogle's list, "buck," referred to sexually potent African American males, often stereotyped as sexually threatening. D. W. Griffith's *The Birth of a Nation* (1915) gave sustenance to the myth of the African American male rapist. Griffith's landmark of American silent cinema is set during Reconstruction following the American Civil War. In a famous scene, Flora Cameron (Mae Marsh) jumps or stumbles off a cliff to her death in fear of rape after an African American soldier named Gus (Walter Long, a white actor) asks her to marry him. The Ku Klux Klan, formed by Flora's brother, Confederate veteran Colonel Ben Cameron (Henry Walthall), lynches Gus. The NAACP protested, trying repeatedly to have the film banned, but to no avail.

At the time *The Birth of a Nation* was released, marriage between African Americans and whites was illegal in twenty-eight states.[18]

The Production Code's ban on miscegenation corresponded to the states' antimiscegenation laws. The PCA suppressed any implication of African Americans having sex with, much less being married to, white Americans. The ban on miscegenation foregrounds the Code's racism and one of American society's longstanding sexual taboos throughout most of the twentieth century. In films that were largely distributed outside the mainstream industry, African American director Oscar Micheaux dealt with miscegenation in *The Exile* (1931) and *The Betrayal* (1948), employing the same conceit that appeared in *Showboat* (1951), when an ostensibly "white" character, Julie (Ava Gardner), discovers she is biracial.

Guess Who's Coming to Dinner (1967) examined the experiences of an African American doctor, John Prentice (Sidney Poitier), and his white fiancée, Joey Drayton (Katharine Houghton). The couple tells their parents about their engagement only six months after the United States Supreme Court ruled that antimiscegenation laws violated the equal protection clause of the Fourteenth Amendment.[19] *The Great White Hope* (1970) looked back at the bitter experiences of an African American boxer, Jack Jefferson (James Earl Jones), based on the legendary boxer Jack Johnson, and his white lover, Eleanor (Jane Alexander), in 1910. *Mandingo* (1975) and its sequel *Drum* (1976) resembled sexploitation films in their sensational depiction of sex between slaves and whites in the antebellum South.

Spike Lee's *Malcolm X* (1992), starring Denzel Washington in the title role, included scenes of the African American nationalist's sexual exploits as a young man. Despite the emergence of African American male stars such as Danny Glover, Eddie Murphy, and Denzel Washington, *Ebony* magazine could still note Hollywood's stubborn resistance to portraying African Americans' sex lives in productions at the beginning of the 1990s.[20] Independent African American women directors also made impressive revisions of the sexual past. Julie Dash's *Daughters of the Dust* (1992) tells the lives of Eula Peazant (Alva Rogers), who is pregnant after being raped by a white man, and Yellow Mary (Barbara O), a former prostitute, on the Georgia Sea Islands in the early 1900s. Another family member, Iona Peazant (Bahni Turpin) has a Native American lover. Kasi Lemmon's *Eve's Bayou* (1997) looks back at segregated Louisiana during the 1960s: a young girl, Eve Batiste (Jurnee Smollett), discovers that her father, Louis Batiste (Samuel L. Jackson), is unfaithful.

Ray (2004), the story of the musical career of Ray Charles (Jamie Foxx, who won an Academy Award for Best Actor), included a fair amount of nonmarital sexuality. The film focuses on three themes of Ray's career and private life: his incredible musical genius, his heroin addiction, and his sexual promiscuity. The film begins with Ray moving to Seattle in the 1940s to meet up with his partner, Gossie McKee (Terrence Howard). He gets a job playing at a small club called The Rocking Chair. The film's sexual themes are introduced even before he auditions when the club's manager, Marlene (Denise Dowse), complains to him that Gossie had been "catting' around" with one of her waitresses. Ray auditions and impresses Marlene. She tells Gossie Ray "can flop at my place." Gossie smiles knowingly and tells her, "You don't never change." Marlene becomes Ray's lover, and they live together in a bungalow.

In a scene emblematic of her sexual insatiability, Marlene is topless, her breasts covered by the bedding as she beckons Ray back to the bedroom. Although Ray is exhausted from their sexual bouts, she tells him "mama ain't finished yet." The scene cuts to a montage of the trio's onstage success and another scene of Marlene calling to Ray from the bedroom: "Mama's got some more blackberry cobbler for you, baby." A worn out Ray simply says, "Damn." Their relation ends after Ray complains about not receiving his fair share from his performances, and he realizes Marlene is using him both sexually and financially.

Ray utilizes jazz clubs, not least African American jazz clubs, to create social environments with sexual mores quite different from middle-class America (white or African American). Sexual relations are casual, discussed openly, and part of a social cocktail that often includes drug use as well as the music and dancing.[21] For Hollywood, the social universe of the club scene motivates Ray's sexual promiscuity when he adopts its sexual code just as it makes his success with women plausible. He is in a social environment where sexual promiscuity is practiced and accepted.

A few scenes later, Ray's talent in a new band is established, and he performs alone with a row of women sitting at the stage and admiring him. Later that evening, seen from the perspective of three band members in a long shot across a bar, Ray hits on a female companion at the far end of the bar. Fathead Newman (Bokeem Woodbine) explains to the other two what Ray is doing, explaining to the viewer, as well, that Ray is determining whether the woman he is flirting with is attractive or not by feeling her wrist. The camera cuts to a close up of Ray sliding his hand along her wrist and arm. A montage of Ray using this tactic on a series of women (the last of whom he can feel is overweight) establishes this move as a running motif in the film, signaling to the viewer that Ray is picking up a woman.

After Ray marries Della (Kerry Washington), it functions as a sign of infidelity. The movie ends on a positive note, though, suggesting that Ray Charles stopped philandering and reconciled with Della. Genre—and the Hollywood happy ending—triumphed over the reality of Ray's continued infidelity and his divorce from Della. The film deserves credit, though, for its willingness to represent the sex life of an African American male, a step forward in "proceed[ing] to fill the empty space in representation with movies about the deeply complicated and brilliant black men that populate the African American narrative tradition.... "[22] In contrast to the African American males in *The Color Purple*, Ray Charles's sexuality is not portrayed in stereotypical terms. Ray Charles was simply a person who engaged in the sexual affairs that he engaged in, his race playing no more of a role in his sexuality than his musicianship.

The Code often forced filmmakers to create undersexed diegetic worlds that bore little resemblance to either mainstream or bohemian sex lives. The limits on sexual content imposed by the Production Code from the 1930s until the 1960s clearly led to the creation of an image of Americans' sex lives that did not correlate with the role that sex played in society. Since the late 1960s, Hollywood has revised American history on-screen to include the libidinous. Revisions have resulted from filmmakers' conceptions of what succeeds at the box office, their presumptions about public morality, and the willingness of actors and actresses to perform sexual roles. However tenuous films' connection to historical reality, Hollywood films' representations of the sexual past have become more plausible. In revising the past as it was presented under the Code, Hollywood has also slowly begun to include African American sexual history in films. Motion pictures play a major role in chronicling sexual diversity in American society throughout the nation's history. Hollywood has been referred to as a "dream factory" more often than as a national archive.[23] Film accentuates the mythical qualities of history as a component of a society's collective memory. As the tagline for *The English Patient* (1996) would have it: "In memory, love lives forever." So, too, in movies, does sex.

7

From the Closet
to the Screen

INTRODUCTION

One chapter can only sketch salient issues in the historical experiences of gays and lesbians in the United States and their fragmentary representations on-screen.[1] It focuses on the ways gays and lesbians have been treated and perceived since the 1930s and represented in American films. From sodomy laws to psychiatric diagnoses, legal and medical sanctions kept "the closet" closed that forced gays and lesbians into the shadows of American life until the late 1960s. Parallel with these social sanctions that kept homosexuality transparent in the American mainstream, the Production Code served to limit the visibility of gays and lesbians in mainstream film. The Code was amended in the early 1960s, and Hollywood began peaking inside the closet. Throughout the 1960s, films typically reflected widespread antigay sentiments.

The modern gay liberation movement began in the late 1960s, and more and more gays and lesbians came "out," increasing their political and legal efforts to change their status in the United States. The efforts of the 1970s bore the fruit of the homophile movement of the 1950s. In the 1970s, attitudes toward homosexuality gradually became more positive both off-screen and on-screen. With the discovery of AIDS in the early 1980s, though, the gay community faced a new ordeal and a backlash. Throughout the 1980s and 1990s, Hollywood went from peaks to valleys in having gay and lesbian protagonists in films. Nonetheless, by the early

1990s, identity politics had contributed to a relatively successful spate of independent films grouped together as New Queer Cinema.

CLOSING THE CLOSET

In the early twentieth century, as homosexuality was viewed more and more as a form of psychopathology, control mechanisms shielded straight Americans from the threats religious leaders, psychologists, and politicians believed homosexuals posed. Sodomy laws made same-sex sexual behavior illegal. Some of the laws were old and very vague, prohibiting "crimes against nature." Now, older statutes were brushed off, new ones passed with more specific prohibitions, and vice squads established. Although inconsistently enforced, sodomy laws dampened the willingness of gays or lesbians to be publicly open about their sexual orientation.[2]

Vice squads also kept a watchful eye on popular culture. Obscenity charges were raised against novels, magazines, photographs, plays, burlesque shows, or motion pictures deemed to have offensive sexual content, with same-sex portrayals frequently singled out in the 1920s. By 1930, when the Code was drafted, gays and lesbians found themselves in a contradictory situation. They risked getting arrested and being ostracized. Yet, urbanization fostered gay and lesbian community networks and provided the anonymity needed to lead double lives: straight in public and homosexual in private. The view of homosexuals as either sinners performing crimes against nature or potentially dangerous pathological sexual "inverts" dominated American attitudes toward gays and lesbians.

The wording of the Code's prohibitions against homosexuality reflected both the antihomosexual beliefs of the Catholic Church and the dominant pathological view of homosexuality at the time as a "sex perversion." The Production Code forbade the representation of "sex perversion or any inference to it." During the first four years of the Code's existence, Hollywood filmmakers occasionally ignored its injunctions against homosexuality just as they had disregarded restrictions on representing heterosexual sex behavior. Indeed, lesbianism was implied by two famous cinematic kisses during the first years of the Code. In *Morocco* (1930), cabaret performer Amy Jolly (Marlene Dietrich), dressed in a tuxedo, kisses a female spectator (uncredited) on the lips before beginning her seduction of Tom Brown (Gary Cooper), who is also in the audience.

In *Queen Christina* (1933), Greta Garbo's eponymous character has an active, if not ambiguous, sex life. Christina Vasa, who had briefly been Queen of Sweden (1644–1654) before abdicating her throne, had been bisexual, and this part of her sexuality made it into MGM's film. At one point, Christina affectionately kisses Ebba Sparre (Elizabeth Young), her lady-in-waiting. When Countess Ebba comes in, the Queen's male attendant, Aage (C. Aubrey Smith), warns her not to "dally" because she has a "busy day." His implication is clear: the Queen indeed sometimes does "dally" when Ebba comes to her room. She welcomes Ebba with a full kiss on the lips, cupping her face in her hands. The androgynous Queen is dressed like a cavalier, Ebba in very feminine attire. They make the perfect butch-femme couple, which fit a stereotype of lesbian relationships.

Lesbian kisses were banished once the PCA strictly enforced the Code. Gone too were indications of the existence of a homosexual subculture as in *Call Her Savage* (1932), which included a scene with same-sex couples sitting together in a Greenwich Village gay and lesbian bar. Along with homophobia in American society, including in the film industry, the Code helped keep homosexuals a nearly invisible sexual minority.[3] During the Code era, filmmakers resorted to a gay and lesbian equivalent of the cinematic shorthand that developed to circumvent the Code's restrictions on representing heterosexual sexual behavior. While not as frequent, homoerotic implications between ostensibly straight male (and sometimes female) characters were part of film's inferential codes. *Gilda* (1946) involves a love triangle between two men, Johnny Farrell (Glenn Ford) and Ballin Mundson (George Macready), and Mundson's wife Gilda (Rita Hayworth). Gilda sleeps around and Johnny, who was her lover before she married Mundson, knows it. He tells her one night he will take her to and from her assignations but only, he sneers, in the same spirit that he would pick up Ballin's laundry. Gilda points out to him that any psychiatrist would find his "thought associations very revealing."

In addition to such word plays, films developed an iconography of *homoeroticism*.[4] Typical iconography included the effeminate mannerisms of the "sissy" or pansy often played by character actors such as Franklin Pangborn and Edward Everett Horton. Another stereotype was a combination of fastidious attire and excessive primness, exemplified by Waldo Lydecker (Clifton Webb) in *Laura* (1944) or Brandon Shaw (John Dall) and Phillip Morgan (Farley Granger) in *Rope* (1948). Finally, homosexuals were depicted as suffering from psychological confusion, such as college student Tom Robinson Lee's (John Kerr) in *Tea and Sympathy* (1956). The PCA forced Robert Anderson to modify his screenplay for *Tea and Sympathy* and resolve Tom's conflicted homosexuality by having him sleep with Laura Reynolds (Deborah Kerr), a married woman who sympathizes with his plight. The film ends with Laura entreating Tom to return her sympathy when he gets older: "When you speak of this in future years . . . you will . . . be kind." Adultery, it seems, was more tolerable than homosexuality.

In October 1961, the Code was amended. "Sex aberration" was now allowed but had to be handled with "care, discretion, and restraint."[5] "In keeping with the culture, the mores and values of our time, homosexuality and other sexual aberrations may now be treated with care."[6] The Code had been amended following a formal request lodged by Arthur Krim of United Artists. Krim wrote the PCA that United Artists had three films that dealt with homosexuality in the pipeline—*The Children's Hour* (1961), *Advise and Consent* (1962), and *The Best Man* (1964). The Code was amended in time for the release of Wyler's remake of his earlier 1936 film, *These Three*, this time with the lesbianism of Lillian Hellman's original play intact.

Advise and Consent notably included a subplot with a scene set in an important venue in gays' and lesbians' semihidden public lives: the gay bar.[7] Gay and lesbian bars had sprung up in American cities throughout the twentieth century, but especially during the Roaring Twenties. Sporadically raided by vice squads and harassed by undercover policemen, the bars nonetheless survived. Bars provided gays and lesbians with a social environment that helped sustain a social network as well as a relatively safe place to meet potential sexual partners. Alternatives to bars had been attic parties, parks, bathrooms, and the street. Bars, like bathhouses, gave sexual encounters greater privacy and dignity than parks and streets.

Gay and lesbian bars also functioned as a node between the homosexual minority and the heterosexual majority, with tourists occasionally coming in to see the clientele. More frequently, though, straights did not frequent gay or lesbian bars, which had reputations for being dangerous and seedy since being there was potentially illegal. The most frequent charges were disorderly conduct or disturbing the peace, unless someone was actually caught performing a sexual act, which would warrant a sodomy charge. Proprietors of gay or lesbian bars risked having their liquor license revoked. Threats of legal action were intended "not only to suppress gay culture from public view, but also to disrupt normal socialization among people considered sublegal."[8]

Preminger's *Advise and Consent* takes place during Senate committee hearings for the confirmation of the president's nomination for Secretary of State, Robert Leffingwell (Henry Fonda). A freshman senator on the committee, Brigham "Brig" Anderson (Don Murray) is being blackmailed because of a homosexual experience he had during World War II. Distraught, he goes to a gay bar in New York City, Club 602, to find his former lover, Ray (John Granger). As he enters the bar, Frank Sinatra sings of "a secret voice" on the jukebox. The bar is dark and filled with shifting shadows created by spotlights, almost noir-like in its imagery. Anderson runs from the bar when he sees the man he was looking for. The film blends the anticommunism of the McCarthy era with the threat of blackmail for homosexuals. During the early Cold War, homosexuals had been fired from government positions because it was believed they were susceptible to subversion because their sexuality placed them at the mercy of blackmailers.[9] Both Congress and the White House had homosexuals, or "sex perverts," as President Dwight Eisenhower's Executive Order described them, removed from positions in the government.[10]

Far From Heaven (2002) revisited the gay bar of the 1950s. "What imprisons desires of the heart?" asked the advertisements for Todd Haynes's film. *Far From Heaven* begins by undermining upper-middle-class suburban security as an anxious wife, Cathy Whitaker (Julianne Moore), worries about her husband, Frank (Dennis Quaid), normally very punctual but who has not come home after work. The telephone rings, the police put her husband on the line, and he says he has been arrested because of a mistake and an overzealous police officer. As they ride home from the station, Frank mentions loitering, and Cathy mentions intoxication, but nothing specific is explained.

Some time later, one evening after dinner at a downtown steak house with a group of colleagues from Magnatech International, the large television and radio manufacturer he works for, Frank wanders through Hartford's night streets bathed in lavender light, ignoring the entreaties of a prostitute (Jezebel Montero). He stops across from a movie theater, The Ritz, where *Three Faces of Eve* (1957) is playing. Frank goes into the theater and is seen in the lobby with an ironic poster behind him advertising cold drinks that reads, "We promise to satisfy your ... hunger, thirst, sweet tooth." The theme of multiple personalities in *Three Faces of Eve* comments nicely on Frank's predicament of having two personalities, if not in a psychological sense then in a lifestyle sense. Frank is of course looking to have a certain sexual hunger or thirst quenched. He tries discretely to attract the attention of another man who is simultaneously equally attempting to avoid detection by anyone else. Unsuccessful, Frank leaves. He watches two men disappear around a corner laughing, and he follows them into what turns out to be a gay bar.

He orders a scotch and drinks, looking around at the all-male clientele. He quickly catches the eye and returns the glance of a man at the end of the bar who orders "the same." The man moves around the back of the man between him and Frank, who is framed tightly in profile and pensively smoking a cigarette as the screen fades to black. The oldest of Hollywood's elliptical implications suggests that Frank's earlier arrest, which he claimed resulted from his being mistaken for a "loiterer," had not been a mistake after all. The legal risk involved in public cruising is clear.

Gay bars have been shown from other perspectives. Gay S&M bars play a central role in William Friedkin's much criticized *Cruising* (1980).

Steve Burns (Al Pacino) is a policeman recruited to go undercover to investigate a string of gruesome murders because he is "right for the job"—the victims of a recent series of murders resemble Burns. Steve takes on the identity of a gay man named "John Forbes" and moves into an apartment. As Forbes, Steve cruises sidewalks and bars lined with gay men. The cruising scenes emphasize the role of the gaze in establishing contact and desire, with a great deal of intercutting between Steve looking and shots of gays. Inside the bars, the camera often tracks along men lined up at the bar or dancing. In its scenes along New York City streets and in city parks, the film captures the difference between the semiprivacy of the bar and the openness of streets and parks as places to meet sexual partners.

ANTIGAY SENTIMENTS

Recent films have also represented homophobia as it has been expressed in a variety of ways at different periods in American society. At one end of the spectrum, there are mild, but oppressive, bigoted comments and insults. At the other end, there is violence and murder. Examples of both ends of the spectrum can be found in American cinema over the last few years. They range from calling characters (whether they are gay or not) "fags" or other insulting terms to what is perhaps the most grotesque example of murderous homophobia, the cannibalization of a young man by a group of local boys after they discover he is gay in *Suddenly, Last Summer* (1959).

Far From Heaven depicts the insult end of the spectrum. Frank comes to terms with his sexuality in a society in which gender roles and sexual norms are clearly defined. Homosexuality violates both. It was also associated with stereotypes. By the 1950s, gays had long been represented as sissies and pansies in popular culture, with Hollywood contributing to the view of gay men as effeminate. As Cathy's best friend, Eleanor Fine (Patricia Clarkson), puts it, "Call me old-fashioned, I just like all the men I'm around to be all men." She is elaborating on her view of gays after telling Cathy about Morris Farnsworth (J. B. Adams), Mona Lauder's (Celia Weston) uncle, who is an art dealer in New York, another cinematic cliché—associating gay men with either the art world, interior decorating, or fashion. Farnsworth attends the reception for the modern art show and apparently lives up to Eleanor's idea of "flowery" and a "touch light on his feet."

Ironically, from the perspective of this narrow-minded community, Frank is anything but flowery. He reminds his colleagues as he leaves Sammy's Steakhouse, he had been "second in command of the U.S.S. McMillan," indicating that he had been masculine enough to succeed in the United States Navy. The horticultural analogy is also on display in *Brokeback Mountain* (2005). Jack Twist (Jake Gyllenhaal) comes back to the mountain looking for work in 1963, the year after he had been there with Ennis Del Mar (Heath Ledger). Joe Aguirre (Randy Quaid) refuses to hire him again because he had seen Jack and Ennis together and had deduced that they had "stemmed the rose," as he puts it. The insult is combined with employment discrimination.

That homophobia is ingrained in the social fabric can be seen in *Boys on the Side* (1995), which begins as a road movie, turns into a death-from-AIDS melodrama, then shifts to a trial drama set in contemporary America. It is the story of the relationships of three women, Jane (Whoopi Goldberg), Robin (Mary-Louise Parker), and Holly (Drew Barrymore). Jane is a down-and-out singer looking for a final break, while Robin is a middle-class woman dying from AIDS (she alludes to having caught HIV from a bartender, but no details ever emerge).[11] Jane is lesbian and falls in love with Robin. Holly, the youngest of the three, has (without realizing it) killed her sleazy, abusive boyfriend and is eventually put on trial for it.

The clearest disparaging attitudes toward homosexuality in the film are on display in a courtroom during Holly's trial for murder. Massarelli (Dennis Boutsikaris), the state's prosecutor, makes Jane's sexual orientation an issue when Jane testifies on behalf of Holly. At first he dances around Jane's sexuality in a manner befitting the Production Code: "How would you characterize your friendship?" Jane answers his question with a question that could be read as a challenge to the Code's insistence on silence concerning sex: "What is this 'friendship' stuff about?" As if he were mentioning something unfathomably dark and sordid, he counters, "Let me put this delicately to avoid offending the court. Is there a 'romantic' character to your friendship?" Jane answers that her relationship with Holly is not "romantic." The reason for the euphemism is made clear in his rephrasing of the question: "You are, however, one of these gay women that we read about, or do you prefer lesbian?" The reference to the mediated presence of lesbianism— "read about"—is telling and double-edged. It reveals the growing visibility of sexual minorities in the media (including, self-referentially, the film itself) as well as the discomfort many heterosexual Americans had with that visibility. More pointedly, the representative of the state would have the jury base Jane's credibility as a witness on her sexual orientation.

Homophobia can be much more destructive than insults or even job discrimination. Sodomy had been a capital offense in Colonial America. Even today, many individuals still believe that it should be punished by death, and they have appointed themselves judge, jury, and executioner. *Brokeback Mountain* shows the ways in which the threat of homophobic violence can make any public display of same-sex desire dangerous. It also raises a basic question: how does a film evince attraction with the medium's conventional methods—glances, facial expression, and body language—when the characters are forced to keep their attraction to themselves within the diegetic world of the film?

The dilemma facing *Brokeback Mountain*'s director, Ang Lee, occurs in the early stages of the two cowboys' time together on the mountain in 1962. In the beginning, neither character is able to express his same-sex desire verbally without being sure that the other one will not react violently. The problem on the mountain, mostly for Jack it seems, is one of sending mixed or no signals at all. Ennis's first reaction to Jack's arm on him in the tent is indeed furious, although it morphs quickly into passion.

Later in the film, after it has been established that Jack occasionally picks up other men, Jack confronts another danger: coming on to the wrong person. An example of the need to send mixed signals can be seen in the scene in the bar following the shot of Jack riding a bull at the rodeo. Jack starts up a friendly conversation with the rodeo clown (Tom Carey) and offers to buy him a beer for his help with the bull. The difficulty of conveying what is happening is captured in Larry McMurtry and Diana Ossana's screenplay to the film, which was adapted from a 1998 *New Yorker* short story by Annie Proulx. In the screenplay, the stage directions read: "There is something, a frisson, a vibe, that gives the Clown an uneasy feeling ... although he remains perfectly friendly...."[12] The clown turns him down and walks away, going to talk to a group of men shooting pool. Jake looks nervously over his shoulder and leaves in fear that the clown may have understood his intentions and be telling the others. The film manages to express the character's desire to the audience even though that desire is forbidden in the diegetic world of the film. Later, Ennis would ask Jack if he ever worried about being outed (in so many words).

The threat of violence is palpable and expressed succinctly by Ennis: "this thing, it grabs hold of us again, at the wrong place, at the wrong time and we're dead." For an audience well aware of the death of Mathew Shepard in 1998 in Wyoming, Ennis's words have a special resonance. For those who do not realize the seriousness of the threat, the film provides brief, graphic shots of the effects of homophobic rage, first in Ennis's flashback to his childhood when he tells Jack about a man who had been killed for having an intimate relationship with another man, and second, in his mental image of how he believes Jack died—at the hands of vicious rednecks.

The psychiatric establishment in the United States offered scientific "evidence" to support Americans' homophobia. When Quigley and Lord wrote the Production Code in 1930, the most widespread American views of homosexuality were a blend of psychoanalysis and older quasi-biological theories of congenital homosexuality or religious views of homosexuality as sinful. In either case, gays and lesbians were widely perceived to be sexual perverts or degenerates and considered dangerous. Many Americans associated homosexuality with pedophilia, which added to their anxiety about the sexual practices of this deviant subculture. Psychiatry in the postwar years did little to help, since the American Psychiatric Association (APA) maintained that homosexuality was a sexual psychopathology, but one that could possibly be cured. One of the side effects of this psychiatric conception of homosexuality, intensified by the legal efforts to punish homosexual practices or repress public accounts in the media, was that homophobia was sometimes internalized. In public discourse, including films, internalized homophobia was portrayed as self-loathing or self-hatred, and it became a staple of the image of gays and lesbians.

Punitive measures were used to achieve what psychiatrists believed were noble aims—the straightening out of the homosexual's sexual inversion—that led to the use of therapy that included electroshock therapy. *Far From Heaven* portrays the lure of psychiatric treatment in the 1950s. Frank decides to go into treatment and begins therapy with Dr. Bowman (James Rebhorn). In their initial meeting, Dr. Bowman summarizes the dominant psychiatric position at the end of the 1950s: "Today, the general attitude regarding this sort of behavior is naturally more modern, more scientific than it ever has been before. But for those who do seek treatment, who possess the will and desire to lead a normal life, there still remains only a scant five to thirty percent rate of success for complete heterosexual conversion." Frank's options are basically Freud's "talking cure" or electroshock aversion therapy or hormonal rebalancing procedures. He chooses talk. Frank's reaction and his expression of determination to be "cured" capture the way in which dominant attitudes toward sexual orientation could be adopted by members of the sexual minority: "I can't let this thing destroy my life, my family's life. I, uh . . . I . . . I know it's a sickness, because it makes me feel despicable. I promise you, Dr. Bowman, I'm going to beat this thing. I'm gonna break it. So help me God." Frank's confusion about his sexuality can be read as synecdochic of the divisions within the gay community at the time between those who accepted the diagnosis of homosexuality as a form of mental illness and those who rejected that diagnosis.

Homosexuality continued to be diagnosed as pathological in the DSM until 1973, when gay activists finally managed to convince the APA that their diagnosis was wrong. That change was a major event since it ended a century-long categorization of homosexuals as insane.[13] The change came about as the result of an at least twenty-year-long struggle that began as the homophile movement in the 1950s. Beginning with the founding of the Mattachine Society in 1950 in Los Angeles and the Daughters of Bilitis in 1955 in San Francisco, the homophile movement emphasized accommodating the majority culture while trying to improve straight America's knowledge about homosexuality. Within a decade, the homophile movement was split between members like Edward Sagarin who supported the pathological model of homosexuality and those like Frank Kameny. Kameny lost his job at the U.S. Army Map Service in 1957 because of his sexual orientation. With no career prospects, Kameny became an activist and rejected the pathological as homophobic and promoted confrontational tactics to achieve its demise.

Before gay liberation eradicated or at least reduced the incidence of homosexual self-hatred, Hollywood used it as a staple in its films. In *The Children's Hour*, Martha Dobie's (Shirley MacLaine) lesbian self-hatred leads her to confess but also deride her love for Karen Wright (Audrey Hepburn). Martha tells Karen hysterically, "Oh, I feel so damn sick and dirty! I can't stand it anymore!" She eventually commits suicide out of despair. The turmoil had begun after a vicious little student at Dobie and Wright's private school for girls, Mary Tilford (Karen Balkin), lies to her elderly aunt Amelia Tilford (Fay Bainter) that Martha and Karen have an "unnatural relationship." In *Advise and Consent*, Brig Anderson kills himself, presumably to avoid a political scandal and because he cannot accept his own latent homosexual desires.

The Boys in the Band (1970) was criticized by gays and lesbians when it was released in 1970 for replicating stereotypes and suggesting that the men suffer from self-loathing, a form of internalized homophobia. The film was an adaptation of playwright Mart Crowley's successful 1968 off-Broadway play, which predated Stonewall and the onset of the gay liberation movement. The film features an ensemble cast and takes place in the Upper East Side of Manhattan apartment of one of the characters, Michael (Kenneth Nelson), who is throwing a birthday party for Harold (Leonard Frey).

Allusions to self-doubt or low self-esteem and negative psychoanalytic theories about homosexuality pepper the men's conversations. They talk about the need to be drunk to have gay sex. When Michael describes himself as a Catholic who gets drunk and sins all night, Emory says, "It all depends on what you think sin is," angering Michael. They also refer to one another repeatedly as *fags*, especially Bernard (Reuben Greene) when addressing Emory (Cliff Gorman). The name-calling seems to be nothing more than the self-deprecating irony of a repressed minority.

It gets serious, though. Harold tells Michael he is "a homosexual and you don't want to be. But there's nothing you can do to change it," including his religion and psychoanalysis therapy. Michael is the character who seems most divided against himself, because of his Catholicism and because he has internalized the pathological model of homosexuality. After the guests leave, Michael becomes hysterical and cries, begging one of the men, Donald (Frederick Combs), not to leave him. Donald gives him a valium to calm him, a hint at the need for drugs to numb the closeted experience and the self-hatred. In therapy so he can stop hating himself, Michael tells Donald it would be nice if gays could learn not to hate themselves so much. Who was it, Michael asks, that used to say, "You show me a happy homosexual, and I'll show you a gay corpse." Quoting his dying father's words, Michael says to Donald before leaving for midnight Mass, "I don't understand any of it. I never did."

OUT

Inspired by the New Left and the civil rights movement, the homophile movement evolved into the gay liberation movement in the 1960s and 1970s. One event, the culmination of a growing resistance to police raids of gay bars that had begun in San Francisco in the 1950s and 1960s, is still considered an important boost to the gay liberation movement. On June 27, 1969, the New York City police carried out one of their periodic raids on a gay bar in Greenwich Village, the Stonewall Inn. Much to the surprise of everyone involved, the men in the bar erupted rather than acquiesce in the harassment and rioted for three days. Although the closet was not eradicated, it would never again be mandatory: gays and lesbians demanded the right to be different.

They had been aided legally by the Supreme Court's discovery of a right of privacy in the Constitution in its decision of *Griswold v. Connecticut* in 1965.[14] Although the decision concerned heterosexual married couples, gay activists and civil rights organizations quickly saw the implications of a right of privacy for same-sex behavior between consenting adults. The right of privacy that has since evolved out of *Griswold* has been expansive and laid the groundwork for Supreme Court decisions providing constitutional protection for gay sex and outlawing sodomy laws. Fittingly, Todd Haynes, who also wrote the screenplay, set *Far From Heaven* in Connecticut, a bastion of moral conservatism in the postwar era.

Armed with the right of privacy and inspired by the success of the civil rights movement and the women's movement, organizations like the leftist Gay Liberation Front and the more moderate Gay Activists Alliance worked for the rights of homosexuals and for ending discrimination and the laws that kept same-sex desire in the closet and encouraged homophobia. After Stonewall, gays and lesbians became more and more visible in American life, if not in American cinema. Criticized for its clichés, *The Boys in the Band* at least displays the growing visibility of gays in New York's public spaces. In the film's opening montage sequence, the main characters move between private and public spaces, including a brief scene in a gay bar that notably enough is not in a back alley. The party also tracks gays' movement from closet to visibility.

In the beginning of the film, Michael does not want to be outed. So when his guests arrive, he tells the others that his friend from college, Alan (Peter White), is straight and will never be ready to "know about me." Emory asks if Alan has had a "lobotomy," since he does not realize that Michael is gay. When the doorbell rings announcing Alan's arrival, Michael asks his friends to "cool it" while his straight friend is there. He tells Emory "no camping." Before Alan comes in, Emory "acts" straight, lowering his voice and asking one of the others whether he thinks "the Giants are going to win the pennant this year." In other words, the cinematic signs of homosexuality were to be hidden. Michael keeps his self-doubts largely to himself when Alan is present.

After introductions, Alan and Michael go to Michael's bedroom and talk. Michael offers to explain about his party (all male guests), but Alan tells him there is no need. He says he likes all of them except Emory, who "seems like such a goddamned little pansy." He says he is "effeminate" and acts like a "butterfly in heat." Alan is pacing around the room, shot from below, making him look more like a menace, while Michael reclines on his bed. Alan says it was no coincidence Emory was showing them a dance because he "probably wanted to dance with you." The shot cuts to Michael, who looks stern.

Alan seems to understand and apologizes for his remark, saying that Michael's "private life" is his "own affair." The parallel development between the legal development and the understanding that sex between consenting adults is a private matter was slowly expanding for many Americans to include homosexuality, as Alan's defense indicates. Michael says he does not know what Alan believes. Alan assures him, "I don't give a damn what people do as long as they don't do it in public or try to force their ways on the whole damn world." When the men stop pretending to be straight in front of Alan, they are not apologetic or in any sense groveling. They are all shown as confident about and comfortable with their sexuality.

Where is the boundary between going public and "forcing one's ways on others"? How far, in other words, would gays and lesbians be allowed to come out of the closet?

That boundary was one of the constant battle lines for gay and lesbian rights in the twentieth century. Homosexual rights evolved out of legal cases involving various aspects of gay and lesbian life. In their initial move toward granting greater equality to homosexuals, courts began distinguishing between self-identifying as a homosexual—status—and engaging in same-sex sexual behavior. As status gradually lost power as a legal category, it was thus no longer sufficient to prosecute homosexuals simply for being homosexual. Courts were not yet willing, though, in the 1950s to grant same-sex behavior the same legal protections. In its opinion for its decision in *Vallegra v. Department of Alcoholic Beverage Control* (1959), the California State Supreme Court sounded like the PCA in its description of the visible signs of homosexuality: "Conduct which may fall short of aggressive and uninhibited participation in fulfilling the sexual urges of homosexuals ... may nevertheless offend good morals and decency by displays in public which do no more than manifest such urges. This is not to say that homosexuals might properly be held to a higher degree of moral conduct than are heterosexuals. But any public display which manifests sexual desires, whether they be heterosexual or homosexual in nature may, and historically have been, suppressed and regulated in a moral society."[15]

The courts sanctioned the closet, and echoing them, in *The Boys in the Band*, Alan, a Georgetown lawyer, wants gays to remain in the closet. Michael's facial expression in the medium close-up reveals that he has heard such sentiments more times than he cares to remember.

Alan comes downstairs and says he is leaving, but taunted by Emory's openly gay humor, he attacks him. The others quickly attempt to pull the two men apart. There is chaos, with Emory hysterical and Alan enraged. Alan goes upstairs after the fight is subdued. When he comes down again, Michael describes Alan's—the straight world's— relationship to gays like "watching an accident on the highway"—"you can't look at it and you can't look away." Yet, the men no longer hide their sexual orientation, and they force Alan to look. The dual nature of the right of privacy—that consenting adults could do what they wanted in privacy and let knowledge of what they do in privacy emerge in public—was a central component of early gay rights advocacy. The point about the importance of privacy is underlined when Larry (Laurence Luckinbill) and Hank (Keith Prentice), a couple who have been arguing, go upstairs to Michael's bedroom to have make-up sex. Michael taunts Alan, asking him what he imagines the two men are doing. Emory invokes the harm principle, saying, "Whatever they're doing, they're not hurting anyone." Harold adds, "They're minding they're own business." Earlier, Larry and Hank had introduced themselves euphemistically as "roommates." After the men have revealed their homosexuality, Michael tells Alan that Hank and Larry are "lovers," not roommates, and that heterosexual men do not live together after they turn thirty.

Just as it had been with representations of heterosexual sexual behavior, the mainstream film industry was a house divided. For example, *Midnight Cowboy* (1969) included same-sex scenes as would-be male gigolo Joe Buck (Jon Voight) ends up hustling on Forty-Second Street and letting a young man (Bob Balaban) fellate him in a movie balcony. Buck also had sex on-screen with women. The nudity and the sex led CARA to rate the film X. Yet, the film was the first X-rated film to win Best Picture. The Academy awarded Valerie Perrine a Best Actress Oscar for her portrayal of Honey Bruce in *Lenny* (1974), which included a scene of Honey Bruce making love to another woman. Al Pacino was nominated for Best Actor for his portrayal of Sonny, a man who robs a bank to get the money to finance a sex change operation for his lover, Leon (Chris Sarandon), in *Dog Day Afternoon* (1975).

By the 1980s, Hollywood had become somewhat emboldened, even if gay or lesbian characters remained infrequent as lead characters. Three notable exceptions appeared in 1982. Warner Brothers' *Personal Best* (1982) is the story of two track stars, Chris Cahill (Mariel Hemingway) and Tory Skinner (Patrice Donnelly), who become lovers while preparing for the Olympics. The women kiss and make love in the nude. By the end of the film, Chris has dropped Tory for a male athlete, a swimmer named Denny Stites (Kenny Moore). Although Twentieth Century-Fox felt compelled to include a warning before the start of *Making Love*, the film did not confine a married doctor named Zack (Michael Ontkean) and a writer named Bart (Harry Hamlin) or their sexuality to the closet. Nor did it shy away from showing two males kiss on-screen.

Victor/Victoria (1982) takes place in Paris in the 1930s, where Victoria (Julie Andrews) poses as a man named Victor to get a job as a female impersonator. She is aided in her trickery by her gay friend, Mr. Todd, or Toddy (Robert Preston). At her performance of "Le Jazz Hot," she catches the eye of an American gangster King Marchan (James Garner). His attraction does not go unnoticed by his mistress, Norma Cassady (Lesley Ann Warren).

Toddy does not conceal his homosexuality. When he agrees to mingle at a backstage gathering with Norma and lavishly compliments her, she says, "I just love Frenchmen," to which Toddy replies, casting a knowing glance and raised eyebrow at Victor, "So do I." Later, leaning against a wall, Norma exclaims, "You really are queer?" He laughs and corrects her, "We prefer 'gay.'" She tells him that "the right woman could reform you." Toddy laughs and jokes, "The right woman could reform you too!" She squeals with laughter at the thought of giving up men. In a twist, King's macho male bodyguard Squash (Alex Karras) takes King's period of self-doubt as an opportunity to come out. When Victoria goes to her suite one night, she finds Squash in bed with Toddy.

The Academy showered *Victor/Victoria* with seven Oscar nominations. Cross-dressing was all the rage at the Oscars that year, as *Tootsie* (1982) was nominated for ten. In Sydney Pollack's updated story of a performer gender bending to get work, Michael Dorsey (Dustin Hoffman) disguises himself as Dorothy Michaels to get work on a soap opera, becoming a cultural phenomenon along the way. Finally, that year, John Lithgow received a Supporting Actor nomination for his portrayal of the transsexual Roberta Muldoon in *The World According to Garp* (1982).

Independent director John Sayles released *Lianna* in 1983, the story of a thirty-year-old mother of two, Lianna (Linda Griffiths), who falls in love with one of her university professors, Ruth (Jane Hallaren). After her husband, Dick (Jon De Vries), is unfaithful, Lianna discovers that she is lesbian, which she tells Dick. He kicks her out and the film traces her as she starts over. The Samuel Goldwyn Company also released a story about a straight woman who falls in love with a lesbian, Donna Deitch's *Desert Hearts* (1985). Vivian Bell (Helen Shaver) arrives in Reno, Nevada, from New York City on an afternoon train around 1961. Frances Parker (Audra Lindley) meets her at the train and takes her to her ranch, where Vivian will live to get Nevada residency so she can get a Reno divorce and put an end to a marriage she describes as "professional."

Vivian meets Frances's adopted daughter, Cay Rivvers (Patricia Charbonneau), when she comes by Cay's house with some mail. The film follows the usual romantic drama trajectory of establishing animosity between the two potential love interests (not unlike, for example, between Kathleen and Joe in *You've Got Mail*). Cay and Vivian eventually bond. Cay tells her best friend and colleague from work, Silver (Andra Akers), that she believes she has "found somebody who counts." She tells her it is Vivian, who is ten years her senior. Silver asks, "You sleeping with her?" and Cay answers no and she "probably won't." Cay adds, "It's not about that." *Sex* is not the goal; *love* is, a point often obscured because of the emphasis on *sexual* in sexual orientation.

Vivian is kicked off the ranch after she and Cay cause a scandal by sharing a kiss and being out all night. She moves into a hotel room, and Cay eventually shows up at Vivian's. Vivian dismisses kissing Cay as "a moment's indiscretion, a fleeting lapse of judgment" that was beyond the pale for a "respected scholar" such as herself. Vivian goes into the hallway to pour a drink and describes everything since she arrived in Reno as "a blur." She turns back toward the motel room and sees Cay naked in her bed. Cay is shown topless from Vivian's point of view, with rack focus bringing her into and out of view as Vivian turns away muttering, "Oh, God." Vivian tells her to leave, but Cay refuses. She tells Vivian she loves her and asks her to put a "do not disturb" sign on the door. Vivian complies. They make love, with shots of them kissing and of their bare breasts. They become a couple but Vivian must return to her work in New York. Cay (implausibly) turns down Vivian's offer to go with her, saying she has too many "loose ends." As the train pulls out of the station, Vivian asks for "another forty minutes," and Cay hops on as the screen fades to black.

By contrast, Warner Brothers' *Boys on the Side* had an ambivalent attitude toward lesbianism. On the one hand, one of the three main characters is a lesbian who is portrayed sympathetically. On the other hand, both she and other characters sometimes sound homophobic. Jane tells Robin in the hospital that she is lesbian but assures her that she "is safe with [her]." The assurance sounds like a throwback to an earlier era when homosexuals were viewed as threatening. Jane also responds inconsistently to other characters' reactions to her homosexuality. She rejects some insults with snappy comebacks but becomes mute when Holly reminds her that Robin is straight. Furthermore, except for numerous comments about her lesbianism, Jane's sexuality is barely visible after she is shown flirting with a woman at the beginning of the film. Near the end of the film, she confesses her love for Robin.

Far From Heaven is more forthright about Frank's sexuality: He comes out. After work one evening, he breaks down in front of Cathy and the children, destroying as he does the fragile protective shield between a happy family life and the threats—some of them sexual—that besiege the family. After the children are dispatched upstairs, Frank tells his wife he has fallen in love with someone who wants to be with him. He sobs, "I never knew what that felt. . . ." This motif is not uncommon in films with gay themes or heterosexual adultery films. Narratives often justify and explain actions that the character does not even understand or perhaps did not expect (as with Ennis in *Brokeback Mountain*) by tying it to love, which in turn is tied to sex and its importance for identity and contentment. In this scene, as they are throughout the film, Frank and Cathy are together in their living room in the dark. As Cathy will later explain to her friend Eleanor, "The endless secrecy . . . Our entire lives just shut in the dark."

Todd Haynes's work linked Hollywood to a movement that was influential in removing gay lives from the dark, New Queer Cinema. New Queer Cinema, which had gained momentum at film festivals in the early 1990s, was an oppositional, highly politicized cinema that represented gay and (eventually) lesbian experiences much more explicitly than Hollywood had before or since. These films, emerging in film festivals and art houses, extended the legacy of gay American underground films from the 1960s and 1970s. These films ranged from *Scorpio Rising*, with its use of images of bikers, which had become a staple of physique and other magazines targeting gay male audiences, to the avant-garde documentary from Jonas Mekas's Film-Makers' Cooperative, Shirley Clarke's *Portrait of Jason* (1967), which was based on an interview with a young African American male prostitute. The difference between Hollywood and the underground is clear in the contrast between the male hustler Joe (Joe Dallesandro) in Paul

Morrissey's *Flesh* (1968) and Joe Buck in *Midnight Cowboy*. Like the under-ground films before them, New Queer Cinema films made no concessions to mainstream heterosexual expectations or prejudices. They often targeted gay and lesbian audiences. Representative titles include Haynes's *Poison* (1991), which was attacked by the religious conservative Reverend Donald Wildmon's American Family Association for receiving funding from the National Endowment of the Arts and won the Grand Jury Prize at the Sundance Film Festival in 1991. Another director who successfully bridged New Queer Cinema and Hollywood was Gus Van Sant, whose *My Own Private Idaho* (1991) starred two young Hollywood straight male stars, River Phoenix (as Mike Waters) and Keanu Reeves (as Scott Favor) as two gay hustlers.

While New Queer Cinema was originally dominated by gay film-makers, lesbians gradually gained recognition. One breakthrough film, Rose Troche's low-budget *Go Fish* (1994), used alternative narrative techniques, including dream sequences and fragmentary images of women's bodies, black-and-white film stock, and ensemble acting to tell the off-beat story of two opposites who eventually attract.

The Wachowski brothers' *Bound* has a lesbian lovemaking scene early in the narrative. Two women who met by chance and shared a single kiss one afternoon, meet again that same night when Violet (Jennifer Tilly) comes down to Corky's truck. When Violet apologizes, Corky rebukes her, "Don't apologize, please. I can't stand women who apologize for wanting sex." But Violet assures her "I'm not apologizing for what I did—I'm apologizing for what I didn't do." They begin kissing and feel-ing each other's breasts. Violet asks, "Do you have a bed somewhere?" In a nice little cinematic trick, the camera pans up from the truck to Corky's bedroom, where the two women are lying on the bed naked and kissing. The camera tracks in on them. It pans down one side of their bodies and up the other. Violet is again fingering Corky and their breasts are bare. The shot resembles a brief soft-core shot. It cuts to a high angle shot look-ing straight down on the bed at the two women tangled in the sheets. The sexually spent couple is a standard Hollywood shot to connote sexual fulfillment and compatibility. Underscoring the importance of sex for personality and identity, Corky utters, "I can see again."

Gays more often appeared in various supporting roles in major films. Harvey Fierstein played Frank, a gay make-up artist who helps disguise his brother, a cross-dressing actor Daniel Hillard/Iphegenia Doubtfire (Robin Williams), in *Mrs. Doubtfire* (1993). A new cinematic cliché emerged in the 1990s, a woman's gay best friend, in films such as *My Best Friend's Wedding* (1997), *The Object of My Affection* (1998), and *The Next Best Thing* (2000). There were films with gay lead characters as well. Robin Williams played a gay lead in the comedy *The Birdcage* (1996). Hollywood even tried its hand at spoofing the closet in *In & Out* (1997), starring Kevin Kline.

AIDS

After the struggle for recognition, the gay community confronted a new obstacle: HIV, which was originally associated with a syndrome called Gay-Related Immune Deficiency. Because of its initial discovery among gay men and found to be most common among sexually active homosexual or bisexual men, the virus was initially framed as a concern for gays. When it became clear that transmission of the virus also occurred in ways unrelated to homosexual sexual behavior, the term AIDS was introduced in 1982. Major debates ensued during the late 1980s and early 1990s as new knowledge about how HIV was transmitted emerged and mingled with tenacious myths. Politically, gays and lesbian tended to gravitate toward the Democratic Party. The Republican Party was closely aligned with the Moral Majority and other conservative Christian groups who saw AIDS as a sign of God's retribution for the sin of homosexuality.

For social and cultural conservatives, AIDS was the sexual equivalent of leprosy. The lethalness of AIDS made the dangers of unsafe sex so threatening that for many Americans the days of unsafe sex, associated by many with the sexual revolution, were over. The term *safe sex* became a part of Americans' sexual vocabularies.

Hollywood did not rush to create films dealing with AIDS. The film industry was shaken, though, when long time matinee idol Rock Hudson died as a result of AIDS in 1985. The first wave of films that dealt with the epidemic came from independent filmmakers. Arthur J. Bressan, Jr., directed *Buddies* (1985), while *Parting Glances* (1986) starred upcoming independent film stalwart Steve Buscemi as Nick, a young man with AIDS in Manhattan. *Parting Glances* was co-directed by Bill Sherwood, who died as a result of AIDS in 1990. One of the successful films of New Queer Cinema, the avant-garde *Postcards from America* (1994), was based on the life of artist and AIDS victim David Wojnarowicz, who died in 1992. For its part, Hollywood finally dealt with AIDS head-on in *Philadelphia* (1993).

HOLLYWOOD GETS AIDS

The success of New Queer Cinema paved the way for Jonathan Demme's *Philadelphia* (1993), the first big-budget, mainstream film to deal with gays and AIDS. The film was criticized by some critics for its tame portrayal of the relationship between Andrew Beckett (Tom Hanks) and Miguel Alvarez (Antonio Banderas), as well as for having the gay hero die at the end of the film, a faint echo of the Production Code's "compensating moral values." The film is also reticent in showing or implying gay sex. The closest Andrew gets to Miguel is dancing with his head against him at their costume party. Despite its timidity, which ends up making Andrew and Miguel seem more like best friends than lovers, *Philadelphia* presented a positive view of their relationship and of the two men.

The film begins with a survey of the streets of Philadelphia panned by a roving camera and accompanied by Bruce Springsteen on the soundtrack. Images of City Hall and a close-up of the cracked Liberty Bell lend the establishing sequence political gravitas: Philadelphia becomes the symbolic cradle of Western democracy and liberal constitutionalism, the birthplace of the freedom and equality that have become centerpieces of American politics. Yet, all is not well, as the panning camera often picks up the poor and destitute with its wandering eye. Political ideals and the eloquence that promotes them are not enough to secure justice, the film suggests. This point is reiterated in the first sequence, which shows Andrew, a successful lawyer with the prestigious Philadelphia law firm of Wyant, Wheeler, Hellerman, Tetlow, and Brown, plying his trade. He is arguing against Joe Miller (Denzel Washington), small-time personal injury lawyer, in front of a Judge Tate (Roberta Maxwell) about a case. Justice, Andrew will explain later, occurs only occasionally.

Philadelphia is, and was marketed by TriStar as, two films, a melodrama about an AIDS victim and a courtroom drama about that victim's discrimination case. With regard to both AIDS and civil rights, the film is a liberal film that attempts to mainstream both issues and does so by drawing on two larger developments within American society. With regard to AIDS, the film follows the pattern of medical science that looks at disease in terms of physical evidence and brackets any moral or religious concerns.

With regard to rights, the film positions the rights of gays and lesbians in general, and AIDS victims in particular, within the gambit of the American rights revolution of the postwar era. This can be seen in the protests outside the court during Andy's antidiscrimination lawsuit. On one side are cultural conservatives with placards that read things like "AIDS Cures Homosexuality." Such sentiments echo those voiced by Moral Majority leader Jerry Falwell, who rejoiced in a sermon broadcast on his "Old Time Gospel Hour" television program in 1987 that "what we [preachers] have been unable to do with our preaching, a God who hates sin has stopped dead in its tracks by saying 'do it and die.' 'Do it and die.'"[16] Conservative Christians attempted to exert their influence with the Reagan Administration to prevent funding for AIDS research. That the protestors are conservative Christians is made clear later when a man (Jim Roche) yells, "It's Adam and Eve not Adam and Steve" at Andrew when he comes out of the courthouse.

In the late 1980s, radical activist groups such as ACT UP (AIDS Coalition to Unleash Power) targeted organized religion as one of the impediments to AIDS research and tolerance for AIDS victims. For example, the group disrupted services at St. Patrick's Cathedral in New York in December 1989. While Christian conservatives gained considerable media attention because of controversial statements such as Falwell's, the response of organized religion was complex and multisided.

Andy's supporters are average-looking Americans who locate his battle in the time-honored tradition of human rights. From their perspective, the battle for gay rights is analogous to the African American civil rights movement, which influenced the gay liberation movement. The film's use of average Americans as spokespersons for liberal American political principles is epitomized by Sarah Beckett (Joanne Woodward), Andy's mother. She tells her son that he should not "sit in the back of the bus. Fight for your rights." The allusion is to the segregation of public transportation in the Jim Crow South. The Montgomery, Alabama, bus boycott, considered the opening salvo in the modern civil rights movement, was precipitated by the refusal of Rosa Parks, an African American woman, to yield her seat to a white man on December 1, 1955. The successful boycott brought Dr. Martin Luther King, Jr., to national prominence.

Together with the women's rights movement, centrist activists in each of these movements appealed to traditional American political ideals. In Philadelphia, Joe Miller reminds television reporter Angela Medina (Donna Hamilton) that "we're standing in Philadelphia, the City of Brotherly Love, the birthplace of freedom, where our Founding Fathers authored the Declaration of Independence. And I don't remember that glorious document saying 'All *straight* men are created equal.' I could have sworn it says, 'All men are created equal.'" Just as freedom of expression expanded during the postwar era, the understanding of civil rights became more inclusive as groups long excluded from the promises of freedom and equality demanded that America's political values be applied to them.

The trial also becomes a forum for portraying homophobia as counter to rather than tolerated and even fostered by the American legal tradition. Before the two sides enter the courtroom, the importance of the American civil rights tradition to ending discrimination against gays is made a part of the legal discourse of the film, both in dialogue and images. First, Andrew has hired a lawyer who must come to terms with his own homophobia to represent his client. That the law can transcend individual attitudes is expressed in an exchange Joe has with homophobes in a local bar. Joe's tone of voice suggests the elevated place in American culture that the Bill of Rights has as a political ideal: "Those people make me sick.... But a law's been broken, okay? The *law.* Remember the law?" The narrative further grounds the importance of the law with references to federal law (the Rehabilitation Act of 1973) banning discrimination and to Supreme Court decisions.

The film is ambiguous in its portrayal of homophobia during the trial. Although, Judge Garnett (Charles Napier) pointedly informs everyone that justice is blind in his courtroom, the film allows for gay stereotypes. For example, the defense is allowed to present Andrew as promiscuous and slightly deviant because he once had sex with a man at the Stallion Showcase Cinema, the pick-up shown in flashback. Although Andrew has clearly never been promiscuous, the implications do more than hang in the air. The law firm's counsel, Belinda Conine (Mary Steenburgen), tells the jury that Andrew's reckless "lifestyle" has cut short his life. When Joe objects to the line of questioning, Belinda insists it is relevant for appraising Andrew's credibility.

At the same time, the most homophobic of the law partners who have ousted Andrew, Walter Kenton (Robert Ridgely), is shown in an unfavorable light throughout the film. Joe Miller also has an outburst in courtroom, badgering his own witness, demanding to know whether he is gay with derogatory terms, and demanding that it is time to "get [homophobia] out in the open, get it out of the closet." The story is not just about AIDS but about the climate of fear and hatred of homosexuals that led to Andrew Beckett's firing.

Philadelphia was part of a larger discourse taking place in the United States. The AIDS epidemic had lasted over ten years by the time it was released. Debates over funding AIDS research and homosexuality were pitting moral terms against scientific terms. In the film, the virulence of the protesters or, even more pointedly, Joe Miller's extreme homophobia at the beginning of the film, is contrasted with the rationalist and empiricist approach of medical science. The rhetoric of sin and retribution was countered by one of epidemiology.

The political effects of framing AIDS in terms of scientific knowledge are depicted in the film's meta-narrative treatment of the myths that underlie Joe Miller's homophobia and fear of AIDS. He is shown consulting his doctor in fear of having possibly contracted the contagious disease through a handshake. Joe's doctor's response weaves together the medical and political developments: Dr. Armbruster (Bill Rowe) tells Joe that he does not care about his sex life (the right of privacy) and that the "HIV virus can only be transmitted through the exchange of bodily fluids, namely blood, semen, and vaginal secretions"—not handshakes. Reference to specific fluids helps demystify the contagion, as does the dialogue in two other scenes.

In an early scene, Andrew discusses the results from his most recent doctor checkup with his mother. He tells her that his "T-cells are up" and that his "platelets look good too." The terms refer to bodily components that can be empirically verified. Shortly after his conversation with his mother, Andrew has to go to the emergency room. While he is there, he and Miguel discuss his options in terms of medical procedures such as a colonoscopy with the intern, Dr. Klenstein (Paul Lazar). Through the exchange, various terms common to the experience of an AIDS patient are used. Dr. Klenstein wants to conduct the colonoscopy in order to see whether the lesions on Andrew's body were caused by KS (Kaposi's sarcoma). Andrew and Miguel suggest that they might be a side-effect of the medication Andrew is taking, AZT, which slows the disease's progression. Besides giving the dialogue a sense of realism, such language also typifies the triumph of the epidemiological model over the moral model of (potentially) sex-related diseases.

In the end, Andrew wins his lawsuit and the jury awards substantial punitive damages. In the following scene, he is on his deathbed in the hospital. Joe visits him and sits on the edge of his bed, indicating that he has gotten rid of his homophobia. After Joe leaves, Miguel kisses Andy's hands near the end in the hospital as he is dying, after which Andy says he is "ready." At Andrew's memorial service, the guests are a mix of straight and gay America, a sign of the film's appeal for acceptance. *Philadelphia* ends with scenes from home movies from Andrew's childhood, with young Andrew (Philip Joseph "PJ" McGee) on a beach with his mother and siblings as well as in other typical childhood situations. The shots of Andrew in his childhood underline the *everyman* quality of, well, every man, straight or gay.

Americans remain divided in their attitudes toward gays and lesbians. While they seem to accept same-sex behavior as part of some people's sex lives, many still believe homosexuality is morally wrong.[17] The Supreme Court ruled in *Lawrence v. Texas* (2003) that sodomy laws were unconstitutional not just because of the sexual acts they punished, but because they also robbed gays of the right to live together with dignity.[18] Same-sex marriage in particular has proven particularly divisive, with religious and cultural conservatives proposing bans on same-sex marriage. By contrast, legal recognition of same-sex partnerships garners widespread support. The success of *Brokeback Mountain* in 2005 has raised the hopes of many gays and lesbians that big-budget Hollywood films might forthrightly represent gay and lesbian characters that have sex lives in mainstream films targeting mainstream audiences.

8

Mainstream Adultery

The importance of adultery as a social issue is self-evident. Historically, adultery has been illegal in most states. As a crime, it violates social morality. Within a marriage, it violates personal trust. Adultery has periodically risen to national attention, as it did following Kinsey's 1948 report that "about half" of American men had been unfaithful.[1] Five years later, Kinsey reported that slightly more than a quarter of American women had affairs before they turned forty.[2] *Newsweek* put adultery on its cover in 1996 and then revisited the topic in 2004, spotlighting an increase in wives' adulterous affairs.[3] Interestingly, a testimony to the impact of film on American self-perception, *Newsweek*'s article on cheating wives included a still of Mrs. Robinson from *The Graduate*, as did John Gagnon's late 1970s sociological study of adultery.[4]

Caryn James observed in the *New York Times* in 1990 that "what Jane Austen did for marriage in the 19th century, film makers are doing for adultery today. In the past few weeks alone, eight films from seven countries have offered a view of infidelity around the world. It is an unmistakable sign of a turbulent social era."[5] If fictionalized accounts of infidelity signal social turbulence, they have a long pedigree. The faithless spouse was a staple of American literature long before motion pictures appeared. From Nathaniel Hawthorne's *The Scarlet Letter* (1850) to Kate Chopin's *The Awakening* (1899) to John Cheever's writings in the 1950s and 1960s and John Updike's since the 1950s, literary fiction has examined unfaithful spouses from every conceivable perspective as well as provided source material for film adaptations. Saul Bellow once compared a novel without adultery to "a circus without elephants."[6] What does the elephant look like in film? This chapter looks at basic narrative

conventions of adultery that correspond to current sociological understanding of infidelity. It looks closely at Adrian Lyne's *Fatal Attraction*
(1987), a box office hit that raised interesting questions about commitment in both marital and adulterous relationships. Finally, it looks at
how Ang Lee's *The Ice Storm* (1997), a critical success, represented the
effects of both traditional and nontraditional forms of extramarital sex
on marriages.

THE ELEMENTS OF THE ADULTERY NARRATIVE

If Hollywood film "presents psychologically defined individuals who
struggle to solve a clear-cut problem or to attain specific goals," as David
Bordwell explains, then adultery offers the filmmaker with a theme that
often combines the problem (sexual desire for someone legally and
morally out of reach) with the goal (sex with that person).[7] Adultery narratives have followed common patterns and included standard elements.
Most of these elements are true to life, even if occasionally strained to fit
narrative needs. One advantage for the filmmaker is the inbuilt dramatic
elements that accompany deceit: the tension between commitment and
betrayal, between getting away with or being caught cheating, between
moving forward or staying put in either relationship. The emotions generated by infidelity suit the silver screen—sexual passion and desire,
sometimes uncontrollable; guilt, jealousy, and anger.

Such drama and emotions are familiar from psychological or sociological studies of adultery.[8] Adulterous relationships have common narrative elements: the initial encounter between potential lovers, initial
attraction, the opportunity to carry on an affair, sex, emotional reactions
of the adulterers, exposure, the effect of the affair on the marriage, and,
finally, motivation. The Production Code attempted to control these as
elements in narratives. Because of the Code's influence, it is important
to begin by considering a narrative's attitude toward the affair.

The Production Code specifically targeted adultery, yet, unlike some
state censorship statutes, did not forbid it completely. Instead, it limited
Hollywood's rendition of marital life to the ideal based on a traditional
Christian view of marriage. From that perspective, love and sexual fidelity were united and exclusive to the marriage. In a sense, the Code did
little more than enforce official attitudes in popular motion pictures. The
biblical injunction against marital infidelity was so strong in the American
legal tradition that adultery was the only ground for divorce in jurisdictions that otherwise completely forbade divorce. Traditionally, both male
and female infidelity was condemned, but as in most matters sexual, a
double standard existed. Indeed, some jurisdictions recognized the right
of a husband to kill his wife and her lover if he caught them in the act.

The Code did not require husbands to murder unfaithful wives, but it did stipulate that adultery, while "sometimes necessary plot material, must not be explicitly treated, or justified, or presented attractively." Filmmakers were not allowed to make adultery "seem right and permissible" or to let love triangles "throw sympathy against marriage as an institution." From the perspective of the Code, all breaches of marital fidelity were immoral and no situational pressures could justify them. Adulterers were dissemblers who maintained a countenance of morality in public while acting on base sexual urges in private—without paying a social or personal price. When permitted in films, affairs were often implied but always immoral, and the cheaters were punished or denigrated by the end of the film.

No sooner had the enforcement mechanisms of the Code been improved than MGM released *Anna Karenina* (1935), starring Greta Garbo as the title character, Fredric March as her lover, and Basil Rathbone as her husband. While Anna committed suicide, pangs of conscience sometimes sufficed, as in *Intermezzo* (1939). Not only dramas examined infidelity. Although the Code forbade filmmakers to use adultery as "the subject of comedy or farce, or treated as material for laughter," romantic comedies often did so anyway. It is perhaps fitting, since, ironically, romantic love has its roots in the adulterous behavior of bachelor knights and married aristocratic women of the European court in the fifteenth century. Originally chaste, such relationships eventually became sexual. Comedies in the 1940s sometimes included adultery in their narratives. Alfred de Carter's (Rex Harrison) suspicion that his wife Daphne (Linda Darnell) is having an affair drives the narrative forward in Preston Sturges's *Unfaithfully Yours* (1948). George Cukor's *Adam's Rib* (1949) put the double standard on trial after Doris Attinger (Judy Holliday) tries to shoot her husband Warren (Tom Ewell) and his lover, Beryl Caighn (Jean Hagen).

While the MPAA struggled to eliminate or curb adultery on-screen, the Academy rewarded it, lavishing eight Oscars on Fred Zinnemann's *From Here to Eternity* in 1953, including Best Picture. Zinnemann's critical and box office success marked a watershed in how far American cinema could go with this taboo subject. Americans flocked to cinemas to see the adulterous love affair between Sergeant Milton Warden (Burt Lancaster) and Karen (Deborah Kerr), the wife of Warden's commanding officer, Captain Dana Holmes (Philip Ober). In giving *From Here to Eternity* a Seal of Approval, the PCA's Joe Breen inched toward accepting that infidelity might sometimes be justified. The PCA felt pressure from the MPAA's own members as well as from foreign competition.

European imports during the 1950s and early 1960s were especially influential in making adultery an acceptable theme, an influence that was tested in American courts. In an important obscenity case, *Kingsley*

Pictures Corp. v. Regents (1959), the Supreme Court ruled that the French import *Lady Chatterley's Lover* (1955) could not be censored because it dealt with *ideas* about adultery, even if those ideas offended viewers or legislators. The idea of adultery, including its representation in motion pictures, was not obscene.[9] In another case, the adultery in Louis Malle's *The Lovers* (1959) conflicted with Ohio state law. The Supreme Court decided the fate of Malle's film in *Jacobellis v. Ohio* in 1964.[10] Although the apex of the American legal system removed legal barriers to its treatment in film, the Court was not condoning adultery on- or off-screen. While the idea was protected, adultery itself remained a key ground for divorce in most American states even at the time of *The Graduate*, and opinion polls demonstrated that a large majority believed it was morally wrong.

Once the ratings system was in place and the Code's "moral compensation" no longer necessary, filmmakers represented a wider range of attitudes toward adultery. Through the 1970s and 1980s, Hollywood films expressed an array of attitudes toward infidelity. Peter Bogdanovich's *The Last Picture Show* interwove the tales of three adulterous affairs, none of which are condemned by the film. *An Unmarried Woman* dealt not only with the painful consequences of adultery, but also with a divorced woman's ability to find strength in herself. In *Dressed to Kill* (1980), a therapist, Dr. Robert Elliott (Michael Caine), advises a patient, Kate Miller (Angie Dickinson), to have an extramarital affair. Some films split the difference. *Terms of Endearment* (1983) presented Flap Horton's (Jeff Daniels) affair as inappropriate, while presenting his wife Emma's (Debra Winger) affair with Sam Burns (John Lithgow), a sympathetic, married banker with a moribund sex life, as a pardonable search for emotional sustenance, not least in the eyes of Emma's mother, Aurora Greenway (Shirley MacLaine). Films also invited the audience to empathize with adulterers despite their sexual peccadilloes. A light-hearted romantic comedy like *Desperately Seeking Susan* (1985) has Roberta Glass (Rosanna Arquette), a middle-class Long Island housewife suffering from amnesia, sleep with Dez (Aiden Quinn), a man she has met and become attracted to, thereby signaling their growing intimacy.

Even under the ratings system, filmmakers continued to portray affairs as morally wrong and adulterers in a negative light. *Presumed Innocent* (1990) made the fruits of adultery lethal. Attorney Rusty Sabich (Harrison Ford) has a passionate and very physical affair with a colleague, Carolyn Polhemus (Greta Scacchi). After Carolyn is murdered, Sabich is tried for her murder but found not guilty. In the film's final moments, Sabich discovers to his horror that his wife Barbara (Bonnie Bedelia) murdered Carolyn and implicated him. He chooses to keep his discovery to himself and presumably stay with his wife, although the film makes clear from the beginning that the two do not love each other.

A justice of sorts, the narrative insinuates wryly, has been served. Code authors Martin Quigley and Daniel Lord would have been pleased.

The Bridges of Madison County (1995), by contrast, would have had the two turning in their graves. Francesca Johnson (Meryl Streep), a lonely and neglected housewife isolated in the Iowan countryside, seduces a willing Robert Kincaid (Clint Eastwood). Kincaid, on assignment for *National Geographic*, meets Francesca when he asks for directions to bridges he has come to photograph. The film portrays the illicit relationship as being therapeutic, with Francesca claiming that it saved her marriage, her memories of her time with Kincaid having given her the strength to maintain a façade in an unfulfilling marriage.

To have an affair, lovers like Francesca Johnson and Robert Kincaid obviously must meet at some point. What brings them together varies. In *Citizen Kane* (1941), Charles Foster Kane (Orson Welles) runs into his future mistress and later wife, Susan Alexander (Dorothy Comingore), on a New York City street as she comes out of a drug store. Martha met Nick at her father's annual faculty party in *Who's Afraid of Virginia Woolf?* Mrs. Robinson had known Benjamin his whole life in *The Graduate*. In *An Unmarried Woman* (1978), Erica Benton's (Jill Clayburgh) husband, Martin (Michael Murphy), becomes infatuated with a woman who is much younger than Erica that he met while shopping in Bloomingdales. Elliott (Michael Caine) lusts after and has an affair with his wife Hannah's (Mia Farrow) sister, Lee (Barbara Hershey), in *Hannah and Her Sisters* (1986). In each of these films, the two characters have already met when the film begins.

Narratives employ various strategies to bring lovers together. Sometimes films take the easy way out and let the two "meet cute." In Malle's *The Lovers*, Jeanne Tournier (Jeanne Moreau) meets Bernard Dubois-Lambert (Jean-Marc Bory) when her car breaks down along a country road, while in *The Scarlet Letter* (1995) Hester Prynne (Demi Moore) meets Arthur Dimmesdale (Gary Oldman) when her carriage bogs down in mud.

More realistically, two people often meet at work. During the 1970s and 1980s, women entered the workforce during a period of rising divorce and increased rates of adultery. Many social commentators saw a connection between these social phenomena. Greater social contact between the sexes increased the likelihood of both meeting someone of the opposite sex and having an affair. For example, in Spike Lee's *Jungle Fever* (1991), Flipper Purify (Wesley Snipes), an architect, has an affair with a temporary worker at his firm, Angie Tucci (Annabella Sciorra).

After establishing contact, a film must represent the characters' initial attraction, sometimes mutual, sometimes not. The allure usually morphs into temptation and then grows to the point that one or both of the characters want to express it sexually. In *From Here to Eternity*, Warden

approaches Karen after the two have exchanged small talk and suggestive glances. He has been emboldened by Sergeant Leva's (Mickey
Shaughnessy) remark that she sleeps around. Leva warns his colleague,
"Better keep your mind off her. What do you wanna do, wind up in
Leavenworth?" Joe Breen could not have put it better. The glances
shared in shots/reverse shots are part of cinema's basic editing codes to
indicate feelings, including desire.

One of the most powerful qualities of cinema is its ability to embody
emotions in actions. Hollywood has long relied on the lovers' gaze as a
key cinematic code of attraction and desire. Adultery films use the
standard conventions of romance films—potential lovers see one another
from afar, exchanging glances and smiles—to imply captivation. On-
screen bodily actions can embody thoughts: a glance or a kiss or lovemaking become signs of passion, overwhelming desire, a submission to fate, a
lack of control.

Adultery sometimes requires on-screen behavior that the audience
must be able to see but that others in the diegetic world must either
miss or perceive as ambiguous. Sometimes, the audience must be willing to suspend disbelief. This occurs, for example, in comedies when
the identity of a disguised character is easily discernible to viewers, but
an enigma to other characters. In adultery narratives, filmmakers deal
with the gaze of desire in a variety of ways. In the company of others,
the unfaithful have to express their desire furtively. Lovers can keep
their eyes to themselves, successfully concealing their desire, as in *Fatal
Attraction*. By contrast, lovers can peek at one another, with the audience privy to the affectionate looks but not the spouse, whose attention
is elsewhere. Finally, the spouse might see the eye contact, interpret it
just as the audience does, and realize what is going on.

Once two people have made clear their mutual attraction to one
another, they must have an opportunity—time and place—to be together
and to have sex without being detected. In *From Here to Eternity*, Warden
goes to Karen's and has a drink with her when he knows the captain is
away. In *Same Time Next Year* (1978), two married people, Doris (Ellen
Burstyn) and George (Alan Alda), carry on a long-term affair that consists of annual trysts while they are away from home. In *Coming Home*
(1978), another Hal Ashby film set in 1968, Sally Hyde (Jane Fonda) has
a love affair with Luke Martin (Jon Voight), a cynical and embittered
paraplegic veteran she meets at a V.A. hospital. Sally volunteers there to
keep busy when her husband, career Marine Corps officer Captain Bob
Hyde (Bruce Dern), completes his tour of duty in Vietnam.

In *Adaptation* (2002), writer Susan Orlean (Meryl Streep) has an affair
with a man she is writing about, John Laroche (Chris Cooper). Susan
lives in New York while John lives in Florida, conveniently providing
them with opportunities since they spend considerable time together

when she travels to Florida to do research for her book. Although the two become lovers in this movie about screenwriting, exploiting the role of adultery as a narrative device, the screenwriter, Charlie Kaufman (Nicolas Cage), had originally rejected the idea over a business lunch as "fake." As the film ends, Kaufman seems to succumb to the demands of either his imagination or Hollywood's commercial interests and include the affair and its sex scenes.

An adulterous relationship is sexual by legal definition. Since adulterous sex in film is represented as it is in any other relationship, a few examples should suffice here, beginning with an example from the Code era. Warden and Karen in *From Here to Eternity* soon meet again when the soldiers have a little R & R. She reveals she is wearing a bathing suit under her dress. They go, famously, to the beach. The nighttime beach scene begins with the camera capturing the surging energy and rolling power of the waves, symbolizing the tumultuous passion of their affair. As with any affair, passion is dual-edged. It propels the relationship, pushing the two lovers together. At the same time, passion can be dangerous, wrong moves can be made, the relationship exposed and destroyed, the lovers forced to pay a heavy price. Like the force of the sea, passion is always potentially beyond the lovers' control even as it washes over them in their ecstasy. The two climb over the rocks onto the sand and begin undressing. Although they are only stripping down to their bathing suits, they are stripping nonetheless, a point driven home by the camera remaining on Karen and her sultry look as she yanks her dress off with a flourish.

After crosscutting with the film's other couple slowly becoming more intimate, the beach scene continues with another shot of the powerful waves, with the camera tracking up to the shore following a breaker that washes over the kissing couple—one of American cinema's most famous images. The two lovers risk drowning in their passion, but the kiss on-screen lasts only a moment before Karen runs up to her beach towel and collapses with Warden behind her. He falls to his knees and they kiss passionately again. She finally speaks, confessing, "I never knew it could be like this." Her faithlessness is a matter of unfortunate timing: had she met the right man before, had she known love, she would not be cheating on her husband.

Post-Code, the sex could be on-screen. The love scene in *Coming Home* is shot with a soft-porn degree of explicitness. Glimpses of Fonda's and Voight's bare skin indicate they are indeed nude. There is a shot of Luke licking Sally's breast. In the spirit of growing sexual equality, she tells him *how* to perform cunnilingus "softly" to enhance her sexual pleasure. There is a long take of her face with her eyes open as if to symbolize that she is seeing her sexual self through sexual pleasure for the first time. In contrast with Karen in the earlier film, who bases her exclamation on a kiss, Sally responds to sexual intercourse, telling Luke, "That's never happened to me before."

In the adultery narrative, lovers are typically sexually compatible, a compatibility equated with emotional and spiritual affinity. The ability to satisfy a lover sexually becomes metonymic for satisfying a lover in all ways. The reverse is often the case in adultery narratives as well, as in the shot early in *Coming Home* of an unresponsive Sally making love to her husband, Bob. The lack of sexual compatibility is also metonymic for a lack of compatibility in other ways. At the other end of the sexual ethics spectrum, adultery is driven by lust.

In 1981's neo-noirs *Body Heat* and *The Postman Always Rings Twice*, married femme fatales used sexual bait to lure saps into killing their husbands. In *Body Heat*, Matty Walker (Kathleen Turner) seduces Ned Racine (William Hurt), who kills her husband Edmund (Richard Crenna). The sex scenes and nudity in *Body Heat* emphasized the erotic appeal of the illicit or taboo. While not as explicit, *The Postman Always Rings Twice* limned the passionate nature of sexual lust in a famous scene in which drifter Frank Chambers (Jack Nicholson) and the married Cora Papadakis (Jessica Lange) make love on the kitchen table. In both cases, the sex is lust-driven, and the men risk losing self-control. This is one of adultery's threats to marriage and social order. Uncontrollable lust leads sex to intrude where it should not be, providing film with a dramatic release of a narrative's sexual tension. The lack of sexual control can be seen in *Fatal Attraction* when Alex Forrest (Glenn Close) performs oral sex on Dan Gallagher (Michael Douglas) in an elevator. It overtakes Chris Wilton (Jonathan Rhys-Meyers) and Nola Rice (Scarlett Johansson) in *Match Point* (2005), when they can no longer control their sexual urges and begin making love while walking on the grounds of a family estate. In *Jungle Fever*, a film that suggests that sexual lust in interracial sexual affairs is heightened by racial taboos, Flipper begins his affair with Angie on his drafting table at work. Finally, although she does not consummate her desire in *Eyes Wide Shut* (1999), Alice Harford (Nicole Kidman) coolly reveals to her husband William (Tom Cruise) that she had been tempted to risk everything to have sex with a naval officer who had only cast a glance at her in the lobby of their Cape Cod hotel. She says, "If he wanted me, if only for one night, I was ready to give up everything. You. Helena. My whole fucking future." Because uncontrollable passion threatens marriage, it is incompatible with social order.

In the middle of the moral spectrum was adultery devoid of lust or love as in *The Ice Storm*. The film takes place in 1973 in suburban New Canaan, Connecticut, where much of the movie was shot, and where in the diegetic world of the film, Ben (Kevin Kline) and Elena Hood (Joan Allen) lead a materially successful life. Not all is well, though. Ben is having an affair with Janey Carver (Sigourney Weaver), an icy, married woman who lives nearby. The adulterous lovemaking scene begins with a camera tracking slowly past the Carver's house. The shot cuts to silk sheets and a couple making love. Seen from an overhead shot, Janey responds to the sex without passion. The man rolls over. It is Ben.

The camera lingers for a moment on the emotional distance between them, even though they are physically close, before cutting to them still lying in bed, but Janey now smoking a cigarette and Ben talking about golfing. *The Ice Storm* avoids justifying the deception: Janey and Ben's relationship seems no more satisfying than their marriages.

In *Adaptation*, Susan and John make love the first time in the back of John's van parked in a parking lot at the beach or on the bay. The scene begins with a shot of the van with a row of palms and the water in a bluish tint in the background and Laroche's voice on the soundtrack continuing a telephone conversation that presumably led to their amorous encounter. The shot cuts to the two lying naked on the floor of the van shot in profile from the shoulder up, with Laroche on top of Susan. A few close-up shots/reverse shots of their faces and then a cut to Susan lying in the grass on a sunny day. An adulterer's tranquility is rarely permanent in American cinema.

More often than not, adulterers struggle not only with their relationships but also with themselves. Feelings of guilt are often expressed through a staple of adultery films: the fear of being seen. In *From Here to Eternity*, Karen and Warden are having drinks at an outdoor restaurant, holding and caressing each other's hands. Underscoring the deceitfulness of their assignation, they leave quickly and discreetly—"run out like jailbirds"—as Karen will say afterwards, when other officers come in. Karen realizes sooner than Warden that they cannot keep meeting secretively. The island is too small to keep secrets, a geographical symbol of the spatial limits to any covert affair. There is always the danger of being seen and thus caught. The film reiterates why adultery works well cinematically: the relationship is by definition strewn with obstacles.

Karen and Warden meet one last time before the attack on Pearl Harbor, this time with a calm, glassy ocean lying dormant in the background and concrete beneath their feet. Because of the Code's injunctions, their relationship is preordained to fail. Karen tells him, "It's no good with us, Milt. It could never have been any good. Hiding, sneaking. It had to wear out." When Warden reaches to take her by the arm, she moves it away from him, a sign that intimacy is no longer possible. *Coming Home*'s Sally and Luke realize they face a moral dilemma from their first kiss. Whereas the Code would have either sublimated the two's passion for one another and hinted at it, post-Code Hollywood allowed them to express their attraction and then develop it.

After the couple has developed their relationship, an affair must run its course, leading eventually to either exposure or termination without detection. Films vary in the way they expose adulterous relationships. While *Coming Home* is relaxed in its portrayal of the couple's sex and presents their relationship as a good thing, it makes clear that the state still frowns on adultery. Because he protests the Vietnam War by chaining himself to the port of a recruitment center, the FBI places Luke under surveillance. His affair with Sally is exposed not through telltale signs, missteps, or a confession, but through government surveillance. Betraying a spouse is analogous to betraying one's nation. More mundanely, traces of another person's presence lead to discovery. Steven Soderbergh's independent success *sex, lies and videotape* (1989) draws on this convention. While vacuuming, Ann (Andie MacDowell) finds an earring that belongs to her sister, Cindy (Laura San Giacomo), in her bedroom. Ann quickly figures out that her husband, John (Peter Gallagher), is sleeping with her sister. The discovery has a major impact on their marriage.

Sex, lies and videotape exams how adultery and adulterous sex drive the final nails into the coffin of a shaky marriage. Like *Who's Afraid of Virginia Woolf?* before it, Soderbergh's film portrays the detrimental effects of illusion on a marriage. It is the story of four people who are related to one another in a complex web of relationships. Ann and John Millaney are a well-off, childless young married couple expecting the visit of John's college roommate, Graham Dalton (James Spader). Neither John nor Ann is happy in their marriage, but both are eager to keep up appearances. Graham arrives and settles in the small town, further disrupting Ann and John's marriage.

An extremely unfortunate outcome occurs in *The World According to Garp* (1982), when Garp (Robin Williams) crashes into a car in which his wife Helen (Mary Beth Hurt) is fellating her lover, Michael Milton (Mark Soper). Walt (Ian MacGregor), Garp and Helen's son, is killed in the accident, Helen's jaw is broken, and Michael loses his penis. More typically, in *Jungle Fever* (1991) Drew kicks Flipper out of their home when she discovers his affair with Angie.

Election (1999) comically portrays the effects of exposed adultery on two marriages. Jim McAllister (Matthew Broderick) teaches civics at George Washington Carver High School in Omaha, Nebraska. The first adulterous affair is between a teacher and an underage student. In a voice-over and flashback montage, Jim tells us how an overachiever named Tracy Flick (Reese Witherspoon) had ruined the career of a former colleague and best friend, Dave Novotny (Mark Harelik). During the voiceover, there is a shot of the couple kissing and one of Novotny pulling Tracy into his bedroom. The latter shot frames Tracy walking down to the end of the hallway in deep focus. Ironically, as he pulls her into the bedroom, she says in her voice-over that what she missed most about their relationship was their "talks." The consequences of Tracy's affair with Novotny during her junior year come quickly after she tells her mother, who in turn tells the school principal. Novotny is fired and his wife divorces him.

Jim explains in a voice-over that he and his wife, Diane (Molly Hagan) were helping Novotny's ex-wife, Linda (Delaney Driscoll), through her postdivorce period, "giving her a lot of love," as the shot cuts from a close-up of his face to a close-up of Linda's derriere in blue jeans as she walks past him. When Jim has sex with Linda, it is after he has just removed a glob of hair from her bathtub drain. After Jim and Linda have sex at her house, they agree to meet at a local motel—aptly called The American Family Inn—and Jim goes during one of his classes, giving the students a pop quiz to buy time. He primes the room for their date. He returns, but Linda never shows up. When he finally goes home, he finds her at his house telling Diane, her best friend, what happened. Diane divorces Jim.

Since the demise of the Code, some films have contended that even though adultery may be morally indefensible, it makes little sense to remain in the wrong marriage. Sometimes people make the wrong decision, including the decision to get married. No-fault divorce laws reflect a modified social contract that institutionalizes the notion that people should not pay for making such mistakes for the rest of their lives. *Wonder Boys* (2000) presents a strong case for leaving an unsatisfying marriage for a relationship that is more rewarding.

When the film begins, English professor Grady Tripp (Michael Douglas) has been having an affair for five years with Sara Gaskell (Frances McDormand), a chancellor at the University of Pittsburgh and the wife of Walter Gaskell (Richard Thomas), head of the department where Grady teaches. Grady has been married three times, but his current wife, Emily, has left him the day the film begins. Disillusioned by his previous failed marriages, he is hopeful about his relationship with Sara. In contrast to the more typical adultery film storyline, their affair has been going on for some time before the film begins. In fact, an unplanned pregnancy forces Grady and Sara to make tough decisions.

The film ends with a redeemed Grady telling viewers in a voice-over as he sits and types in an office with large glass windows overlooking a lovely wooded area that he lost everything—his book, job, and wife, the things he had thought were important. He now knew, he says, where he wanted to go. He turns and looks out the window and sees Sara getting out of her car. She then takes their baby out of the backseat and looks up at Grady smiling. In a shoulder shot, he says in a voice-over, "And now I had someone to help me get there." Grady and Sara have the ideal companionate marriage in which love and the lover are guiding beacons. Innocence is not something that is lost irretrievably; instead, it goes dormant waiting to be rejuvenated by love. His creativity revived, he is writing on a portable computer. He saves the file he is working on, the screen goes black, and the credits role to Bob Dylan singing "Things Have Changed."

Remaining in an unsatisfactory relationship is no longer widely perceived to be a moral or social obligation. It has become a personal option. The shift in attitudes and behavior has been most visible in the rising divorce rate and the eroded hegemony of marriage. The focal point of fidelity has moved from the institution of marriage, once very widely perceived to be permanent and sanctioned by strongly held religious beliefs, to oneself. Yet, as *Wonder Boys* makes clear, the decision to abandon a marriage is rarely flippant.

Nonetheless, for conservatives, this shift in values has placed the marital institution at risk since a given marriage's stability and endurance is now potentially at the whim of either spouse at any given time. Liberals, by contrast, see the change as one that makes the institution more viable. From the liberal perspective, relationships that are unrewarding or actually detrimental to the psychological or physical well-being of one of the spouses—usually the wife—are not worth salvaging and do more to demean marriage than divorce. It would be unfair to conservatives to suggest that the cultural debates over marriage's new status in American society are fought over whether physically or emotionally battered women (or men) should remain in dysfunctional marriages. Liberals and conservatives argue about the more mundane concern with individual fulfillment in a consumerist culture that has long emphasized the individual's continual search for happiness and contentment. In their views on marriage, conservatives and liberals draw the line between narcissism and legitimate self-interest at different places.

People have been trying to explain the cause of adultery as long as it has existed, not least unfaithful spouses caught in the act. It has been examined from the perspective of religion, law, sociology, psychology, biology, and sexology. Intermittently receiving the attention of the media, adultery becomes a contentious subject of debate among religious leaders, sociologists, psychologists, and politicians. Some blame secularization and the lack of a moral compass while others believe sex before marriage paves the way morally for sex outside of marriage. Some believe that the growing acceptance of divorce has made attitudes toward infidelity more lenient, since individuals sometimes find themselves getting involved in a new relationship before they abandon a deteriorating marriage. In such cases, adultery was not seen as the cause of divorce as much as a sign that divorce was in the cards.

Explanations for having an affair are as various as the excuses offered by snared adulterers. Sometimes an affair is motivated by a deep love for a lover and a lack of love for a spouse. Sex often represents such shifting feelings. *Coming Home* renders Sally's lack of marital contentment and her estrangement from Bob through their unfulfilling sex life. Early in the film, Sally stares blankly at the ceiling as Bob makes love to her.

Another frequently stated cause is that love has died because of neglect by a callous or emotionally unavailable spouse. The narrative of *From Here to Eternity* partially justifies Karen's promiscuity by framing it as refuge from a cruel and unfaithful husband who abides strongly by the double standard. Oscar-winning screenwriter Daniel Taradash emphasized Captain Holmes's character traits to placate Joe Breen, who accepted them as a form of compensating moral values.[11] In *Diary of a Mad Housewife* (1970), Tina Balser (Carrie Snodgress), emotionally abused by her husband, Jonathan (Richard Benjamin), seeks, unsuccessfully, solace in an affair with George Prager (Frank Langella). Sometimes, the spouse is too busy with work or friends and indifferent to the other's needs. Sometimes a husband and wife have just grown apart, "going," as Elliot claims to Lee in *Hannah and Her Sisters*, "in different directions."

LUST CAN KILL YOU: *FATAL ATTRACTION*

In America, conservatives and liberals, although they understand the institution in different ways, repeatedly hail marriage and the family as a cornerstone of civilization. *Fatal Attraction* begins with the small, nuclear family at home, all dressed in white but only half-clothed, symbols of innocence and purity, the home as the Garden of Eden before temptation. Beth (Anne Archer), the mother, walks around in a small white shirt and white panties, the couple's six-year-old daughter Ellen (Ellen Hamilton Latzen) watches television wearing an oversized white shirt, while Dan Gallagher works on the couch in a white dress shirt and underwear, a law book on the edge of the couch back indicating his profession.

Interestingly, while all seems idyllic, such as the friendly banter with Beth's friend on the telephone and the couple's affectionate address to their child, there is a curious disorder in the home. First, this idyllic image of the home includes Ellen being babysat by the television set as the parents concentrate on their own lives. Second, Dan stubs his toe and the pain knocks him off balance, causing him to swear as he hops around. Finally, moments later, Beth is unable to get Ellen to obey her, and when Ellen drops something, Beth too starts swearing.

In another early scene, after the party at which Dan first meets Alex Forrest, Dan and Beth arrive home, Beth very attractive in her strapless evening gown and Dan seemingly ready to make love. First, though, he has to walk the dog, and when he returns, Ellen has climbed into their bed. His frustration is palpable. The film has established a likeable male protagonist with a sympathetic and sexy wife that he loves. The inconveniences of daily family life—pets and kids—prevent him from attaining sexual satisfaction. That family can be a burden is visualized in the next scene, as the family goes out to their station wagon with their arms overflowing with luggage and Dan awkwardly walking Ellen's bike. Dan and Beth are also bickering. Paradise is not perfect. Marriage is hard work, petty details, and compromise.

The family idyll is established at the end of the film, as the adulterous Dan is forgiven and welcomed back into his wife's arms and into the home. After Dan and Beth embrace and walk out of the frame, the film ends with the camera facing a family portrait in the hallway. The only one of the nuclear family who remains in white, who remains innocent, is Ellen. Family portraits are meant to be read as moments of contentment frozen in time, but Ellen's image of innocence is misleading. She has had her pet boiled by a mentally unstable woman, been abducted by that same woman, watched her mother kick her father out of their home, and heard her mother shoot and kill a woman. What madness we invite into our lives when we venture outside that frame.

Dan's journey beyond the framework of the safety of the family begins subtly in the second scene. At a work-related party he attends with Beth, Dan briefly sees Alex for the first time, and then bumps into her moments later while getting a glass of champagne. Relaxed in the company of strange women, Dan is made attractive to the audience by simultaneously being self-confident, suave, and self-deprecating. He introduces himself and learns Alex is an editor at a publishing company that his law firm represents. He leaves when Beth waves him over, Alex teasing him, "Better run along."

Beth and Ellen leave for the weekend, ironically enough, to look at a house that will become the new family *home*. In narrative terms, Beth and Ellen's exit, Dan's staying behind because of a work meeting, and Alex's attendance at that meeting provides Dan and Alex with *opportunity*, an important social aspect. The narrative brings them together again after the meeting, and uses the common device of placing them in a shared predicament that can bring them closer together: they are caught in a downpour and cannot get a taxi. Dan invites her for a drink, and over drinks and coffee, they begin opening up and flirting with one another. He lights her cigarette, and the camera lingers on him for a moment to symbolize his inkling that he might be playing with fire. Her eyes, facial expression, and a slight nod of her head indicate she is enticed.

When she asks about his wife and learns that Beth is away, the two of them cut to the chase. Alex coyly says, "And you're here with a strange girl being a naughty boy." Dan protests, saying he does not "think having dinner with anybody is a crime." Alex comes back smoothly, "Not yet." Intrigued, Dan asks, "Will it be?" When she says she does not know and asks what he thinks, he answers, "I definitely think it's gonna be up to you." Alex then does the adulterer's calculus: "We were attracted to each other at the party. That was obvious. You're on your own for the night. That's also obvious. We're two adults." He immediately calculates the solution to her calculus: "Let's get the check." Throughout their dialogue, reaction shots have shown Alex smiling and in control and Dan growing more and more sexually agitated.

The shot at the bar cuts to Dan and Alex kissing and undressing frantically. There is a brief shot of Alex removing her panties from beneath her white dress. Dan pulls his underwear down to his knees, revealing his derriere from the side. He helps her up on the kitchen counter and then enters her forcefully. Their lovemaking is on the verge of being out of control. She reveals a breast and he appears to lick it, although it is not clear whether the act is real or simulated. Dan carries Alex to the bed, presumably still inside her, and the shot cuts to a boiler symbolically about to boil over. After a trip to a salsa club and more lovemaking, Dan leaves without saying goodbye the next morning. He goes home and calls his wife, successfully accounting for his whereabouts the night before and planning to see her the next day. When he hangs up, the phone rings and it is Alex, who will not take no for an answer when he tries unsuccessfully to squirm his way out of seeing her again.

The remainder of their weekend together exposes the hypocrisy of a philanderer. Over dinner in her apartment, Alex asks Dan about his family. When she says his situation "Sounds good," he concurs, "I'm lucky." Alex then poses the question that has to be on most viewers' minds: "So what are you doing here?" Psychologists and sociologists have uncovered numerous reasons for *not* cheating: the marriage contract, religious beliefs, internalized social customs or sexual mores, a feeling of companionship or love, fear of being caught, and a satisfying sex life. Yet, for all of the veneration and regulation Americans accord marriage, they have affairs and flings.

Recent research confirms the complaints that many social conservatives have had about the overwhelming emphasis placed on self-expression as essential to personality and self-fulfillment. A husband or wife is less likely to remain faithful if they do not find the marriage or intimate relationship fulfilling or if it keeps them from growing.[12] Dan evades the issue and does not answer Alex's query. Yet, since the Gallaghers' dog does not prevent Dan from having sex with Alex, it seems that inconveniently having to walk the dog when Dan appears to be in the mood for sex is more a symptom than a cause.

Alex realizes the sex is transgressive and seeks Dan's acquiescence in justifying what they are doing. She says she wants to see him again and asks the inevitable question, the moral equivalent of her earlier adultery calculus: "Is that so terrible?" He replies, "No." It is hard not to wonder why their affair is not terrible. The film lays bare the adulterer's hypocrisy: from his perspective, the affair is not wrong because the attraction is not wrong and anyway it is beyond his control, since he is the casualty of uncontrollable sexual urges. Dan agrees that their chemistry justifies his betraying his wife, but he adds that he does not "think it's possible" for them to keep seeing each other. The problem for these two is not morality or other people's feelings: it is expediency. Dan is not willing to sacrifice his marriage or his relationship with his child to enter into a fully committed relationship with Alex. In fact, he is not interested in anything beyond the weekend. When she asks where she stands, he can only muster, "I think you're terrific. But I'm married. What can I say?" When she replies, "Just my luck," Dan smiles as if he feels like he is getting away with something.

They make love again and when he realizes he has to go, she gets upset for a moment and tries to stop him. She is topless. He offers a solution: "Jesus Christ. I mean, let's be reasonable." From this point on the film turns into the psychological drama, with Alex attempting suicide before he leaves. He remains with her and helps her recuperate. From this point, the film traces the trajectory of Alex's growing madness. She plagues his secretary with phone calls. The audience is expected to sympathize with Dan when he tells her on the phone (her responses cannot be heard): "I'm sorry. I thought you understood. If I misled you in some way, I apologize. But I don't think it's a good idea if we talk to each other anymore. Okay?" One has to wonder, though, at what point during their lovemaking he was misleading her.

Alex changes tactics and calls Dan at home. She calls in the middle of the night and forces him to agree to meet with her the next day. He tells her it is over and scolds her for clinging to what he calls their "imaginary love affair." If she were not so maniacal, it is hard to see how anyone could sympathize with him. Dan remains in total denial. She tells him she is pregnant. He expresses surprise that she had not been on the pill (he had apparently not bothered to ask). The birth control pill provides a good example of women's contradictory sexual freedom since the 1960s. On the one hand, the pill had freed women from worries about unwanted pregnancies or the need to interrupt foreplay to take care of contraception. On the other hand, the responsibility for not getting pregnant had gotten even heavier for women. With the empathy of the enchanting person he is proving to be, Dan magnanimously offers: "The abortion. I'll take care of it. I'll pay for it."

Although she is clearly mentally unstable, she rightfully responds to his assertion that she is "sick" by asking "Why? Because I won't allow you to treat me like some slut you can just bang a couple times and throw in the garbage? I'm gonna be the mother of your child. I want a little respect." As is often the case in adultery movies, the film does not concentrate on the predicament of the woman who is party to the affair or the threat to the spouse, who is the real victim, but to the unfaithful spouse who will stop at nothing to escape undetected and unscathed from a clandestine affair. When Alex threatens to reveal their affair to Beth, Dan threatens to kill her. The central moral dilemma that the adulterer cannot explain away is why he or she must keep the affair a secret if it not so terrible. Adultery is always haunted by questions of commitment, responsibility, and disclosure.

When the incessantly ringing phone (a common motif in adultery films) proves ineffective, Alex retaliates by pouring acid on Dan's Volvo, giving him a cassette recording of a long diatribe, and boiling Ellen's pet rabbit, which forces Dan to confess his misdeed. Beth is devastated. He, of course, assures her, "The last thing I ever wanted to do was to hurt you." When she asks if he is in love with Alex, he again downplays what he has done, lying in the process, "No, it was one night. It didn't mean anything." When he explains that Alex is pregnant, Beth understandably kicks him out of their house.

Before he leaves, Dan calls Alex to let her know that he had told Beth everything. He puts Beth on the line, and she, too, threatens to kill Alex, a promise she makes good on in the final sequence of the film. Alex appears, kitchen knife in hand, and tries to murder Beth. Dan saves Beth and appears to have drowned Alex when she springs out of the water. Beth shoots Alex through the heart, fulfilling her earlier pledge to kill her. The family that kills together stays together. The object of sexual desire will kill you, if your spouse does not kill it first. By killing this woman, who becomes a symbol of temptation and the wages of lust, the family's safety is reestablished.

Fatal Attraction is both a crass thriller and an interesting probe of the double standard that questions tolerating adultery. The film's treatment of the double standard is clearest in its development of Dan's character. The narrative very slyly cues the audience to sympathize with Dan. While nothing informs the viewer as to whether his fling with Alex is the first time he has taken advantage of his wife's absence or whether he has done so before, his smooth operation with Alex suggests that he has probably done this before. He deftly flirts with her at the bar at the party. He does not hesitate to invite her for a drink when they are caught in a downpour. He takes control of the conversation when she begins turning up the heat, making the decision that they leave together. His shrewdness in covering his tracks at their apartment to make it look like he has been home while Beth and Ellen were away hints at more experience than a rookie. Finally, when he discusses his legal predicament later with Jimmy (Stuart Pankin), a colleague and friend, he is not distraught about having behaved naughtily but worried about losing his family. The absence of moral qualm insinuates he has already wrestled with his conscience.

At the same time, the narrative lets a single woman question the right of a married man to decide single-handedly when his affair with her has ended. By doing so, the film raises troubling questions about commitment and responsibility among consenting adults. Unfortunately, a homicidal character suffering from something like borderline personality disorder asks them. Because the narrative does what it can to maintain audience sympathy with Dan and ensure we experience Alex's vicious insanity from Dan's perspective, it ultimately remains ambiguous about infidelity and the problems it causes. By contrast, *The Ice Storm* portrays infidelity as a personal and social catastrophe.

ANOTHER KIND OF INFIDELITY: *THE ICE STORM*

A critical success, *The Ice Storm* did not do well at the box office. Critics praised the film's representation of the suburban personal and social masquerade. As in *The Graduate*, there is very little communication between any of the family members in either the Hood or Carver families. The couples barely talk. As in Mike Nichols's second film, the adulterers also find it difficult to communicate, drawing into question one of the standard causes of adultery—the search for greater fulfillment than one is getting out of a marriage. In *The Ice Storm*, the search for fulfillment leads beyond traditional extramarital sex to experimental mate swapping that enjoyed a brief vogue in the media in the early 1970s. Always a very small minority, swingers tended to be highly educated, white, middle-class suburbanites between the ages of twenty and forty, not unlike the characters in Lee's film.[13] This reading will examine the film's representation of consensual extramarital sex in the *key club* sequence.

In featuring ostensibly consensual extramarital sex, the film captures a paradox of adultery: it is as universal and nearly as old as monogamy and very widespread. Proponents of open marriages and swinging were quick to point out adultery's longevity and frequency to justify their behavior in 1970s. The film maintains a moral distance from the experimentalism of the key party by illustrating the devastating consequences of the lure of alternative sexual moralities, as well as the emotional impact of adultery on the Hoods and the Carvers.

While their teenage daughter, Wendy (Christina Ricci), watches Richard Nixon on TV, a hint at Watergate, an event that exemplifies the decline in respect for authority and civic institutions in the United States during the early 1970s, the Hoods head off for dinner with their friends and neighbors, Jim (Jamey Sheridan) and Janey Carver. The three couples, all in their late thirties or early forties, are served by the Carvers' two sons, Mikey (Elijah Wood) and his younger brother, Sandy

(Adam Hann-Byrd). Jim regales them with a story of seeing Harry Reems, the star of *Deep Throat*, at a freedom of expression benefit. It is the year of porno chic (the American Civil Liberties Union actually defended Harry Reems on obscenity charges several times during the 1970s).

The other couple, Dorothy (Kate Burton) and Ted Franklin (Jonathan Freeman), has seen *Deep Throat*. Dorothy tells the others that she felt "something in the air" being in a theater filled with "horny young college boys." Her talk excites Mikey, who spills wine on Ben's crotch. Janey coolly wipes the wine with a napkin, coyly watching the others as she does so. The sexual tension under the surface in the dinner party's talk rises uncomfortably close to the surface.

When the conversation resumes, Ted and Dorothy are talking about their experiences in group therapy. Ted says there are a "couple of lookers" in the group. It emerges that Ben and Elena had been in couple's therapy as well, but Ben says they do not really get into the "histrionics." The film hints that the two are no longer close, assuming they ever were, both through the way Elena says they decided to drop therapy and her muted facial expression. The two are also spaced at some distance from one another. The psychotherapy they were unable to attend together was supposed to bring them closer.

Various psychotherapies commonly grouped under the rubric *human potential movement* also appealed to the burgeoning middle-class desire for self-improvement. Self-improvement and self-expression were considered integral to self-fulfillment. For conservatives, a particularly deplorable manifestation of what they considered Americans' new self-absorption was the swelling in the ranks of self-improvement methods, originating largely in California, such as Frederick Perls's Gestalt Therapy, which had begun in the 1940s, and the Esalen Institute, which was founded in 1962. Another typical self-improvement therapy that caught the media's attention was est (Erhard Seminar Training), the brainchild of Werner Erhard (né Jack Rosenberg), who had begun his seminars in the early 1970s. The baby boom generation was often depicted in the media in the 1970s as having come of age, in the words of Tom Wolfe, during the "me decade."[14] Self-discipline, it was asserted, had been undermined by the demands of and desires catered to in a consumer society.

Later, over cigarettes and cognac, Dorothy tells the others (who sit nearly expressionless) about one of her friends who met her current husband at a key party, "one of those California things." Dorothy's comment suggests one idea about why a couple would attend a key party: the desire to experiment. From this perspective, extramarital sex, like other forms of taboo sexual behavior, blended erotic temptation with the exoticness of a novel encounter. Another motivation was a lack of affection between spouses.

The Ice Storm establishes Ben and Elena's sexual and emotional estrangement when they go to bed after the dinner party. Elena keeps her back turned to him. In several scenes in the film, married life consists of inattention and small tasks and being tired and a lack of time for real companionship. For reasons the film never makes clear, but surely including Ben's affair, Elena seems at a loss for how to move forward. The key party seems to offer an opportunity to be jolted back to life.

Ben and Elena drive to the party without speaking in the drizzling rain, arriving at the home of their overly ebullient host, Dot Halford (Allison Janney). Guests mill about and socialize. Just as the Hoods are about to remove their coats, Dot appears with a glass bowl cupped in her hands and asks, "Would you care to play? It's new this year. It's strictly volunteer, of course." Taken by surprise, Elena says she left something in the car. They go out and Dot puts the bowl of keys on a hall table. The camera lingers on the keys. The shot match cuts on an empty ignition and the key being put into it in the car.

Shaken, Ben and Elena look at one another, alarmed, as the rack focus divides the audience's attention between them. This strain of the sexual revolution frightens them. Back in their car, Ben denies knowing it was a key party. Elena pushes him on his affair with Janey, and Ben confesses. She storms back inside the house (parallel with her storming out of rooms earlier in the film). She throws the keys to Dot, who smiles.

While mingling, Ben accosts Janey, but she blows him off. He is upset that she had abandoned him during one of their trysts. In that earlier scene, Ben had told Janey that he and Elena seemed to be "on the verge of saying something" to one another—hinting that they may be getting a divorce. Janey hopped up, telling Ben, "I'll be back." Ben had walked around the house in his underwear and socks until he realized she was not coming back. The audience realizes that she had been put off by the thought of Ben getting a divorce since she knows he might want to be with her, something that does not interest her. Janey now tells Ben, "I mean, one or two good-natured encounters—that doesn't mean I'm— I'm not just some toy for you." She tells him she had disappeared because she had things to do. He is stunned. Coldly informing him, "How you take it isn't all that interesting to me, Benjamin," Janey turns away from him.

She is in the spirit of the party, its decadent ambiance symbolized by close-ups of ice cubes clinking into drink glasses and Gordon's Vodka pouring over them. Mark Boland (John Benjamin Hickey) notes that one of the women, Maria Conrad (Donna Mitchell), brought her son Neil (Glenn Fitzgerald) to the party. He adds creepily that he wishes "some of the gang had brought their daughters." Ben, a young girl's father, is visibly (although subtly) upset by Mark's remark, which throws what he and Elena and the others—as parents—are doing into relief. The sequence crosscuts between the party and the Hoods' and Carvers' unchaperoned children, who are attempting to explore their own sexuality in various ways. The scenes of the key party are also interspersed with images of the effects of the ice storm of the film's title, windows blurred, power lines and railroad tracks—the technology of communication and contemporary society—weighted down by ice.

Ben asks Elena if she would like to leave when the time comes to draw keys from the bowl. The women begin drawing keys, with the focus shifting between the adults as a group and the specific reactions of individuals. As if to underscore how far the behavior of these upper middle-class suburbanites is cut off from their daily lives, the camera shoots one of the draws from outside the house, cutting to an extreme close-up of a leaf and twig. The men and women cheer as if they were playing a childish game of charades. Not everyone is lighthearted, though. The assortment of guests reflects the diversity within the swinger community, ranging from those who wished to change societal norms to those who were content to violate sex norms temporarily for sexual pleasure. The guests at the key party seem to fall readily into the category of recreational sexual deviants. In fact, the film visually contrasts the enthusiasm of some guests with the hesitancy others express about what they are about to do. One woman draws her own husband's keys, and they quickly take advantage of their luck and disappear together.

The narrative also focuses on individual reactions to what is transpiring. The camera isolates Ben, who is disconcerted, and Neil. Seen earlier telling Janey about his experiences with est, Neil is intent on getting with her, and Janey obviously intends to fulfill his desires. As individuals, they defy any monolithic image of the swinging 1970s. Jealous, Ben wants his relationship with Janey to be exclusive. Janey has already stopped caring what others think about her sexuality, signified earlier by the way in which she sponged the wine off Ben's crotch in front of her husband, children, and dinner guests. Elena is trying to emerge from her passive shell. Jim does not even know why he is there.

To Neil's delight, Janey draws his keys. Ben stands up to stop him but crashes drunkenly to the floor. Elena looks on despondently. In the end, Jim and Elena are alone. Neither is enthused, and they sit separately on the couch. Jim explains it would be strange to sleep with a neighbor and close friend, asking if she would like a cup of coffee. His question is doubly ironic. First, neither his wife nor Elena's husband share his qualms. Second, Ben had earlier used Jim's mustached coffee cup as a pretense for being at the Carver's in the middle of the afternoon. Elena recommends they keep each other company. Oblivious to the severity of the storm, Jim suggests going for a ride. Once in Jim's Cadillac, the two begin making out and eventually make love.

After the party, the adults go home, including Janey, who curls up alone in a fetal position on her waterbed. Ben discovers Mikey dead in the road on the way home, a fallen power line having taken his life. While the parents had walked on slippery ice metaphorically, Mikey had foolishly done so literally. Like the child's death, ice storms come suddenly with devastating consequences. Ironically but tragically, the adults in the film are aware of neither the impending natural disaster nor the familial one they are causing themselves.

Short of the death of a spouse, few events in a relationship are as traumatic as sexual infidelity. Outside of the small minority of Americans who practice swinging, swapping, open marriages, and other alternative forms of relationships, there is a very strong assumption that intimate relationships are monogamous. If sex is the most intimate aspect of interpersonal relationships and trust is taken to be essential to the sustenance of a relationship, infidelity can be seen as doubly damaging to the offended spouse or partner. In legal terms, the marriage contract has been violated. At the interpersonal level, it is trust that has been undermined, for many irrevocably. Furthermore, since relationships are widely accepted to be the center of self-fulfillment for many people, infidelity robs the cheated partner of a great deal of self-esteem since a commonly given and accepted reason for being unfaithful is unfulfilled needs. Once the cuckolded partner is aware of his or her status, he or she must contemplate forgiving the unfaithful spouse or ending the relationship. Given the severity of the impact adultery can have on a marriage, it seems safe to say that in real life Saul Bellow's elephant is more nearly in a china shop than a circus.

In polls, Americans have overwhelmingly disapproved of adultery.[15] In conclusion, it is safer to say that movies are more like Bellow's circuses than mirrors, with elephants something that intrigue audiences. Just as with literature, film audiences accepted extramarital affairs as a narrative device and adulterers as the main protagonists in movies, even if they did not accept it as readily in their own lives. There is a discrepancy between the extramarital sexual behavior Americans say they find intolerable in real life and what they accept from movie characters, just as there is with many Americans' own behavior. The difference seems analogous to acceptance of screen violence. Americans accept violent acts (by good and bad characters) in cinema that they would usually not accept in real life. Indeed, Americans have watched on movies screens violent and other deviant sexual behaviors that have never gained widespread acceptance in American society.

9

Children in the Dark

DEVIANCE, PERVERSION, AND DESIRE

In *Postmodern Sexualities* (1996), William Simon defines sexual *deviance* as "the inappropriate or flawed performance of conventionally understood sexual practices," which Simon exemplifies with rape. Simon classifies deviant sexual behavior as *a disease of control* and sexual *perversion* as *a disease of desire*. Sexual perversion violates both *"sexual practices"* and *"common understandings that render current sexual practices plausible"*; perversions *"tend to be forms of desire too mysterious and sometimes too threatening ... to be tolerated."*[1] Pedophilia is a sexual perversion. Not only is it nonvolitional, pedophilia is a sexual perversion that sometimes combines with another perversion: incest. Anthropologists, psychologists, and sociologists agree the incest taboo is universal. Nonetheless, like other sexual taboos, incest has a long history. When a form of pedophilia, incest differs from adultery or other forms of sexual behavior discussed in this work since it does not involve two consenting adults. When the incest victim is underage, he or she cannot consent, and the sex is nonvolitional as well as abusive. By far the most prevalent form of parent-child incest involves the abuse of daughters by their fathers or stepfathers.

For more than two decades, the sexual abuse of children has been a major topic of social debates in the United States. From the trial and acquittal of staff of the McMartin preschool in Manhattan Beach, California, on charges of child molestation in the mid-1980s, to the Michael Jackson trial, which ended with an acquittal in 2005, pedophile scandals have kept the issue in the mass media. Legal responses include the passage in 1996 of the federal Megan Law, which required convicted sex offenders to register with the state they live in and required the states to notify the public about those offenders. Congress passed Megan's Law in the wake of the rape and murder in New Jersey of seven-year-old Megan Kanka by a pedophile that lived across the street. Some liberals derided the saliency of the debates and the strict punitive measures as evidence of a moral panic that overestimated the extent of the problem.

INCEST

The Production Code did not single out incest; it was forbidden by the blanket prohibition against "Sex perversion or any inference to it." Indeed, dialogue suggesting an incestuous relationship between gangster Tony Camonte (Paul Muni) and his sister, Cesca (Ann Dvorak), in *Scarface* (1932), much of the suspicion being voiced as a warning to Cesca by the siblings' mother (Inez Palange), was one of the reasons Will Hays improved the enforcement mechanism of the Production Code in 1934. The PCA generally kept implications of incest out of its members' films, although *Rebel without a Cause* (1955) hinted at an incestuous relationship between Judy (Natalie Wood) and her father (William Hopper). Robert Aldrich's *The Last Sunset* (1961) was a western with a romantic subplot about Brendan O'Malley's (Kirk Douglas) attraction to a teen named Missy Breckenridge (Carol Lynley), who, O'Malley is shocked to discover, is his daughter. Although it appeared in *The Color Purple* and *The Cider House Rules*, father-daughter incest has generally been as taboo on-screen as off-screen. One of the darkest, most cynical portrayals of incest in a Hollywood film was in Roman Polanski's *Chinatown*.

Chinatown is a tale of power and greed involving water rights in Los Angeles as well as the investigation of a police officer turned private detective. With his background in sexual intrigue, it is no surprise that Jake's investigation uncovers sexual secrets. As John Belton and other critics have noted, "The desire for knowledge which characterizes the detective genre as a whole is translated by Polanski into virtually pornographic interest in sexual misconduct."[2] First and foremost a detective film in the *film noir* tradition, Roman Polanski's *Chinatown* trails a detective who journeys between the world of social norms and that of social deviance. As a motivating agent, private detective Jake Gittes leads the viewer into the darker recesses of social and private life. The detective, by the nature of the job at hand, can penetrate into areas cordoned off from those who are not participants in the deviant behavior, be it gambling, drug abuse, or sexual infidelity.

Jake is asked to investigate an adultery case by a woman identifying herself as the wife of Hollis I. Mulwray (Darrell Zwerling), the chief engineer for the Los Angeles Department of Water and Power. He photographs Mulwray together with a young woman. Jake later discovers that the "Mrs. Mulwray" who initially hired him was an imposter named Ida Sessions (Diane Ladd). The real Evelyn Cross Mulwray (Faye Dunaway) hires Jake to find out who murdered her husband and why. Jake is also hired by Evelyn's father, Noah Cross (John Huston), an immensely wealthy and powerful man who controls the water supply to Los Angeles, to find the young woman he photographed spending time with Hollis. Jake's journey leads him to uncover the darkest of hidden sexual secrets when a father's rape of his teen daughter turns out to be an ugly piece of a complicated criminal jigsaw puzzle.

Rather than immediately make the crime explicit, the film plants several clues to Evelyn's dark sexual secret. The first clues come when Jake has a drink with Evelyn to learn more about her relationship with her husband. He tells her he believes she is "hiding something," and she admits she is but concocts a story about Hollis having an affair. Before saying that, though, she looks anxious, as if she fears Jake has unearthed her secret. The next clue comes when Evelyn shows up at Jake's office to retain his services to investigate Hollis Mulwray's death. When he mentions her father, Noah Cross, Jake notices that Evelyn becomes flustered and lights a second cigarette; so he asks her, "Does my talking about your father upset you?" She says "no," then admits it does, claiming it is because her father, an epithet Evelyn can barely bring herself to use, and Hollis had "a falling out." Jake, without realizing his prescience, asks if the two men had a falling out over Evelyn. Ever fearing exposure, she nervously asks, "Why should it be over me?" Jake assumes it was over the water department. Finally, another clue comes much later after Jake and Evelyn make love. The phone rings, and Evelyn sits up topless in the bed. After she hangs up and tells him she has to leave, Jake tells her he recently met with her father. Evelyn covers her breasts with her arms, again visibly shaken by the mere mention of her father.

The narrative continues to retain its secret although it begins to gradually lose its grip on the secret. One of film's most powerful devices is the creation of lacunae of meaning that forces viewers and characters to reconsider what they believe they have learned so far. Sometimes the meaning implied by such gaps only becomes clear in retrospect, but they are there like gaping wounds that symbolize an unspoken violence. One such gap surfaces very subtly after Jake trails Evelyn to a house where he sees the young woman Hollis Mulwray supposedly had an affair with. When Evelyn comes outside, Jake tells her she will have to turn herself in to the police. Evelyn tries to explain why the young woman is there, but Jake replies, "That's not what it looks like." "What does it look," she asks, hesitating slightly, "like?" The briefest of pauses, it turns her question into a remarkably self-reflective line about film narrative. As Evelyn's father had warned Jake earlier, "You may think you know what you're dealing with, but believe me, you don't." Jake, who takes pride in his experience—which is the detective's source of knowledge—is unable to fathom what confronts him. He overlooks the clue buried in Evelyn's hesitation.

He overlooks it because he believes Evelyn is keeping the young woman she claimed Hollis had an affair with prisoner. To keep Jake from turning her over to the police, Evelyn explains that the woman is her sister, Katherine (Belinda Palmer). Jake asks, "Why all the secrecy?" Secrecy conceals behaviors and attitudes that would not be tolerated if made public. For that reason, incest, more than most sexual behaviors, is usually hidden from public view. The detective's job is precisely to expose secrets, bring to the light of day behavior that cannot endure the light, but Jake has yet to pierce the darkness. Too concerned with saving his career, Jake draws the most obvious conclusion for a man who does "matrimonial work," as he earlier described his business to Evelyn. He concludes the secrecy must be because the younger sister had an affair with Hollis, which Evelyn is relieved to let him believe.

After Ida Sessions is murdered, though, Jake concludes Evelyn killed her husband. The narrative shifts from trying to tip Jake off and brings Noah and Evelyn Cross's secret into the open. When Jake calls the police, Evelyn is forced to confess to him. She repeats her earlier claim that Katherine is her sister, but Jake slaps her. Evelyn's face is completely drained of emotion. Although the scene has been much parodied since, it retains its power in Evelyn's indifference to the violence she is subjected to, an indifference born of victimization. "My father and I—.... Understand? Or is it too tough for you?" Shot from slightly above, framed in the side of the screen, Evelyn cannot answer when Jake asks if her father raped her. Her facial expressions and the turn of her head fill in the blanks. Evelyn was only fifteen when she had the baby, which means she was only fourteen or fifteen when her father raped her.

A particularly disturbing form of sexual abuse, incest had only recently begun to gain widespread media attention when *Chinatown* was released, not least because of the efforts of feminists to bring the issue to light.[3] Parent-child incest had remained sequestered from public view. One impediment to the public acknowledgement of incest as a social problem stemmed from psychiatrists' conviction that their patients' accounts of having been sexually abused as children were nothing more than oedipal fantasies.[4] This was problematic since one source of information about this form of child abuse was the accounts of teenage girls or women in therapy. The failure to mention or see incest was also influenced by the unwillingness of medical and mental health professionals to diagnose it. In the United States, during the

1890s, argues Lynn Sacco, medical doctors confronted with inexplicable outbreaks of venereal diseases like gonorrhea among underage white middle- and upper-class girls deigned to change their understanding of the etiology of sexually transmitted diseases rather than admit the possibility of widespread incest among middle- and upper-class whites. Health care workers at the time believed incest was a phenomenon among poor African Americans or immigrants.[5] Besides establishing the myth of infectious lavatory seats, the denial of an incestuous cause of sexually transmitted diseases contributed to the wall of silence around the sexual crime that lasted well into the 1960s. Furthermore, incestuous relationships are almost totally shrouded in secrecy, a secrecy reinforced by social denial. It seems, as many commentators have noted, "there is only one taboo about incest—mentioning it."[6] There seems to be a general unwillingness to accept that such offenses occur, since the family has generally been viewed as the cornerstone of civilization. Just as it threatens the defenseless child as an individual victim, incest threatens social order by threatening the family. The perpetrator is guilty of subverting the most basic of relationships. Guilt, though, is not an emotion that Evelyn's father feels.

"I don't blame myself," Cross explains to Jake. "You see, Mr. Gittes, most people never have to face the fact that at the right time and right place, they're capable of anything." Cross feels no guilt for his behavior. Feeling neither empathy for his victim nor remorse for his behavior, Cross justifies raping his daughter by invoking an abstract notion of his being beyond the bounds of right and wrong. Because his wealth and power have placed him beyond the reach of the law in his business dealings, Cross believes they have raised him above sexual morality as well. Cross finds himself in "the right time and right place"—the wrong time and place for Evelyn—because of his position at the top of the social ladder rather than near its bottom rung, in contrast to Celie's stepfather in *The Color Purple*. In both cases, though, the community ignores the plight of victims, either out of disregard for a poor, disenfranchised African American woman or subservience to a powerful and highly respected perpetrator like Cross. Another film that portrays sexual immorality among the wealthy and powerful is Milos Forman's tale of debauchery in eighteenth-century French aristocracy, the import *Valmont* (1989), which includes a pedophiliac subplot.

A fifteen-year-old girl is seduced twice, once by her aunt. Both scenes rely on implication through editing. At the opera with her fifteen-year-old niece, Cecile de Volanges (Fairuza Balk), the Marquise de Merteuil (Annette Bening) runs into the Vicomte de Valmont (Colin Firth). The Marquise smiles wantonly as she tells Valmont Cecile's age, but warns him to stay away from her. Ignoring her, Valmont later seduces Cecile in a scene that highlights the psychological manipulation involved in pedophilia. Valmont dictates a letter for Cecile to the young boy she wants to marry. Cecile lies on her bed fully clothed writing, her legs crossed in the air. As Valmont walks around, shots alternate between his glances and close-ups of Cecile's calves and feet moving with a child's restless energy. He dictates softly as he sits on the edge of the bed, caressing her foot and leg. Cecile looks nervously over her shoulder. Taking advantage of an adult's authority over a child, Valmont tells her to keep writing. Valmont caresses her leg and slides his hand under her dress. Cecile glances back nervously but obediently keeps writing. He lifts her dress and begins kissing her stocking-covered buttocks. Confused and nervous, Cecile keeps writing as Valmont applies psychological pressure. Undressing, Valmont spreads Cecile's legs slightly and dictates the ending of her letter. He puts out the candles, and there is a cut to the Marquise lying in her bed looking pensive. In the next shot, Valmont comes out of Cecile's bedroom, his clothes and hair in disarray.

Distraught and disheveled, Cecile runs down to the Marquise's bedroom and in tears tells her "something awful has happened." Although Cecile has been raped by an older man, the Marquise's reaction is far from shock or disgust. Instead she smiles, caresses Cecile's face, and murmurs, "Monsieur Valmont is quite a writer, isn't he?" This brings a smile to Cecile's face, but she says she had repeatedly said no even as she did his bidding. Cecile begins to sniffle, emphasizing that she does not love Valmont. The film suggests that Cecile's greatest concern is that she does not love Valmont.

Telling her she is a woman now, the Marquise explains romantic love to Cecile. Throughout the scene, Cecile kneels at the side of the Marquise's bed, shot from a high angle. The Marquise is shot from a low angle, emphasizing the older woman's power, which comes from their age difference and her greater sexual experience. Sexual innocence is powerless in the face of immorality it seems. The Marquise asks Cecile whether she enjoyed the experience; Cecile smiles and nods yes, so the Marquise tells her she has "nothing to worry about." The film has created a diegetic world in which victims are easily recruited into sexual debauchery through pleasure that overrides their victimization. The Marquise tells Cecile that she loves her as the scene cuts to a carriage arriving the next morning.

The next scene begins with Cecile's mother (Sian Phillips) looking into Cecile's empty bedroom, followed by the Marquise raising her head from her pillow at the sound of a door shutting. She turns her head further on hearing a knock at her door, two bodies clearly under the sheets. After she says, "Yes," her door opens, and she is seen lying in bed with Cecile sitting up beside her. Cecile's mother's face registers both surprise and suspicion. Cecile and the Marquise look uneasy about being caught in bed together but smile at one another before Cecile jumps out of bed and runs to her mother. The implication is clear: the aunt's profession of love for her niece had been spoken to seduce the young girl, and the Marquise and the girl have had sex. Although female abuse of children is an extremely rare form of pedophilia and incest, it has appeared in films, perhaps most famously in Louis Malle's *Murmur of the Heart* (*Le souffle au cœur*; 1971), a French sex comedy about a young teen, Laurent Chevalier (Benoit Ferreux), who loses his virginity to his mother, Clara (Lea Massari).

Although it appears occasionally in films, incest remains relatively taboo in American cinema. In Oliver Stone's *Natural Born Killers* (1994), Mallory Knox (Juliette Lewis), who joins her husband Mickey (Woody Harrelson) on a cross-country killing spree, is sexually abused by her father (Rodney Dangerfield). Stone presents the abuse in a darkly comic sequence. Anjelica Huston's *Bastard out of Carolina* (1996) portrays the physical violence that sometimes accompanies the sexual abuse of children. Atom Egoyan's *The Sweet Hereafter* (1997), a Canadian import, poignantly captures the tragic consequences of a father's sexual abuse of his daughter. Two of the three adult sisters in the melodrama *A Thousand Acres* (1997) discuss being beaten and "fucked" by their father, Larry Cook (Jason Robards), when they were growing up. In the preposterous psychological thriller *Wicked* (1998), Ellie Christianson (Julia Stiles) is the aggressor in her relationship with her father, Ben (William R. Moses). While Hollywood shies away from incest, it has been slightly less hesitant to portray nonincestuous pedophiliac relationships.

PEDOPHILES

While implications of pedophilia rarely slipped past the PCA, the sexualization of child stars had long concerned critics of Hollywood. The sexual appeal of the most famous child actress, Shirley Temple, was the subject of a scathing film review in the British magazine *Night & Day*, by English film critic and author, Graham Greene. Greene attacked the eroticization of the nine-year-old Temple in John Ford's *Wee Willie Winkie* (1937) and the leering male adults potentially in the audience: "Her admirers—middle-aged men and clergymen—respond to her dubious coquetry, to the sight of her well-shaped and desirable little body, packed with enormous vitality, only because the safety curtain of story and dialogue drops between their intelligence and their desire."[7] Greene assumed, of course, the images of Temple were erotic, raising the question of where the line between cute or pretty and erotic might be drawn. Critics have continued to argue over the sexualization of young girls in Hollywood films, debating whether the industry purposively attempted to commercialize the attractiveness of child stars as sexual and whether images of young actresses were fodder for pedophile fantasies.[8] Such debates, as with similar debates today, intersected with debates about the sexuality of teenage girls off-screen. In the 1930s, Temple and Deanna Durbin helped keep Universal solvent during the Great Depression. In the 1990s, there were pedophiliac themes or undertones in *The Crush* (1993), with Alicia Silverstone, *Léon: The Professional* (1994), and *Beautiful Girls* (1996), with Natalie Portman. Similar starlets and similar debates about child sexuality surfaced periodically in the decades between.

During World War II, psychiatrists, social workers, and public officials worried about the sexual behavior of young women labeled *victory girls*. The victory girls had sex with servicemen, and many of them were underage. Billy Wilder's *The Major and the Minor* (1942) spoofed pedophiliac attraction. Susan Applegate (Ginger Rogers) disguises herself as a preteen so she can get a cheaper fare on a train trip from New York City to Iowa. During the journey, she meets Army Major Philip Kirby (Ray Milland), who finds himself strangely attracted to what he believes is an eleven-year-old girl. Shirley Temple grew from child star to teen star, and in *Kiss and Tell* (1945), her character pretends to be a pregnant unwed teen. Two years later Temple played a teenage girl who dates an older playboy played by Cary Grant in *The Bachelor and the Bobby-Soxer* (1947). In the emboldened 1950s, Elia Kazan's *Baby Doll* (1956) adapted a Tennessee Williams play about Archie Lee Meighan (Karl Malden) and his teenaged wife, Baby Doll (Carroll Baker), a film the Legion of Decency condemned.

The flagship of cinematic pedophilia was the adaptation of Vladimir Nabokov's critically acclaimed novel *Lolita*, published in France in 1955. When it was finally allowed through U.S. customs in full in 1958, *Lolita* was considered too objectionable for the screen even though it became a best seller. Eventually, Stanley Kubrick directed the film, and MGM released it in 1962, marketing it with the teaser, "How did they make a movie out of *Lolita*?" Rather than being seen as a bulwark against vulgarity, the PCA and the Legion were being mocked in the advertising campaign as unnecessarily prudish.

In Kubrick's adaptation as in Nabokov's novel, Humbert Humbert (James Mason) becomes hopelessly infatuated on first sight with Lolita Haze (Sue Lyon), whose age was increased from twelve in the novel to fifteen in the film. He takes a room as a boarder with Lolita's mother, Charlotte (Shelley Winters). He marries Charlotte, who discovers Humbert's sexual obsession with her daughter, but she runs in front of a car and is killed. Humbert retrieves Lolita from summer camp, and they spend a night at the Enchanted Hunters Hotel. The following morning, Humbert has sex with Lolita, which she initiates. Later that day, he tells

Lolita her mother is dead. She is distraught, but he convinces her to stay with him. Humbert's plans for settling down with Lolita are disrupted by Clare Quilty (Peter Sellers), a playwright who had sex with Lolita before Humbert met her and while he lived with her. Eventually, the young girl he labeled a "nymphet" escapes and runs away to New Mexico with Quilty. She was in love with Quilty but put off by his "bunch of weird friends staying there.... painters, nudists, writers, weight lifters." Quilty sent Lolita packing when she refused to be in "an art movie" he was making. She met and married Dick Schiller (Gary Cockrell), a young man closer to her age. When she writes asking for money, Humbert tracks her down to find out who his nemesis had been. Lolita tells him, and out of despair, Humbert murders Quilty, the film ending where it had begun. Although the Code had been modified to insure that Kubrick's film could be given a Seal, it would be an exaggeration to claim that the floodgates had been opened. It would be fair, though, to say that a steady trickle of pedophiliac themes in movies has flowed since.

In *The Last Picture Show*, a minor character named Joe Bob Blanton (Barc Doyle), a preacher's son who had earlier explained the importance of the Christian faith to the other teens, is arrested for "kidnapping" a little girl named Molly Clarg (uncredited). Outside the courthouse, a group of locals discusses the arrest. One man says a doctor's examination proved Joe Bob had not molested the child. Another man chimes in, disconcertingly, that Joe Bob "never had the guts."

Taxi Driver (1976) follows the downward spiral of Travis Bickle (Robert De Niro), a psychopathic New York City cab driver who rescues an under-aged prostitute. When he approaches her for the first time, Iris (Jodie Foster) is wearing hot pants, a shirt tied up like a halter, and red stacks. She directs Travis over to her pimp, Matthew (Harvey Keitel), who catalogues the abusive possibilities for Travis, highlighting her age: "She's twelve and a half years old. You ain't never had no pussy like that. You can do anything with her. You can come on her, fuck her in the mouth, fuck her in the ass, come on her face, man." Matthew's description objectifies the young female.

Travis goes with Iris to her bedroom and offers to take her away from her pimp, but the young girl is unable to comprehend his proposition. Working on autopilot, she massages his crotch (off-screen) and attempts to fellate him. Scorsese shot the scene with greater restraint than Paul Schrader's screenplay, which called for Iris to remove her top and expose her breasts.[9] In the film, Travis asks her to keep her top on, which she does. Eventually, Travis rescues Iris in a bloody shootout and becomes a hero.

Child street prostitution in large urban areas drew considerable national attention in the 1970s. Iris is realistically drawn since child or adolescent prostitution was often accompanied by drug use and the

youth were often runaways, many of whom had suffered sexual abuse
at home.[10] Underage prostitutes today have many of the same characteristics.[11] They shared similar fates in the late nineteenth and early
twentieth centuries as well.

Two years after *Taxi Driver*, French director Louis Malle's *Pretty Baby*
(1978) stirred up a great deal of controversy. Set in Storyville, the infamous red light district of New Orleans, Louisiana, in 1917, the film follows a young *trick baby* named Violet (Brooke Shields) when she meets,
becomes the lover of, and eventually marries hermitical photographer
E. J. Bellocq (Keith Carradine), a character based on a real-life New
Orleans photographer of the same name. One of the main sources for
the film's storyline and many of its images came from a collection of
photographs taken by Bellocq.[12]

Malle purposively kept sexual behavior off-screen, implying it
through pre-sex or post-sex scenes. He reasoned, "If you deal with
whores, you take for granted that the number one activity is sex, so
why show it?"[13] As filmed by cinematographer Sven Nykvist, Malle's
brothel is more aesthetic than demeaning. Malle and screenwriter Polly
Platt based their story on tales of brothel life gleaned from Al Rose's
examination of life in the once-legal red light district, *Storyville New
Orleans*. Malle's portrayal of the experiences of growing up a trick baby
is much more sanitized than the brief vignette the real-life Violet provided Rose about her childhood experiences as a trick baby.[14]

Pretty Baby opens with a fade from black screen to Violet's face
shrouded in darkness and Violet's prostitute mother, Hildegard "Hattie"
Marr (Susan Sarandon), having another trick baby, a little boy. The scene
quickly establishes that neither the brothel nor the commercialized sex in
it have any moral meaning for Violet. She runs from the room and sticks
her head in on a prostitute having sex with a john. The prostitute sends
Violet away without missing a beat, the narrative underlining the impersonal routines of commercial sex. The child runs downstairs into the
main room of the brothel and shares the news.

The narrative depicts Violet's everyday life growing up in the
brothel. She shares a loft bedroom with other children born there.
Despite growing up in the brothel, Violet acts very much like any other
child. She skips rope, wanders around the house aimlessly, and rides a
pony with another young girl. Yet, innocence is an illusion since the
pony could also signal even darker sexual behaviors. According to Al
Rose's *Storyville New Orleans*, the real-life Violet was a part of a "sex
circus," in which her ten-year-old friend Liz performed. Violet told Rose
that her mother performed sexually with a pony for the circus audience.[15] Malle exempts the audience from that part of Violet's recollec-
tion. Instead, he intertwines Violet's tale with the aesthetic aims of
photographer Bellocq.

Bellocq arrives one morning and explains to the house madam, Nell Livingston (Frances Faye), what he wants to do and that he has "photographed in the district many times." Nell is suspicious of sexual images. "Photographs?" she asks, adding, "I don't cater to the inverts." The allusion to early pornographic images is clear. Everyone has a limit and Nell's is modernist technology, but she consents and lets him photograph the prostitutes. Bellocq frequents the brothel and observes the prostitutes as they dance with each other or with customers or make small talk with men in sailor uniforms or well-appointed evening attire. As Bellocq stands at the bar, a passive fly on the wall, Violet quizzes him about his lack of sexual interest. The smallness of the child is caught in a medium shot of Bellocq and Violet talking to one another. Ironically, since the framed image clearly shows otherwise, Violet childishly tells him she is "not a child" when he irritates her.

Despite her age, Violet is allowed to wander among the customers. One evening, a sailor (C. C. Courtney) sets Violet on his lap and begins caressing her arm and asking her questions. Nell whispers something in his ear, and he pushes Violet off him, saying he was only kidding. Another evening, Hattie tells Violet to join her and a john (Joe Catalavetto), assuring the man that Violet is a virgin and "only for friends." Violet joins her mother and the man in another room. The scene is indicative of the way that Malle treats child prostitution. In contrast to more exploitive film genres, the emphasis in Malle's film is on the *idea* of child prostitution as an existential reality with a history rather than the *experience* of the child prostitute. Thus, the moment is less important than the prelude to the moment since the very notion that a mother would ask her daughter to perform with her in a sex act is in itself shocking.

Thus, Malle emphasizes the situation's mise-en-scène. The scene is divided into three planes. Hattie sits on the bed removing her stockings in the background. She looks momentarily at Violet, then looks away, obviously nonplussed. In the middle ground, the man sits in a chair pulling his pants down and staring at Violet. In the foreground with her back to the camera, Violet leans against the door frame watching the other two. The next shot faces Violet, who lingers until she reaches behind her and slides the door closed. An inheritance from the ambiguity of the Code era, the closing door suffices to signal impending sexual behavior. After that night, Violet performs oral sex on johns until her virginity is auctioned off.

The film portrays the absence of conventional sexual morality in the brothel when the prostitutes prepare Violet for her sexual debut. They advise her that she should react to what she believes the customer desires. The scene emphasizes the prostitutes' manipulation of feigned sexual pleasure and appearance for commercial ends. They dress Violet in a fine dress, do her hair, and apply make-up to ready her for "busting her cherry." Promoting the child as a "virgin, bona fide," Nell declines to say how old Violet is but calls her "the finest delicacy New Orleans has to offer." Violet is placed on a stand and auctioned off. Between close-ups of the faces of lustful johns, the brothel's African American piano player Claude (Antonio Fargas) looks ill at ease. His expression suggests he recognizes the clear parallel to a slave auction.

A man (Don K. Lutenbacher) pays $400 to deflower Violet. Looking to be in his forties, he carries the child up the stairs. Violet's deflowering scene takes place in near darkness. The man undoes his cuffs silently as Violet says, "I hope you're gentle," and asks if he wants whisky. Violet backs away from him, and the scene cuts to two small children who live in the bordello. Violet is heard screaming on the soundtrack. Again, Malle focuses on the prelude to the event since the idea itself is shocking enough. Afterwards, Violet laughs about her debut with her mother and the other prostitutes.

In the following scene, Violet is taking a bath when Miss Nell brings in a customer who wants a virgin because he is worried about disease. Violet stands up, instinctively covering herself, when they come in. Nell yanks the towel away, and Violet stands for inspection, smiling. Nell lies, claiming Violet is "pure as driven snow." Innocence is an illusion some men will pay to exploit. The scene ends with the man looking at her. In a later scene, an experienced Violet plies her trade, hitting on a john and dancing with him, her dress short and her thighs bare.

Hattie marries a wealthy customer, Alfred Fuller (Don Hood), and promises to send for Violet, who she has said is her sister. Abandoned, Violet flirts with Bellocq, at one point, kissing him then telling him, "I love you once, I love you twice. I love you more than beans and rice." Nell tells Bellocq that she can see he is in love with Violet. Violet leaves the brothel after being whipped for trying to seduce an African American kid named Nonny (Von Eric Thomas). She goes to Bellocq's. They go upstairs, and she tells him she wants to live with him and wants him to be her "lover man." He starts kissing her, they lean back, and the scene fades to black. In the next scene, Violet wakes up, naked in bed. The shot is framed and the actress positioned so her genitals and breasts are concealed. The film then traces what Malle described as "a weird love story."[16] The affair's strangeness is encapsulated by Bellocq's buying Violet a doll and explaining, "every child should have a doll." Understandably puzzled, Violet asks, "I'm a child to you?" Bellocq photographs her wearing a pretty dress and a flowered bonnet and holding her doll. He also has Violet pose on a divan, completely nude, but she moves at the last second, ruining his photograph.

Bellocq and Violet eventually get married. After some time, though, Hattie reappears with Mr. Fuller. Hattie informs Bellocq that the marriage is not legal without her consent. When Bellocq tells the Fullers he cannot "live without" Violet, Fuller entreats him to give Violet an opportunity to escape her past. Bellocq lets her go. *Pretty Baby* ends with Violet dressed nicely at the train station. The final frame freezes her posing for Mr. Fuller's Kodak Brownie. The snapshot is the antithesis of Bellocq's artistry and, given the girl's childhood in a brothel, the pornographic images that also circulated at the time, and that she may have ended up posing for when she got older.

Another period film that includes pedophilia is Neil Jordan's adaptation of Anne Rice's 1976 novel *Interview with the Vampire* (1994), which is chiefly set in eighteenth-century New Orleans. As is common in vampire films, *Interview with the Vampire* sexualizes the blood lust of its main characters, Lestat (Tom Cruise) and Louis (Brad Pitt), vampires who seduce their victims as if for sexual intimacy but end up biting their necks or wrists and drinking their blood. James B. Twitchell argues that the vampire has "served to explain the dynamics of human social and sexual behavior ... especially as a paradigm of suppressed interfamilial struggles." According to Twitchell, "the modern vampire is not only interested in blood, he is interested in the process of seduction and forbidden possession.... He is a psychosexual leech." Twitchell calls "the connection between incest and vampirism ... the mainstay of the myth, the prime generator of the horror."[17] Indeed, according to Twitchell, "the fear of incest underlies all horror myths in our culture."[18] Lestat and Louis find a young girl, Claudia (Kirsten Dunst), who they turn into a vampire. Lestat takes Louis to Claudia's bed and asks, "Do you remember how you wanted her? To taste her?" The sexual implications of *wanted* and *taste* are reinforced by the image of Claudia lying asleep in bed and a shot/reverse shot of Claudia and Louis, with Louis's facial expression indicating the attraction she holds for him and the feelings he has for her.

Lestat wakes the child, tells her she is ill and needs help, and then cuts his own wrist. In a scene with sexual overtones, he lets Claudia suck blood from his wrist. The blood drips into Claudia's open mouth. She then takes Lestat's wrist into her mouth and sucks forcefully. Lestat can be heard off-screen moaning, "That's it. Yes." There is then a shot/reverse shot of Claudia with Lestat's arm to her mouth, her eyes peering over his arm and Lestat's pained but ecstatic reaction. He then pulls himself away forcefully because Claudia will not stop draining his blood. Claudia's hair changes to golden locks, her vampire fangs appear and she gasps, "I want some more," a nymphet of darkness. Lestat provides her with a woman, but Claudia still wants more. Lestat tells her to take it easy and compliments her for not spilling a drop.

Once Claudia is a vampire, she remains eleven years old eternally. She becomes a ghoulish version of Humbert's frustrated wish in Nabokov's novel that he had eternalized young Lolita by filming her dressed in her white tennis outfit: "Idiot, triple idiot! I could have filmed her! I would have had her now with me, before my eyes, in the projection room of my pain and despair."[19] If Lestat and Louis form a couple and Claudia is their daughter, the men's relationship with the child is incestuous since their sexual proclivities extend to pedophilia. The film pulls back from clear-cut pedophilia, though. In one scene, the child is fitted for clothes in a fashion that conveys parental pampering rather than a lover's indulgence. Throughout the film, the physical consummation of the vampires' sexual desires remains ambiguous. Claudia sleeps with Louis in his coffin, yet Louis makes it sound innocent. Furthermore, when Louis and Claudia are in Europe, Louis meets with the leader of a theater troupe and tells him that Claudia is dear to him and that she is his daughter. The troupe leader corrects him, "Your lover." Louis alters it to "My beloved." The narrative maintains its ambiguity but insists on questioning the nature of their relationship.

Less ambiguous representations of pedophilia are found in Adrian Lyne's remake of *Lolita* (1997), starring Jeremy Irons as Humbert and Melanie Griffith as Charlotte Haze. The combination of Lyne's slightly more explicit and faithful, although his Lolita (Dominique Swain) is fourteen, adaptation of Nabokov's novel, coupled with the difficulties he encountered in securing a distributor for his film, indicates the futility of portraying the history of sex in American cinema as unidirectional. The latter pointed at the political ascendancy of sexual conservatism in the late 1990s while the former made clear that conservatism coexisted with still strong sexual liberalism. Another film from 1997, Paul Thomas Anderson's *Boogie Nights* includes a pedophiliac subplot. A sleazy character known cryptically as The Colonel (Robert Ridgely), who finances the film production of pornographer Jack Horner (Burt Reynolds), appears in scenes with young girls and is at one point arrested for possession of child pornography, which causes Horner to disavow him. Whether for legal or moral reasons, the large majority of pornographers have kept their distance from child pornography, which only first emerged in the 1960s and 1970s.

While Hollywood has shied away from child pornography, two recent films have represented same-sex pedophilia. Todd Solondz's independent black comedy *Happiness* (1998) portrays the exploits of Bill Maplewood (Dylan Baker), a middle-class New Jersey psychiatrist who drugs and molests two of his eleven-year-old son Billy's (Rufus Read) friends. Maplewood is caught and both socially ostracized and arrested.

Clint Eastwood's *Mystic River* (2003) portrays different aspects of child molestation, separated from one another in the narrative's structure, which serves to underscore each aspect. The film portrays the abduction and molestation of a child and two conceptions of the psychological repercussions of the traumatic experience—the darkness

that pervades each day of the victim's adult life and revenge as blood-
letting. The film begins in 1975, which, chillingly, was around the time
serial murderer John Wayne Gacy, Jr., began his spree of raping and
murdering over thirty boys, teens, and young men in Illinois. The
abduction scene in the prologue foregrounds verbal threats and subterfuge to represent the psychological ploys pedophiles often employ. By
portraying both the abduction and its aftermath in terms of crucial
moments leading up to the violation and then fading to black, the film
emphases its randomness, making the horror of abuse even more
chilling.

In a working-class Boston neighborhood, three school boys are carv-
ing their names in the wet cement of a sidewalk. Two middle-aged men
drive up, and one of the men gets out of the car. He identifies himself
as a police officer, harangues the kids, and asks them where they live.
Dave Boyle (Cameron Bowen) lives on a different street, so the man
tells him to get into the backseat of the car so they can talk with his
mother. Dave is reluctant because the floorboard is covered with debris,
but the man forces him into the back seat. A long take of Dave's worried face through the rear view window creates the feeling of time slow-
ing down as the car drives away, heightening the horror of what lies in
store for the defenseless child as the screen fades to black.

The second phase of abuse begins with a shot of a cellar door opening into blackness until the light reveals Dave lying terrified on a mat-
tress in a grubby cellar. Ominous music plays on the soundtrack as a
man in a sleeveless t-shirt descends the stairs while the other sexual
predator passes through the frame in the background and then returns
to the door. The film locates child molestation where it often takes
place: in regular houses in regular neighborhoods across the country.
The basement as an isolated and dangerous space is common to film
narratives, but also known in cases such as that of JonBenét Ramsey,
the six year old who was discovered murdered and possibly sexually
abused in her parents' basement. In *Mystic River*, a frightened Dave
begs, "Please. No more," as the camera tracks in on him and the man's
shadow falls behind him. The screen goes dark; Dave is then seen running in a wooded area from his captors after a four-day ordeal.[20]

Victims of sexual abuse as children often show symptoms of
posttraumatic stress disorder.[21] *Mystic River* depicts a third aspect of
abuse, posttraumatic syndrome, first, through Dave's inability to communicate clearly with others and second, by filming him in semidarkness that symbolizes his darkened state of mind. After the introductory
abduction scene, the narrative jumps forward, and Dave (Tim Robbins),
now an adult, is walking home with his young son, Michael (Cayden
Boyd) along the street where he had been abducted as a child. As the
camera rotates on its axis, Dave looks at the names carved in the

pavement and has a flashback of the man pounding the roof of the car and demanding he "Get in." The drained expression on Dave's face signals that he still suffers.

Being raped as a child caused Dave to turn inward and left him emotionally inarticulate. Trying to communicate with his wife, Celeste (Marcia Gay Harden), he tells her somewhat cryptically, that he thinks about vampires and wants to feel human again. Celeste does not understand what he is trying to tell her. It appears Dave has never told Celeste what happened to him. Now he tells her the names of the two men who assaulted him, Henry and George. He calls them wolves and speaks of himself in third person as the "boy who escaped from wolves." He is bitter that no one came to his rescue and that he had to "pretend to be somebody else" to survive the ordeal. When Celeste tries to comfort him, he tells her "Dave's dead" because Dave never "came out of that cellar." In a medium close-up from a three-quarter angle with only a small ray of light on his temple, he whispers, barely able to bring himself to express it, "It's like a vampire. Once it's in you, it stays." He concludes, "I can't trust my mind anymore."

Dave's two friends on that fateful day are Jimmy Markum (Sean Penn), an ex-con who owns a corner grocery store in Dave's neighborhood, and Sean Devine (Kevin Bacon), a homicide detective assigned to investigate the murder of Jimmy's teenage daughter Katie (Emmy Rossum). By juxtaposing two shots, the narrative insinuates Dave might have murdered Katie. The first tracks in close on Dave in a bar as he tells a fellow drinker (Ken Cheeseman) that he has known Jimmy's daughter "since she was a kid," as they watch her drink and dance with a couple of other women. In the next scene, Dave comes home in the middle of the night covered in blood and concocts a dubious story to explain his blood-soaked clothes.

The final aspect of victimization that *Mystic River* portrays is the postulate that trauma leads to vicarious revenge. Suspecting Dave killed his daughter, Jimmy and three thugs take Dave to a dark spot near the river. When Dave realizes that Jimmy thinks he killed Katie, he confesses that he killed a "child molester. He was having sex with this kid in his car. He was a fucking wolf, he was a vampire." As Dave says this, there is a flashback. A man sits in a parked car with his head thrown back and his mouth slightly open. The camera tracks in and the man's door is opened, causing him to look up. Dave starts slugging him. A teenage boy's head springs up from the bottom of the frame. Dave tells the boy to leave, and he runs off. When Dave turns around, the man slices him with a knife. Dave violently vents decades of rage as the man pays for Henry and George's crimes. As Dave beats the man, there is a brief flashback embedded in Dave's flashback of young Dave running through the woods again. By first implying Dave might have

murdered Katie and then having Dave murder a pedophile, the film
implicates Dave in a cycle of abuse.

After Dave pounds his victim, the narrative returns to the present as
Dave tells Jimmy that he and young Dave killed the child molester.
Although the viewer learns through crosscutting who actually murdered Katie, Jimmy tricks Dave into confessing to a crime he did not
commit. Dave tells Jimmy he would understand if he had gotten in
"that car." Jimmy, hardened by his criminal life and enraged by his
daughter's death, simply replies, "I didn't get in that car," before cold-
bloodedly murdering Dave.

The film ends shortly after Sean tells Jimmy that the police appre-
hended Katie's killers and that the body of a known pedophile had
been discovered. Sean figures out that Jimmy has killed Dave, but does
not pursue it, pointing out that all three of them had been frozen in
time since that fateful day in 1975. Critics were divided over the complex or confused moral messages contained in the film, just as they
were over the portrayal of sex research pioneer Alfred Kinsey in Bill
Condon's *Kinsey*.

In *Kinsey*, Alfred Kinsey (Liam Neeson) and his associate Wardell
Pomeroy (Chris O'Donnell) interview Kenneth Braun (Bill Sadler), a
man who claimed to have had sex with hundreds of preadolescent
males and females. When Pomeroy storms out of the room in disgust,
Braun rationalizes his behavior by saying, "Everybody should do what
they want." Kinsey, believing Braun attributes that conceptualization of
tolerance to him, counters, "I've never said that." Kinsey goes on to
criticize sex with children because it is nonvolitional on the child's part:
"No one should be forced to do anything against their will. No one
should ever be hurt." His reasoning triggers Braun to tell Kinsey,
"You're a lot more square than I thought you'd be." Yet, Kinsey had
failed to address incest in his two monumental studies despite relatively
lengthy discussions of preadolescents' and adolescents' sexual experiences with adults.[22] Indeed, Kinsey was roundly criticized for speculating
that the only reason many children reacted negatively to being molested
nonincestuously was the negative reaction of their parents and other
adults.[23] The cultural conservative organization Concerned Women for
America continues to criticize what it views as Kinsey's indirect negative impact on the lives of children; the organization protested the
release of Bill Condon's biography of Kinsey.[24]

Filmmakers continue to use pedophiliac themes in various ways.
Pedophilia continues to be an element of narratives and has appeared
in a variety of genres: psychological dramas (*The Woodsman*; 2003), independent romantic comedies (*Me and You and Everyone We Know*; 2004),
thrillers (*Hard Candy*; 2004), mysteries (*Birth*; 2004), a cartoon noir (*Sin
City*; 2005) and a comedy drama (*Running With Scissors*; 2006). The

Spanish import, Pedro Almodóvar's *Bad Education* (*La mala educación*; 2004), includes a pedophile priest (Daniel Giménez Cacho) at a Catholic boarding school in Franco's Spain. Amy Berg's *Deliver Us From Evil* (2006), which won Best Documentary at the Los Angeles Film Festival, documents the abusive acts of sexual predator Oliver O'Grady in the 1970s and 1980s while a Catholic priest in Southern California. The film resonated with a public still reeling from the recent child sexual abuse scandals involving Catholic priests in the United States. U.S. Congressman Mark Foley (R-Florida), who resigned from Congress in 2006 after his inappropriate conduct with underage Congressional pages was exposed, was himself abused by a Catholic priest as a young teenager. The most secret of sexual aberrations, incest, has also become more public, with recovered memories of childhood abuse sparking public debates. The *New York Times* has reported on elaborate online pedophile communities as well as child pornography online.[25] With high-profile campaigns led by celebrities like Oprah Winfrey, child sexual abuse remains in the media spotlight in the United States.

Conclusion

This book has examined nudity and sex in American cinema and the interaction between the social and cultural contours of American society at various periods and the sexual content of film. For decades, the Production Code explicitly enforced and privileged a conservative Christian morality that shaped the representation of sex in hundreds of films produced by the mainstream American film industry. Until the 1950s, few of the films produced by MPAA members portrayed sex in a way that resembled the complexity of its role in Americans' lives. Given that industry self-censorship or regulation ultimately determined how sex was portrayed in motion pictures, it makes no sense to claim that sex in films reflected sexual behavior patterns or attitudes in the United States. Yet, the Code alone did not shape the representation of sexual behavior in film until the mid-1960s, no more than the ratings system has since 1968. Thus, while the relationship between film and society *is* somehow reciprocal, mirror metaphors about film reflecting reality prove inadequate. The interrelationship between film production, film reception, and the larger society and culture is too complex for such a simple claim.

Throughout American film history, sexual representations have resulted from a combination of influences just as sex in mainstream film today requires a number of industry, social, and cultural preconditions to coalesce. Not least, there have to be performers (mostly female) willing to remove their clothes or appear in various stages of undress or to simulate any number of sexual behaviors. From screenwriters to directors to cinematographers to producers to marketers and so on, numerous individuals, some representing companies and organizations, have to decide to include sexual representations and how to present them— explicitly or implicitly—in the film narrative. As shown, the film industry has always been a house divided over the issue of sex.

Indeed, of all the subjects depicted in films on American movie screens, few themes are as potentially controversial—or commercial—as sexual themes. The plurality of attitudes and cultural divisions found within the film industry are similar to the rest of the United States and, as shown, have been equally contentious within the industry and the broader society. Across the country and over time, conservatives have repeatedly been offended by Hollywood's licentiousness, liberals unimpressed by its timidity. Although sexual representations have divided conservatives and liberals, both groups have united in their agreement that sex in films is an important social and cultural issue. Despite the polemics, sex sells, as a truism heard and criticized repeatedly throughout cinema history would have it.

Sexual representations in film are not only gratuitous additions for commercial objectives, though. They are also cultural expressions of what filmmakers believe or feel about sex in their society and in individuals' lives. Motion pictures are aesthetic creations that conform primarily to the aesthetic demands of the medium and the objectives of filmmakers who rarely if ever intend their films to be held accountable by the rigorous standards of sociologists or historians. Screenplays are written or adapted more with aesthetic than social or historical goals in mind. There are numerous narrative demands and genre conventions that override considerations of social or historical accuracy. Yet, however tenacious the connection of films to social, cultural, or historical reality, motion pictures have played a major role in chronicling life, including—to widely varying degrees—the myriad roles played by sex in American society. This survey has stressed the sexual pluralism found both on- and off-screen in the United States because, culturally and socially, the film industry, in its sexual conservatism as much as its sexual liberalism, remains a microcosm of the society it is a part of and seeks to entertain.

Notes

CHAPTER 1. DRAWING THE LINE: CODES AND LAWS

1. *Block v. City of Chicago*, 239 Ill. 251; 87 N.E. 1011 (1909).

2. 239 Ill. 251; 87 N.E. 1011 (1909).

3. 236 U.S. 230 (1915).

4. 236 U.S. 230 (1915).

5. Richard S. Randall, *Censorship of the Movies: The Social and Political Control of a Mass Medium* (Madison: University of Wisconsin Press, 1968), 14.

6. All citations from the Production Code are taken from Martin Quigley, *Decency in Motion Pictures* (New York: Macmillan, 1937), 52–70.

7. Gregory D. Black, *Hollywood Censored: Morality Codes, Catholics, and the Movies*, Cambridge Studies in the History of Mass Communications (Cambridge: Cambridge University Press, 1994), 65–70.

8. Raymond Moley, *The Hays Office* (Indianapolis, IN: Bobbs-Merrill, 1945), 250.

9. Will H. Hays, *The Memoirs of Will H. Hays* (Garden City, NY: Doubleday, 1955), 445.

10. Ben Hecht, *A Child of the Century* (New York: Playbill/Ballantine, 1970; reprint, 1954), 455.

11. Lea Jacobs, *The Wages of Sin: Censorship and the Fallen Women Film, 1928–1942* (Madison: University of Wisconsin Press, 1991), 111–15.

12. 334 U.S. 131 (1948).

13. 343 U.S. 495 (1952).

14. 343 U.S. 495 (1952).

15. 177 Kan. 728, 282 P.2d 412 (1955).

16. Quoted in Vito Russo, *The Celluloid Closet: Homosexuality in the Movies*, rev. ed. (New York: Perennial Library, 1987), 121–22.

17. Quoted in Leonard J. Leff and Jerold Simmons, *The Dame in the Kimono: Hollywood, Censorship, and the Production Code from the 1920s to the 1960s* (New York: Grove Weidenfeld, 1990), 252.

18. Murray Schumach, "M.J. Frankovich, New Columbia Boss, Sketches Plan of Positive Action," *New York Times*, March 15, 1964, X9.

19. Leff and Simmons, *Dame in the Kimono*, 246.

20. Quoted in *Roth v. United States*, 354 U.S. 476 (1957).

21. L. R. 3 Q. B. 360 (1868).

22. 354 U.S. 476 (1957).

23. 354 U.S. 476 (1957).

24. *Manual Enterprises v. Day*, 370 U.S. 478 (1962).

25. 378 U.S. 184 (1964).

26. 383 U.S. 502 (1966).

27. 383 U.S. 413 (1966).

CHAPTER 2. SHIFTING BOUNDARIES

1. 3 N.Y.2d 237 (1957).

2. Charles Stinson, "'Immoral Mr. Teas' Ends Era in Movies," *Los Angeles Times*, January 26, 1960, 18.

3. *Dunn v. Maryland State Board of Censors*, 240 Md. 249 (1965).

4. Frank A. Hoffmann, "Prolegomena to a Study of Traditional Elements in the Erotic Film," *Journal of American Folklore* 78, no. 308 (1965): 144.

5. Arthur Knight and Hollis Alpert, "The History of Sex in Cinema Part 17: The Stag Film," *Playboy*, November 1967, 158.

6. Commission on Obscenity and Pornography, *The Report of the Commission on Obscenity and Pornography* (Washington, DC: U.S. Government Printing Office, 1970), 114.

7. Knight and Alpert, "The Stag Film," 170.

8. William Murray, "Porn Capital of America: San Francisco," *New York Times Magazine*, January 3, 1971, 23.

9. Richard Corliss, "Randy Metzger Aristocrat of the Erotic: An Interview by Richard Corliss," *Film Comment* 9, no. 1 (1973): 19.

10. Jonas Mekas, "Notes on Some New Movies and Happiness," *Film Culture* 37 (1965): 19.

11. Louis Botto, "They Shoot Dirty Movies Don't They?," *Look*, November 3, 1970, 58.

12. Alfred C. Kinsey et al., *Sexual Behavior in the Human Female* (Philadelphia: W. B. Saunders, 1953), 329.

13. For a summary of critiques of Kinsey's behaviorist bias, see Regina Markell Morantz, "The Scientist as Sex Crusader: Alfred C. Kinsey and American Culture," *American Quarterly* 29, no. 5, Special Issue: Reassessing Twentieth Century Documents (1977): 578–81.

14. Reprinted in Lionel Trilling, "The Kinsey Report," in *The Liberal Imagination: Essays on Literature and Society* (Harmondsworth: Penguin, 1976), 234.

15. Discussed in David Allyn, "Private Acts/Public Policy: Alfred Kinsey, the American-Law-Institute, and the Privatization of American Sexual Morality," *Journal of American Studies* 30 (1996): 407.

16. Paula England and George Farkas, *Households, Employment, and Gender: A Social, Economic, and Demographic View* (New York: Aldine de Gruyter, 1986), 11.

17. Joel Feinberg, *Rights, Justice, and the Bounds of Liberty: Essays in Social Philosophy* (Princeton: Princeton University Press, 1980), 93 (footnote 8).

18. John Modell, "Historical Reflections on American Marriage," in *Contemporary Marriage: Comparative Perspectives on a Changing Institution*, ed. Kingsley Davis (New York: Russell Sage Foundation, 1985), 189.

19. Quoted in Alice Kessler-Harris, *Out to Work: A History of Wage-Earning Women in the United States* (New York: Oxford University Press, 1982), 300.

20. Tommy Thompson, "Raw Dialogue Challenges All the Censors," *Life*, June 10, 1966, 98.

CHAPTER 3. INSIDE OUT

1. Committee on Commerce, Science, and Transportation, *Effectiveness of Media Rating Systems: The Testimony of Mr. Jack Valenti*, Science, Technology, and Space Hearing, September 28, 2004.

2. Leff and Simmons, *Dame in the Kimono*, 244.

3. *Ginsberg v. New York*, 390 U.S. 629 (1968).

4. *Interstate Circuit v. Dallas*, 390 U.S. 676 (1968).

5. Motion Picture Association of America, "Official Code Objectives," in *The Movies in Our Midst: Documents in the Cultural History of Film in America*, ed. Gerald Mast (Chicago: University of Chicago Press, 1982), 707.

6. Ibid., 704.

7. Jack Hamilton, "Movies: And Everybody's Doing It," *Look*, November 3, 1970, 41.

8. Commission on Obscenity and Pornography, *The Report of the Commission on Obscenity and Pornography*, 82.

9. 394 U.S. 557 (1969).

10. Bruce A. Austin, Mark J. Nicolich, and Thomas Simonet, "M.P.A.A. Ratings and the Box Office: Some Tantalizing Statistics," *Film Quarterly* 35, no. 2 (1981–82): 29.

11. Kinsey et al., *Sexual Behavior in the Human Female*, 329.

12. 413 U.S. 15 (1973).

13. 418 U.S. 153 (1974).

14. Fletcher Knebel, "Mood of America," *Look*, November 18, 1969, 28.

CHAPTER 4. EVERYBODY'S DOING IT—AREN'T THEY?

1. Isadore Rubin, "Transition in Sex Values: Implications for the Education of Adolescents," *Journal of Marriage and the Family* 27, no. 2 (1965): 185–87.

2. "Changing Morality: The Two Americas, a Time-Louis Harris Poll," *Time*, June 6, 1969.

3. Ira Robinson et al., "Twenty Years of the Sexual Revolution, 1965–1985: An Update," *Journal of Marriage and the Family* 53, no. 1 (1991): 219.

4. England and Farkas, *Households, Employment, and Gender*, 10.

5. Andrew J. Cherlin, *Marriage, Divorce, Remarriage*, rev. and enl. ed. (Cambridge, MA: Harvard University Press, 1992), 13.

6. Ibithaj Arafat and Betty Yorburg, "On Living Together without Marriage," in *Intimate Life Styles: Marriage and Its Alternatives*, ed. Jack R. DeLora and Joann S. DeLora (Pacific Palisades, CA: Goodyear, 1975), 308.

7. Robert Towne, "Dialogue on Film: Robert Towne," *American Film* 1, no. 3 (1975): 43.

8. Peter Biskind, *Easy Riders, Raging Bulls: How the Sex-Drugs-and-Rock-'N'-Roll Generation Saved Hollywood* (New York: Simon & Schuster, 1998), 302.

9. Quoted in Ibid.

10. Robert N. Bellah et al., *Habits of the Heart: Individualism and Commitment in American Life* (Berkeley: University of California Press, 1985), 47.

CHAPTER 5. TO HAVE OR NOT TO HAVE SEX

1. Tom W. Smith, "Liberal and Conservative Trends in the United States since World War II," *Public Opinion Quarterly* 54, no. 4 (1990): 498.

2. Jerry Falwell, Ed Dobson, and Edward E. Hindson, *The Fundamentalist Phenomenon: The Resurgence of Conservative Christianity* (Garden City, NY: Doubleday, 1981), 206.

3. For a detailed account of the controversy surrounding the production and release of Scorsese's film, see Robin Riley, *Film, Faith, and Cultural Conflict: The Case of Martin Scorsese's The Last Temptation of Christ* (Westport, CT: Praeger, 2003).

4. Edward O. Laumann et al., *Sex in America: A Definitive Survey* (Boston: Little Brown, 1994).

5. Sam Roberts, "It's Official: To Be Married Means to Be Outnumbered," *New York Times*, October 15, 2006.

6. "R-Rated Films in Decline," *Film Journal International* 108, no. 4 (2005): 4.

7. Susan Wloszczyna, "Extreme Cinema Returns with a Vengeance," *USA Today*, October 26, 2004. For a more pessimistic account of the outlook for R films, see Dade Hayes and Jonathan Bing, "H'wood: R Kind of Town (Cover Story)," *Variety*, March 31, 2003.

8. Stuart Y. McDougal, *Stanley Kubrick's A Clockwork Orange* (Cambridge: Cambridge University Press, 2003), 3.

9. Claude Brodesser, "'Dreamers' Goes NC-17," *Daily Variety*, January 14, 2004.

10. Ibid.

11. Ron Leone and Nicole Houle, "21st Century Ratings Creep: PG-13 and R," *Communication Research Reports* 23, no. 1 (2006): 60.

12. Peter Biskind, *Down and Dirty Pictures: Miramax, Sundance, and the Rise of Independent Film* (New York: Simon & Schuster, 2004), 214.

13. "Trends in HIV-Related Risk Behaviors among High School Students—United States, 1991–2005," in *Morbidity and Mortality Weekly Report*, 2006.

14. André Bazin, "On the Politique Des Auteurs," in *Cahiers Du Cinéma: The 1950s: Neo-Realism, Hollywood, New Wave*, ed. Jim Hillier (London: Routledge & Kegan Paul in association with the British Film Institute, 1985), 258.

15. S. R. Stern, "Self-Absorbed, Dangerous, and Disengaged: What Popular Films Tell Us about Teenagers," *Mass Communication and Society* 8, no. 1 (2005).

CHAPTER 6. PURITANICAL PAST IN A PORNOGRAPHIC LIGHT

1. For discussions of the paucity of historical scholarship examining Americans' sexual behavior in the past through the 1960s, see Vern L. Bullough, "Sex in History: A Virgin Field," *Journal of Sex Research* 8, no. 2 (1972).

2. Alfred C. Kinsey, Wardell Baxter Pomeroy, and Clyde E. Martin, *Sexual Behavior in the Human Male* (Philadelphia: W. B. Saunders, 1948), 21–34.

3. Vern L. Bullough, *Sexual Variance in Society and History* (New York: Wiley, 1976), 3–4.

4. Quoted in Arthur Knight and Hollis Alpert, "The History of Sex in Cinema Part 12: The Fifties—Hollywood Grows Up," *Playboy*, November 1966, 176.

5. Scholars have questioned the stereotype of Victorians as sexual prudes. See Carl N. Degler, "What Ought to Be and What Was: Women's Sexuality in the Nineteenth Century," *American Historical Review* 79, no. 5 (1974); and Peter Gay, *The Bourgeois Experience: Victoria to Freud*, 5 vols. (New York: Oxford University Press, 1984).

6. For an illustrated account of sexual behavior in Berlin during the 1920s and 1930s, see Mel Gordon, *Voluptuous Panic: The Erotic World of Weimar Berlin* (Los Angeles, CA: Feral House, 2000).

7. For a discussion of the musical's irony, particularly in the song lyrics, see Randy Clark, "Bending the Genre: The Stage and Screen Versions of 'Cabaret,'" *Literature/Film Quarterly* 19 (1991).

8. *Attorney General v. Book Named "Tropic of Cancer,"* 345 Mass. 11, 184 N. E. 2d 328 (1962). Miller's reputation as a libertine would be varnished by feminist criticism in the 1970s.

9. See Paul Hammond, *French Undressing: Naughty Postcards from 1900–1920* (London: Jupiter Books, 1976); and L. Z. Sigel, "Filth in the Wrong People's Hands: Postcards and the Expansion of Pornography in Britain and the Atlantic World, 1880–1914," *Journal of Social History* 33, no. 4 (2000).

10. See Sarah Projansky, "The Elusive/Ubiquitous Representation of Rape: A Historical Survey of Rape in U.S. Film, 1903–1972," *Cinema Journal* 41, no. 1 (2001), for an overview of rape in Hollywood films.

11. For a review of the debates, see Jacqueline Bobo, "Sifting through the Controversy: Reading the Color Purple," *Callaloo* 39 (1989).

12. Ishmael Reed, "Stephen Spielberg Plays Howard Beach," *Black American Literature Forum* 21, no. 1/2 (1987): 8.

13. See J. E. Hasday, "Contest and Consent: A Legal History of Marital Rape," *California Law Review* 88, no. 5 (2000); and R. M. Ryan, "The Sex Right: A Legal History of the Marital Rape Exemption," *Law and Social Inquiry* 20, no. 4 (1995). It is worth noting that the Supreme Court of Georgia, the state where *The Color Purple* is set, ruled definitively against a marital exemption for rape in 1985 in *Warren v. State*, 255 Ga. 151, 336 S. E. 2d 221.

14. Patricia Godeke Tjaden and Nancy Thoennes, *Extent, Nature, and Consequences of Intimate Partner Violence* (Washington, DC: Department of Justice (U.S.), 2000), 34; and J. A. Neff, B. Holamon, and T. D. Schluter, "Spousal Violence among Anglos, Blacks, and Mexican-Americans: The Role of Demographic-Variables, Psychosocial Predictors, and Alcohol-Consumption," *Journal of Family Violence* 10, no. 1 (1995).

15. Tjaden and Thoennes, *Extent, Nature, and Consequences of Intimate Partner Violence*, 25.

16. Barbara Smith, "Sexual Oppression Unmasked," *Callaloo* 22 (1984): 170.

17. Donald Bogle, *Toms, Coons, Mulattoes, Mammies, and Bucks: An Interpretive History of Blacks in American Films* (New York: Viking Press, 1973).

18. See Albert Ernest Jenks, "The Legal Status of Negro-White Amalgamation in the United States," *American Journal of Sociology* 21, no. 5 (1916).

19. *Loving v. Virginia*, 388 U.S. 1 (1967).

20. Stanley Kauffmann, "Black Love in Movies and on Television: Independent Directors and Producers Are Taking Steps to Bring Black Romance and Intimacy to the Screen," *Ebony*, February 1991.

21. An interesting study by sociologist Howard S. Becker examines deviance among night club performers: Howard S. Becker, "The Professional Dance Musician and His Audience," *American Journal of Sociology* 57, no. 2 (1951). For a recent survey and discussion of the trope in popular culture, including cinema, see Paul Lopes, "Signifying Deviance and Transgression: Jazz in the Popular Imagination," *American Behavioral Scientist* 48, no. 11 (2005).

22. Ed Guerrero, "The Black Man on Our Screens and the Empty Space in Representation," *Callaloo* 18, no. 2 (1995): 397.

23. Hortense Powdermaker, *Hollywood, the Dream Factory: An Anthropologist Looks at the Movie-Makers* (Boston: Little, Brown, 1950).

CHAPTER 7. FROM THE CLOSET TO THE SCREEN

1. For a brief overview of the emergence of gay cinema, see Jack Stevenson, "From the Bedroom to the Bijou: A Secret History of American Gay Sex Cinema," *Film Quarterly* 51, no. 1 (1997). For a more detailed treatment of homosexuality on- and off-screen in Hollywood, see David Ehrenstein, *Open Secret: Gay Hollywood, 1928–1998* (New York: William Morrow, 1998).

2. William N. Eskridge, "Law and the Construction of the Closet: American Regulation of Same-Sex Intimacy, 1880–1946," *Iowa Law Review* 82, no. 4 (1997).

3. There have been recent challenges to the idea that the presence of homosexuals was totally obliterated in American society and culture, including film, during the Code era. See Richard Barrios, *Screened Out: Playing Gay in Hollywood from Edison to Stonewall* (New York: Routledge, 2003), 56–60.

4. See Russo, *The Celluloid Closet: Homosexuality in the Movies*.

5. Jack Vizzard, *See No Evil: Life inside a Hollywood Censor* (New York: Simon & Schuster, 1970), 368.

6. Quoted in Barrios, *Screened Out: Playing Gay in Hollywood from Edison to Stonewall*, 303. The wording of the amendment was meant to be vague enough to allow Stanley Kubrick's upcoming *Lolita* (1962) to be awarded a Seal of Approval despite its representation of pedophilia.

7. For more on gay and lesbian bars before Stonewall, see Nancy Achilles, "The Development of the Homosexual Bar as an Institution," in *Sexual Deviance*, ed. John H. Gagnon, William Simon, and Donald E. Carns (New York: Harper & Row, 1967); and John D'Emilio, *Sexual Politics, Sexual Communities: The Making of a Homosexual Minority in the United States, 1940–1970* (Chicago: University of

Chicago Press, 1983). In *Kinsey* (2004), Alfred Kinsey (Liam Neeson) and his associate Clyde Martin (Peter Sarsgaard) go to a gay bar to find men willing to be interviewed about their sex lives.

8. Eskridge, "Law and the Construction of the Closet: American Regulation of Same-Sex Intimacy, 1880–1946," 1086.

9. David K. Johnson, *The Lavender Scare: The Cold War Persecution of Gays and Lesbians in the Federal Government* (Chicago: University of Chicago Press, 2004).

10. Quoted in Patricia A. Cain, "Litigating for Lesbian and Gay Rights: A Legal History," *Virginia Law Review* 79 (1993): 1566.

11. In making a straight white woman the film's AIDS victim, *Boys on the Side* echoed the Republic National Committee, which invited Mary D. Fisher, who had contacted HIV from her husband, to address the Republican National Convention in 1992.

12. Larry McMurtry and Diana Ossana, "Brokeback Mountain: The Screenplay," in *Brokeback Mountain: Story to Screenplay*, ed. Annie Proulx, Larry McMurtry, and Diana Ossana (London: Harper Perennial, 2006), 35.

13. See Achilles, "The Development of the Homosexual Bar as an Institution"; D'Emilio, *Sexual Politics, Sexual Communities: The Making of a Homosexual Minority in the United States, 1940–1970*; and Jennifer Terry, *An American Obsession: Science, Medicine, and Homosexuality in Modern Society* (Chicago: University of Chicago Press, 1999).

14. 381 U.S. 479 (1965).

15. 347 P. 2d 909 (Cal. 1959).

16. Quoted in National Research Council, *The Social Impact of AIDS in the United States* (Washington, DC: National Academy Press, 1993), 131.

17. Henry J. Kaiser Family Foundation., *Inside-Out: A Report on the Experiences of Lesbians, Gays, and Bisexuals in America and the Public's Views on Issues and Policies Related to Sexual Orientation* (Menlo Park, CA: Henry J. Kaiser Family Foundation, 2001); and Pew Research Center for the People and the Press, *Less Opposition to Gay Marriage, Adoption, and Military Service* (Washington, DC: Pew Research Center for the People and the Press, 2006).

18. 539 U.S. 558 (2003).

CHAPTER 8. MAINSTREAM ADULTERY

1. Kinsey, Pomeroy, and Martin, *Sexual Behavior in the Human Male*, 585.

2. Kinsey et al., *Sexual Behavior in the Human Female*, 416.

3. Jerry Adler and Tessa Namuth, "Adultery (Cover Story)," *Newsweek*, September 30, 1996; and Lorraine Ali et al., "The Secret Lives of Wives," *Newsweek*, July 12, 2004.

4. John Gagnon, *Human Sexualities* (Glenview, IL: Scott Foresman, 1977), 223.

5. Caryn James, "What's Adultery? A Little Sex, a Lot of Politics," *New York Times*, October 14, 1990.

6. W. Doniger, "Sex, Lies, and Tall Tales," *Social Research* 63, no. 3 (1996): 670.

7. David Bordwell, *Narration in the Fiction Film* (Madison: University of Wisconsin Press, 1985), 157.

8. John H. Gagnon broke adultery down into similar components in his analysis of nonmarital sexuality in Gagnon, *Human Sexualities*. For a penetrating look at adultery, see Annette Lawson, *Adultery: An Analysis of Love and Betrayal* (New York: Basic, 1988).

9. 360 U.S. 684 (1959).

10. 378 U.S. 184 (1964).

11. Leff and Simmons, *Dame in the Kimono*, 193. That Breen accepted Dana's cruelty as morally compensating is telling of the shifts within the interpreters of Code morality.

12. Gary W. Lewandowski, Jr., and Robert A. Ackerman, "Something's Missing: Need Fulfillment and Self-Expansion as Predictors of Susceptibility to Infidelity," *Journal of Social Psychology* 146, no. 4 (2006).

13. Betty Fang, "Swinging: In Retrospect," *Journal of Sex Research* 12, no. 3 (1976): 221. For further reading on swinging during the period, see Gilbert D. Bartell, *Group Sex: A Scientist's Eyewitness Report on the American Way of Swinging* (New York: H. Wyden, 1971); and Brian G. Gilmartin, *The Gilmartin Report* (Secaucus, NJ: Citadel Press, 1978).

14. Tom Wolfe, "The Purple Decades," in *The Me Decade and the Third Great Awakening* (London: Penguin, 1983), 276.

15. See Tom W. Smith, "Attitudes toward Sexual Permissiveness: Trends, Correlates, and Behavioral Connections," in *Sexuality across the Life Course*, ed. A. S. Rossi (Chicago: University of Chicago Press, 1994). More than 90 percent of Americans polled described adultery as always or almost always wrong. For recent statistics, see Paul Taylor, Cary Funk, and Peyton Craighill, *A Barometer of Modern Morals* (Washington, DC: Pew Research Center, 2006).

CHAPTER 9. CHILDREN IN THE DARK

1. William Simon, *Postmodern Sexualities* (London: Routledge, 1996), 117–18 (italics in original).

2. John Belton, "Language, Oedipus, and Chinatown," *MLN* 106, no. 5 (1991): 942.

3. Judith Herman and Lisa Hirschman, "Father-Daughter Incest," *Signs* 2, no. 4 (1977): 735.

4. E. Olafson, D. L. Corwin, and R. C. Summit, "Modern History of Child Sexual Abuse Awareness: Cycles of Discovery and Suppression," *Child Abuse and Neglect* 17, no. 1 (1993). While there has been a degree of self-critique within psychiatry for psychoanalysis's role in submerging incest, there has not been a corresponding reassessment of the oedipal complex among Freudian film critics or theorists.

5. Lynn Sacco, "Sanitized for Your Protection," *Journal of Women's History* 14, no. 3 (2002). British health care officials responded similarly; see Carol Smart, "Reconsidering the Recent History of Child Sexual Abuse, 1910–1960," *Journal of Social Policy* 29 (2000).

6. Jeff Aronson, "Incestuous Sheets," *BMJ* 331, no. 7529 (2005).

7. Reprinted in Graham Greene, "Review of *Wee Willie Winkie* and *The Life of Emile Zola*," in *Mornings in the Dark: The Graham Greene Film Reader*, ed. David

Parkinson (Manchester: Carcanet, 1993), 234. Greene and the magazine lost a libel suit brought against them in the English courts by Twentieth Century-Fox on behalf of Temple.

8. For discussions of the issues involved with young female stars in Hollywood films and popular culture in general, see Sarah Hentges, *Pictures of Girlhood: Modern Female Adolescence on Film* (Jefferson, NC: McFarland, 2006); Marianne Sinclair, *Hollywood Lolitas: The Nymphet Syndrome in the Movies* (New York: Henry Holt, 1988); and Valerie Walkerdine, *Daddy's Girl: Young Girls and Popular Culture* (Cambridge, MA: Harvard University Press, 1997).

9. Paul Schrader, *Taxi Driver*, Faber Film (London: Faber and Faber, 1990), 67.

10. Diana Gray, "Turning Out: A Study of Teenage Prostitution," *Urban Life and Culture* 1, no. 4 (1973); and Ivan Gibson-Ainyette et al., "Adolescent Female Prostitutes," *Archives of Sexual Behavior* 17, no. 5 (1988).

11. Ronald B. Flowers, *The Prostitution of Women and Girls* (Jefferson, NC: McFarland, 1998).

12. E. J. Bellocq and Museum of Modern Art, *Storyville Portraits: Photographs from the New Orleans Red-Light District, Circa 1912* (New York: Museum of Modern Art, 1970).

13. Dan Yakir, "Louis Malle's *Pretty Baby.*," *Film Comment* 14 (1978): 65.

14. Al Rose, *Storyville, New Orleans: Being an Authentic, Illustrated Account of the Notorious Red-Light District* (Tuscaloosa, AL: University of Alabama Press, 1974), 148–50.

15. Ibid., 149. Malle and Platt's use of Rose's work was uncredited in the film although both acknowledged its influence in interviews.

16. Antonio Chemasi, "*Pretty Baby*: Love in Storyville," *American Film* 3 (1977): 12.

17. James B. Twitchell, *Dreadful Pleasures: An Anatomy of Modern Horror* (New York: Oxford University Press, 1985), 110–13.

18. Ibid., 93.

19. Vladimir Nabokov, *Lolita* (London: Penguin, 1980), 229.

20. Debra Kalmuss, "Nonvolitional Sex and Sexual Health," *Archives of Sexual Behavior* 33, no. 3 (2004): 197.

21. W. C. Holmes, E. B. Foa, and M. D. Sammel, "Men's Pathways to Risky Sexual Behavior: Role of Co-Occurring Childhood Sexual Abuse, Posttraumatic Stress Disorder, and Depression Histories," *Journal of Urban Health* 82, no. 1 Suppl. 1 (2005); and N. Rodriguez et al., "Posttraumatic Stress Disorder in Adult Female Survivors of Childhood Sexual Abuse: A Comparison Study," *Journal of Consulting and Clinical Psychology* 65, no. 1 (1997).

22. Kinsey et al., *Sexual Behavior in the Human Female*, 121.

23. V. L. Bullough, "Alfred Kinsey and the Kinsey Report: Historical Overview and Lasting Contributions," *Journal of Sex Research* 35, no. 2 (1998): 130.

24. See the organization's Web site at http://www.cwfa.org/kinsey.asp.

25. Kurt Eichenwald, "From Their Own Online World, Pedophiles Extend Their Reach," *New York Times*, August 21, 2006.

Bibliography

Achilles, Nancy. "The Development of the Homosexual Bar as an Institution." In *Sexual Deviance*, edited by John H. Gagnon, William Simon, and Donald E. Carns, 228–44. New York: Harper & Row, 1967.

Adler, Jerry, and Tessa Namuth. "Adultery (Cover Story)." *Newsweek*, September 30, 1996, 54–60.

Ali, Lorraine, Lisa Miller, Vanessa Juarez, Holly Peterson, Karen Springen, Claire Sulmers, William Lee Adams, and Raina Kelley. "The Secret Lives of Wives." *Newsweek*, July 12, 2004, 46–54.

Allyn, David. "Private Acts/Public Policy: Alfred Kinsey, the American-Law-Institute, and the Privatization of American Sexual Morality." *Journal of American Studies* 30 (1996): 405–28.

Arafat, Ibithaj, and Betty Yorburg. "On Living Together without Marriage." In *Intimate Life Styles: Marriage and Its Alternatives*, edited by Jack R. DeLora and Joann S. DeLora, 302–9. Pacific Palisades, CA: Goodyear, 1975.

Aronson, Jeff. "Incestuous Sheets." *BMJ* 331, no. 7529 (2005): 1378.

Austin, Bruce A., Mark J. Nicolich, and Thomas Simonet. "M.P.A.A. Ratings and the Box Office: Some Tantalizing Statistics." *Film Quarterly* 35, no. 2 (1981–82): 28–30.

Barrios, Richard. *Screened Out: Playing Gay in Hollywood from Edison to Stonewall*. New York: Routledge, 2003.

Bartell, Gilbert D. *Group Sex: A Scientist's Eyewitness Report on the American Way of Swinging*. New York: H. Wyden, 1971.

Bazin, André. "On the Politique Des Auteurs." In *Cahiers Du Cinéma: The 1950s: Neo-Realism, Hollywood, New Wave*, edited by Jim Hillier, 248–59. London: Routledge & Kegan Paul in association with the British Film Institute, 1985.

Becker, Howard S. "The Professional Dance Musician and His Audience." *American Journal of Sociology* 57, no. 2 (1951): 136–44.

Bellah, Robert N., Richard Madsen, William M. Sullivan, Ann Swidler, and Steven M. Tipton. *Habits of the Heart: Individualism and Commitment in American Life*. Berkeley: University of California Press, 1985.

Bellocq, E. J., and Museum of Modern Art. *Storyville Portraits: Photographs from the New Orleans Red-Light District, Circa 1912.* New York: Museum of Modern Art, 1970.

Belton, John. "Language, Oedipus, and Chinatown." *MLN* 106, no. 5 (1991): 933–50.

Biskind, Peter. *Down and Dirty Pictures: Miramax, Sundance, and the Rise of Independent Film.* New York: Simon & Schuster, 2004.

———. *Easy Riders, Raging Bulls: How the Sex-Drugs-and-Rock-'N'-Roll Generation Saved Hollywood.* New York: Simon & Schuster, 1998.

Black, Gregory D. *Hollywood Censored: Morality Codes, Catholics, and the Movies,* Cambridge Studies in the History of Mass Communications. Cambridge: Cambridge University Press, 1994.

Bobo, Jacqueline. "Sifting through the Controversy: Reading the Color Purple." *Callaloo* 39 (1989): 332–42.

Bogle, Donald. *Toms, Coons, Mulattoes, Mammies, and Bucks: An Interpretive History of Blacks in American Films.* New York: Viking Press, 1973.

Bordwell, David. *Narration in the Fiction Film.* Madison: University of Wisconsin Press, 1985.

Botto, Louis. "They Shoot Dirty Movies Don't They?" *Look,* November 3, 1970, 56–60.

Brodesser, Claude. "'Dreamers' Goes NC-17." *Daily Variety,* January 14, 2004, 20–24.

Bullough, Vern L. "Alfred Kinsey and the Kinsey Report: Historical Overview and Lasting Contributions." *Journal of Sex Research* 35, no. 2 (1998): 127–31.

———. "Sex in History: A Virgin Field." *Journal of Sex Research* 8, no. 2 (1972): 101–16.

———. *Sexual Variance in Society and History.* New York: Wiley, 1976.

Cain, Patricia A. "Litigating for Lesbian and Gay Rights: A Legal History." *Virginia Law Review* 79 (1993): 1551–1641.

"Changing Morality: The Two Americas, a Time-Louis Harris Poll." *Time,* June 6, 1969.

Chemasi, Antonio. "*Pretty Baby*: Love in Storyville." *American Film* 3 (1977): 8–15.

Cherlin, Andrew J. *Marriage, Divorce, Remarriage.* Rev. and enl. ed. Cambridge, MA: Harvard University Press, 1992.

Clark, Randy. "Bending the Genre: The Stage and Screen Versions of 'Cabaret.'" *Literature/Film Quarterly* 19 (1991): 51–59.

Commission on Obscenity and Pornography. *The Report of the Commission on Obscenity and Pornography.* Washington: U.S. Government Printing Office, 1970.

Committee on Commerce, Science, and Transportation. *Effectiveness of Media Rating Systems: The Testimony of Mr. Jack Valenti,* Science, Technology, and Space Hearing, September 28, 2004.

Corliss, Richard. "Randy Metzger Aristocrat of the Erotic: An Interview by Richard Corliss." *Film Comment* 9, no. 1 (1973): 18–29.

Degler, Carl N. "What Ought to Be and What Was: Women's Sexuality in the Nineteenth Century." *American Historical Review* 79, no. 5 (1974): 1467–90.

D'Emilio, John. *Sexual Politics, Sexual Communities: The Making of a Homosexual Minority in the United States, 1940–1970*. Chicago: University of Chicago Press, 1983.

Doniger, W. "Sex, Lies, and Tall Tales." *Social Research* 63, no. 3 (1996): 663–99.

Ehrenstein, David. *Open Secret: Gay Hollywood, 1928–1998*. New York: William Morrow, 1998.

Eichenwald, Kurt. "From Their Own Online World, Pedophiles Extend Their Reach." *New York Times*, August 21, 2006, A1 (L).

England, Paula, and George Farkas. *Households, Employment, and Gender: A Social, Economic, and Demographic View*. New York: Aldine de Gruyter, 1986.

Eskridge, William N. "Law and the Construction of the Closet: American Regulation of Same-Sex Intimacy, 1880–1946." *Iowa Law Review* 82, no. 4 (1997): 1007–1136.

Falwell, Jerry, Ed Dobson, and Edward E. Hindson. *The Fundamentalist Phenomenon: The Resurgence of Conservative Christianity*. Garden City, NY: Doubleday, 1981.

Fang, Betty. "Swinging: In Retrospect." *Journal of Sex Research* 12, no. 3 (1976): 220–37.

Feinberg, Joel. *Rights, Justice, and the Bounds of Liberty: Essays in Social Philosophy*. Princeton: Princeton University Press, 1980.

Flowers, Ronald B. *The Prostitution of Women and Girls*. Jefferson, NC: McFarland, 1998.

Friedan, Betty. *The Feminine Mystique*. New York: Norton, 1963.

Gagnon, John. *Human Sexualities*. Glenview, IL: Scott Foresman, 1977.

Gay, Peter. *The Bourgeois Experience: Victoria to Freud*. 5 vols. New York: Oxford University Press, 1984.

Gibson-Ainyette, Ivan, Donald I. Templer, Ric Brown, and Lelia Veaco. "Adolescent Female Prostitutes." *Archives of Sexual Behavior* 17, no. 5 (1988): 431–38.

Gilmartin, Brian G. *The Gilmartin Report*. Secaucus, NJ: Citadel Press, 1978.

Gordon, Mel. *Voluptuous Panic: The Erotic World of Weimar Berlin*. Los Angeles, CA: Feral House, 2000.

Gray, Diana. "Turning Out: A Study of Teenage Prostitution." *Urban Life and Culture* 1, no. 4 (1973): 401.

Greene, Graham. "Review of *Wee Willie Winkie* and *The Life of Emile Zola*." In *Mornings in the Dark: The Graham Greene Film Reader*, edited by David Parkinson, 233-35. Manchester: Carcanet, 1993.

Guerrero, Ed. "The Black Man on Our Screens and the Empty Space in Representation." *Callaloo* 18, no. 2 (1995): 395–400.

Hamilton, Jack. "Movies: And Everybody's Doing It." *Look*, November 3, 1970, 41–47.

Hammond, Paul. *French Undressing: Naughty Postcards from 1900–1920*. London: Jupiter Books, 1976.

Hasday, J. E. "Contest and Consent: A Legal History of Marital Rape." *California Law Review* 88, no. 5 (2000): 1373–1505.

Hayes, Dade, and Jonathan Bing. "H'wood: R Kind of Town (Cover Story)." *Variety*, March 31, 2003, 1.

Hays, Will H. *The Memoirs of Will H. Hays*. Garden City, NY: Doubleday, 1955.

Hecht, Ben. *A Child of the Century*. New York: Playbill/Ballantine, 1970. Reprint, 1954.

Henry J. Kaiser Family Foundation. *Inside-Out: A Report on the Experiences of Lesbians, Gays, and Bisexuals in America and the Public's Views on Issues and Policies Related to Sexual Orientation*. Menlo Park, CA: Henry J. Kaiser Family Foundation, 2001.

Hentges, Sarah. *Pictures of Girlhood: Modern Female Adolescence on Film*. Jefferson, NC: McFarland, 2006.

Herman, Judith, and Lisa Hirschman. "Father-Daughter Incest." *Signs* 2, no. 4 (1977): 735–56.

Hoffmann, Frank A. "Prolegomena to a Study of Traditional Elements in the Erotic Film." *Journal of American Folklore* 78, no. 308 (1965): 143–48.

Holmes, W. C., E. B. Foa, and M. D. Sammel. "Men's Pathways to Risky Sexual Behavior: Role of Co-Occurring Childhood Sexual Abuse, Posttraumatic Stress Disorder, and Depression Histories." *Journal of Urban Health* 82, no. 1 Suppl. 1 (2005): 189–99.

Jacobs, Lea. *The Wages of Sin: Censorship and the Fallen Women Film, 1928–1942*. Madison: University of Wisconsin Press, 1991.

James, Caryn. "What's Adultery? A Little Sex, a Lot of Politics." *New York Times*, October 14, 1990, 15, Column 1.

Jenks, Albert Ernest. "The Legal Status of Negro-White Amalgamation in the United States." *American Journal of Sociology* 21, no. 5 (1916): 666–78.

Johnson, David K. *The Lavender Scare: The Cold War Persecution of Gays and Lesbians in the Federal Government*. Chicago: University of Chicago Press, 2004.

Kalmuss, Debra. "Nonvolitional Sex and Sexual Health." *Archives of Sexual Behavior* 33, no. 3 (2004): 197–209.

Kauffmann, Stanley. "Black Love in Movies and on Television: Independent Directors and Producers Are Taking Steps to Bring Black Romance and Intimacy to the Screen." *Ebony*, February 1991, 162–67.

Kessler-Harris, Alice. *Out to Work: A History of Wage-Earning Women in the United States*. New York: Oxford University Press, 1982.

Kinsey, Alfred C., Wardell Baxter Pomeroy, and Clyde E. Martin. *Sexual Behavior in the Human Male*. Philadelphia: W. B. Saunders, 1948.

Kinsey, Alfred C., Wardell Baxter Pomeroy, Clyde E. Martin, and Paul H. Gebhard. *Sexual Behavior in the Human Female*. Philadelphia: W. B. Saunders, 1953.

Knebel, Fletcher. "Mood of America." *Look*, November 18, 1969, 23–32.

Knight, Arthur, and Hollis Alpert. "The History of Sex in Cinema, Part 12: The Fifties—Hollywood Grows Up." *Playboy*, November 1966, 162–85.

———. "The History of Sex in Cinema, Part 17: The Stag Film." *Playboy*, November 1967, 154+.

Laumann, Edward O., John H. Gagnon, Robert T. Michael, and Stuart Michaels. *Sex in America: A Definitive Survey*. Boston: Little Brown, 1994.

Lawson, Annette. *Adultery: An Analysis of Love and Betrayal*. New York: Basic, 1988.

Leff, Leonard J., and Jerold Simmons. *The Dame in the Kimono: Hollywood, Censorship, and the Production Code from the 1920s to the 1960s.* New York: Grove Weidenfeld, 1990.

Leone, Ron, and Nicole Houle. "21st Century Ratings Creep: PG-13 and R." *Communication Research Reports* 23, no. 1 (2006): 53–61.

Lewandowski, Jr., Gary W., and Robert A. Ackerman. "Something's Missing: Need Fulfillment and Self-Expansion as Predictors of Susceptibility to Infidelity." *Journal of Social Psychology* 146, no. 4 (2006): 389–403.

Lopes, Paul. "Signifying Deviance and Transgression: Jazz in the Popular Imagination." *American Behavioral Scientist* 48, no. 11 (2005): 1468–81.

McDougal, Stuart Y. *Stanley Kubrick's A Clockwork Orange.* Cambridge: Cambridge University Press, 2003.

McMurtry, Larry, and Diana Ossana. "Brokeback Mountain: The Screenplay." In *Brokeback Mountain: Story to Screenplay*, edited by Annie Proulx, Larry McMurtry, and Diana Ossana, 29–97. London: Harper Perennial, 2006.

Mekas, Jonas. "Notes on Some New Movies and Happiness." *Film Culture* 37 (1965): 16–20.

Modell, John. "Historical Reflections on American Marriage." In *Contemporary Marriage: Comparative Perspectives on a Changing Institution*, edited by Kingsley Davis, 181–96. New York: Russell Sage Foundation, 1985.

Moley, Raymond. *The Hays Office.* Indianapolis, IN: Bobbs-Merrill, 1945.

Morantz, Regina Markell. "The Scientist as Sex Crusader: Alfred C. Kinsey and American Culture." *American Quarterly* 29, no. 5, Special Issue: Reassessing Twentieth Century Documents (1977): 563–89.

Motion Picture Association of America. "Official Code Objectives." In *The Movies in Our Midst: Documents in the Cultural History of Film in America*, edited by Gerald Mast, 704–7. Chicago: University of Chicago Press, 1982.

Murray, William. "Porn Capital of America: San Francisco." *New York Times Magazine*, January 3, 1971, 8+.

Nabokov, Vladimir. *Lolita.* London: Penguin, 1980.

National Research Council. *The Social Impact of AIDS in the United States.* Washington, DC: National Academy Press, 1993.

Neff, J. A., B. Holamon, and T. D. Schluter. "Spousal Violence among Anglos, Blacks, and Mexican-Americans: The Role of Demographic-Variables, Psychosocial Predictors, and Alcohol-Consumption." *Journal of Family Violence* 10, no. 1 (1995): 1–21.

Olafson, E., D. L. Corwin, and R. C. Summit. "Modern History of Child Sexual Abuse Awareness: Cycles of Discovery and Suppression." *Child Abuse and Neglect* 17, no. 1 (1993): 7–24.

Pew Research Center for the People and the Press. *Less Opposition to Gay Marriage, Adoption, and Military Service.* Washington, DC: Pew Research Center for the People and the Press, 2006.

Powdermaker, Hortense. *Hollywood, the Dream Factory: An Anthropologist Looks at the Movie-Makers.* Boston: Little, Brown, 1950.

Projansky, Sarah. "The Elusive/Ubiquitous Representation of Rape: A Historical Survey of Rape in U.S. Film, 1903–1972." *Cinema Journal* 41, no. 1 (2001): 63–90.

Quigley, Martin. *Decency in Motion Pictures.* New York: Macmillan, 1937.

Randall, Richard S. *Censorship of the Movies: The Social and Political Control of a Mass Medium.* Madison: University of Wisconsin Press, 1968.

Reed, Ishmael. "Stephen Spielberg Plays Howard Beach." *Black American Literature Forum* 21, no. 1/2 (1987): 7–16.

Riley, Robin. *Film, Faith, and Cultural Conflict: The Case of Martin Scorsese's The Last Temptation of Christ.* Westport, CT: Praeger, 2003.

Roberts, Sam. "It's Official: To Be Married Means to Be Outnumbered." *New York Times*, October 15, 2006, A22 (L).

Robinson, Ira, Ken Ziss, Bill Ganza, Stuart Katz, and Edward Robinson. "Twenty Years of the Sexual Revolution, 1965–1985: An Update." *Journal of Marriage and the Family* 53, no. 1 (1991): 216–20.

Rodriguez, N., S. W. Ryan, H. Vande Kemp, and D. W. Foy. "Posttraumatic Stress Disorder in Adult Female Survivors of Childhood Sexual Abuse: A Comparison Study." *Journal of Consulting and Clinical Psychology* 65, no. 1 (1997): 53–59.

Rose, Al. *Storyville, New Orleans: Being an Authentic, Illustrated Account of the Notorious Red-Light District.* Tuscaloosa, AL: University of Alabama Press, 1974.

"R-Rated Films in Decline." *Film Journal International* 108, no. 4 (2005): 4.

Rubin, Isadore. "Transition in Sex Values: Implications for the Education of Adolescents." *Journal of Marriage and the Family* 27, no. 2 (1965): 185–89.

Russo, Vito. *The Celluloid Closet: Homosexuality in the Movies.* Rev. ed. New York: Perennial Library, 1987.

Ryan, R. M. "The Sex Right: A Legal History of the Marital Rape Exemption." *Law and Social Inquiry* 20, no. 4 (1995): 941–1001.

Sacco, Lynn. "Sanitized for Your Protection." *Journal of Women's History* 14, no. 3 (2002): 80–104.

Schrader, Paul. *Taxi Driver.* London: Faber and Faber, 1990.

Schumach, Murray. "M.J. Frankovich, New Columbia Boss, Sketches Plan of Positive Action." *New York Times*, March 15, 1964, X9.

Sigel, L. Z. "Filth in the Wrong People's Hands: Postcards and the Expansion of Pornography in Britain and the Atlantic World, 1880–1914." *Journal of Social History* 33, no. 4 (2000): 859–85.

Simon, William. *Postmodern Sexualities.* London: Routledge, 1996.

Sinclair, Marianne. *Hollywood Lolitas: The Nymphet Syndrome in the Movies.* New York: Henry Holt, 1988.

Smart, Carol. "Reconsidering the Recent History of Child Sexual Abuse, 1910–1960." *Journal of Social Policy* 29 (2000): 55–71.

Smith, Barbara. "Sexual Oppression Unmasked." *Callaloo* 22 (1984): 170–76.

Smith, Tom W. "Attitudes toward Sexual Permissiveness: Trends, Correlates, and Behavioral Connections." In *Sexuality across the Life Course*, edited by A. S. Rossi, 63–97. Chicago: University of Chicago Press, 1994.

———. "Liberal and Conservative Trends in the United States since World War II." *Public Opinion Quarterly* 54, no. 4 (1990): 479–507.

Stern, S. R. "Self-Absorbed, Dangerous, and Disengaged: What Popular Films Tell Us about Teenagers." *Mass Communication and Society* 8, no. 1 (2005): 23–38.

Stevenson, Jack. "From the Bedroom to the Bijou: A Secret History of American Gay Sex Cinema." *Film Quarterly* 51, no. 1 (1997): 24–31.

Stinson, Charles. "'Immoral Mr. Teas' Ends Era in Movies." *Los Angeles Times*, January 26, 1960, 18.

Taylor, Paul, Cary Funk, and Peyton Craighill. *A Barometer of Modern Morals*. Washington, DC: Pew Research Center, 2006.

Terry, Jennifer. *An American Obsession: Science, Medicine, and Homosexuality in Modern Society*. Chicago: University of Chicago Press, 1999.

Thompson, Tommy. "Raw Dialogue Challenges All the Censors." *Life*, June 10, 1966, 92–98.

Tjaden, Patricia Godeke, and Nancy Thoennes. *Extent, Nature, and Consequences of Intimate Partner Violence*. Washington, DC: Department of Justice (U.S.), 2000.

Towne, Robert. "Dialogue on Film: Robert Towne." *American Film* 1, no. 3 (1975): 33–48.

"Trends in HIV-Related Risk Behaviors among High School Students—United States, 1991–2005." *Morbidity and Mortality Weekly Report*, 2006.

Trilling, Lionel. "The Kinsey Report." In *The Liberal Imagination: Essays on Literature and Society*, 224–43. Harmondsworth: Penguin, 1976.

Twitchell, James B. *Dreadful Pleasures: An Anatomy of Modern Horror*. New York: Oxford University Press, 1985.

Vizzard, Jack. *See No Evil: Life inside a Hollywood Censor*. New York: Simon & Schuster, 1970.

Walkerdine, Valerie. *Daddy's Girl: Young Girls and Popular Culture*. Cambridge, MA: Harvard University Press, 1997.

Wloszczyna, Susan. "Extreme Cinema Returns with a Vengeance." *USA Today*, October 26, 2004, 01d.

Wolfe, Tom. "The Purple Decades." In *The Me Decade and the Third Great Awakening*, 265–93. London: Penguin, 1983.

Yakir, Dan. "Louis Malle's *Pretty Baby*." *Film Comment* 14 (1978): 61–66.

Index

Roth v. United States (1957), 15; underground cinema and, 32–33
From Here to Eternity (1951), 11, 153, 155–57, 159, 163

Gay/lesbian bars, ix, 119, 131–34, 139–40, 199 n.7
Gays, x–xi, 87; *American Beauty* (1999), 106–7; Hollywood and, 129–50; *Manual Enterprises v. Day* (1962), 15; pornography and, 25; rights of, 66, 87; *Shampoo* (1975), 66; underground cinema and, 32–33
Gender, 143; *Annie Hall* (1979), 70–71; *Boys Don't Cry* (1999), 102–3; feminists and, 65–66, 120; *An Officer and a Gentleman* (1982), 78; roles, 35–36, 41, 44, 122–23, 134
Genre, 80, 95, 97, 127, 192; detective, 174; pedophilia and, 189–90; romantic comedy, 70, 93; sexploitation, and genre conventions, 18–19, 21–22, 55, 100; sexuality and, x–xi
Ghoulies, 23–24
Gilda (1946), 9, 131
Ginsberg v. New York (1968), 51
Go Fish (1994), 145
Government censorship, x, 29, 109, 191; early, 1–22, 111, 113, 152; film and, 2, 154; pornography and, 24, 56, 58; sexploitation films and, 22–23; underground cinema and, 32
The Graduate (1967), 45–50, 59, 61, 152, 154, 156, 168
Griswold v. Connecticut (1965), 139

Happiness (1998), 89, 186
Hays, Will H., 4–5, 7–9, 102, 110, 174
Henry & June (1990), 88, 91, 117–20
HIV, 95, 100–101, 135, 146, 149, 199 n.11
Holmby Productions v. Vaughn (1955), 10
Homophobia, xi, 102, 130–31, 134–39, 148–50
Homosexuality, xi, 198 n.3; attitudes toward, 64; *Cabaret* (1972), 114;

"closet," 96, 129, 139–42, 145, 149; Hollywood and, 129–35, 137–42, 144, 146–47, 149–50; Kinsey Report and, 34; Production Code and, 6, 9, 11–13; repressed, 106–7; sodomy laws, 36

The Ice Storm (1997), 152, 158–59, 168–72
Identity, 32, 46, 53, 70, 104–5, 117, 119, 144–45
The Immoral Mr. Teas (1959), 21–22
Implication (narrative), 111, 122, 126, 179, 188; adultery, 153, 156; *American Beauty* (1999), 106–7; *L'Avventura* (1960), 29–30; *Blow-Up* (1966), 30–31; CARA and, 75–76, 77, 92; *Chinatown* (1974), 174–75; cohabitation, 88; conventions, 182; editing, 5; erotic noir, 96–99; homoerotic, 124, 130–31, 133, 146, 149; New Hollywood and, 53–54, 58, 67; Production Code and, 6, 9, 114; rape, 7; sexploitation films and, 22; U.S. Supreme Court, 16, 51; *Valmont* (1989), 177–78
Incest, xii, 91, 189–90, 200 n.4; *Chinatown* (1974), 110, 174–77; Hollywood and, 174, 179; Kinsey Report and, 189; sexploitation films and, 23; social problem, 173–74, 176–77; taboo, 173; *Valmont* (1989), 178–79; vampirism, 185–86
Individual autonomy, 33, 38, 45, 57
Infidelity, xi, 94, 127, 174; sexploitation films and, 23; *Shampoo* (1975), 69; social issue, 151–52; *Who's Afraid of Virginia Woolf?* (1966), 41–42. See also Adultery
Interstate Circuit v. Dallas (1968), 51
Interview with the Vampire (1994), 185–86
In the Cut (2003), 98–99
Intimacy, 59, 68, 77–78, 119, 123, 159; *Annie Hall* (1979), 70, 72; marital, 33; race to, 66, 93–94; sexual, 78, 84, 154, 185

About the Author

JODY W. PENNINGTON is Associate Professor in Media and Culture Studies at the Department of English, University of Aarhus, Denmark, where he teaches Media and Cultural Studies as well as American Studies. He has published articles and presented papers on various aspects of film and popular music, as well as American constitutional law. He is currently president of the Danish Association of American Studies.